THE 9 NATURAL LAWS OF LEADERSHIP

THIRD EDITION

REVISED 2011

WARREN BLANK
AARON BROWN

The Leadership Group Press

This book is available at a special discount when ordered in bulk quantities. For more information, please contact Warren Blank, President, The Leadership Group, 505 Beachland Blvd., Suite 223, Vero Beach, FL 32963 Phone: (919) 656-3344

The 9 Natural Laws of Leadership:
Quantum Leadership For the New Millennium

ISBN No. 0-9779737-352995.EPS

3rd Edition, Revised

Published by: The Leadership Group Press

Printing
10 9 8 7 6 5 4 3

E-Mail *LeaderWB@aol.com*

Contents

◆◆◆

Acknowledgments

Second Edition

Warren Blank

At the deepest levels of reality, everything is connected. Existence displays itself as fields of interaction. The first edition of this book could never have been written without the insights and support of many individuals

First, I want to thank the thousands of participants in my leadership training seminars who asked so many penetrating questions about practical issues and challenged me to think through my ideas about leadership.

I would specifically like to thank all those who allowed me to recount their personal leadership experiences: Ray Alvord, David Bell, Dick Frazer, Ron Fisher, Joe Frick, Pat Grysavage, Martha Hahn, Dudley Hanson, Joseph Hoeg, Floyd Hoelting, Louis Katopodis, John Lainhart, Leon Moore, Garry Nelson, Robert Nelson, Ron Opitz, and Alex Stolley.

I also want to thank Terry Fairchild for his help with earlier versions of the original manuscript, and the staff at AMACOM, particularly Adrienne Hickey and Kate Pferdner.

I am indebted to Steven G. Green, an outstanding leadership scholar and good friend, for all he has taught me about leadership.

My deepest gratitude goes to Maharishi Mahesh Yogi, for providing me with knowledge about the meaning of life.

To my mother, Helen Blank, thank you for being a lifelong model of one who always sought to learn and grow.

And to the most important person in my life, my wife, Mary Ann Cooke. Thank you for being my perfect partner.

Aaron Brown

I have been fortunate in my life and career to have had two significant professional and personal relationships that have made the most positive impacts in all phases of my individual development and growth. In the early part of my career, Charles M. "Chuck" Montgomery provided the foundational elements of my ability to help and train others through the Life Skills Developmental Models created by Dr. Robert R. Carkhuff in the 1960's and 1970's. Our co-authorship of the book, *"In the Land of the Blind"* (1982), documented the success of our collaborative efforts for that time in our lives. I am indebted to Chuck as my coach, teacher, and master trainer.

Since 1990, Warren Blank has not only become a respected and trusted professional colleague, but more importantly my closest friend, and the brother I never had growing up. Our collaborations over the years in training, development, and authoring has allowed my mind to expand and my professional skills to grow beyond my own expectations. More importantly though is the true friendship that has developed over the years. Other than my Mother and Father, you are the only person in my life who has never let me down or compromised the trust I've placed in you. That may be the rarest quality of true leadership and true friendship. I can only say thank you, my friend!

Warren and Aaron

Finally, with the publication of the second edition of this book, we need to thank the thousands of trainees, clients, and organizations that have supported our efforts over the years, including: the Federal Executive Institute, the Western Management Development Center, the Shell Oil Company, Fiesta Mart, the IRS, the Department of Defense, the EPA, the DOE, Kroger Foods, and the Federal Bureau of Prisons. Your success is our reward. We look forward to working with each of you in the future, and with new leaders who have read this second edition and who will eventually attend our training programs. May you continue to grow, evolve, and lead "Naturally"!!!

◆◆◆

Preface to the Second Edition

New experience and thoughtful analysis can increase one's knowledge and ability to express it. We have had the good fortune of many insightful experiences since the publication of the first edition of the *Nine Natural Laws of Leadership.* This revised edition includes those insights. It also includes the very positive contributions of Aaron Brown with whom I revised and expanded this second edition.

The second edition also has a new format. Each chapter concludes with a "Field Guide." The Guide contains all the "action ideas" presented in the first edition as well as new action ideas that have been "field tested" and proven to be useful. Each chapter's Field Guide includes a "implementation process plan" (IPP). The IPP's provide a structured approach to applying the action ideas and measuring results.

The world has changed dramatically since 1995. The leadership challenge has not changed. Organizations, in all forms, need more and better leadership at all levels. Leaders must take a holistic and "enlightened" approach. That means leaders must consider the largest context for all their actions and approach every situation seeking to provide benefit for all. The Nine Natural Laws of Leadership and Quantum Leadership Model clarify how to achieve these most important goals.

Preface to the First Edition

The Nine Natural Laws of Leadership answers the questions: What does it mean to be a leader? When and how does leadership occur? How do leaders and managers differ? What is the source of a leader's power? And, perhaps most importantly: How can leaders provide more enlightened, life-supporting direction for their organizations? Answers to these questions will provide practical choices for those men and women who care to take initiative and make a difference in their organizations.

A paradigm shift has occurred in our knowledge about nature's deeper realities. That mind-set offers new insights into our understanding of leadership. This book defines a new way of thinking about leadership. It describes a new leadership paradigm. And, it offers practical action ideas to guide leaders.

Leadership and Natural Law

After almost 100 years of formal study, leadership remains an elusive phenomenon that everyone yearns for but often finds to be in short supply. I believe the problem lies in the way people think about leadership. To date, we still do not have a complete understanding of leadership's most fundamental natural laws.

By natural law, I mean the intelligence or order that explains the patterns of behavior and interaction of leadership. Today, people commonly view leadership by focusing only on the leader. They commonly define leaders by their personal traits, behaviors, or habits. This approach fails to address the deeper reality: that to be a leader means to have willing followers. The focus on the leader alone obscures the interactional quality of leadership. The obsession with individual attributes fails to recognize that such characteristics are important only in relation to followers.

The Nine Natural Laws of Leadership defines the fundamental laws that describe leaders in all contexts and across all scales from leaders of countries and leaders of large and small companies to leaders of quality improvement teams. The nine natural laws spell out the requirements for anyone who is a leader. They show how all leaders influence others and describe the arena in which every leader operates. The laws detail the boundary conditions and realistic consequences faced by anyone who leads. The natural laws of leadership also clarify the source of leadership capability within each person. The nine laws also provide a practical guide for anyone who wants to take the lead.

A New Leadership Paradigm

Knowledge about any phenomenon's natural laws depends on the prevailing paradigm used to make sense of nature. The existing leadership mind-set is based on a set of assumptions developed in the seventeenth century, known as classical or Newtonian physics. For example, the repeated attempts to define leadership in terms of the leader alone and to understand leaders in terms of a set of traits or habits are based on Newton's assumption that nature is made up of separate bits of solid matter. Newton believed nature could best be understood by breaking it down into its separate and independent components. Newton's approach, while valid for material objects, has not helped us to understand leadership.

The discovery of quantum physics at the beginning of the twentieth century shattered Newton's worldview as the definitive portrait of reality. Quantum physics reveals deeper layers of nature's functioning and has provided new and compelling insights into economics, technology, and psychology (e.g., George Gilder's Microcosm: *The Quantum Revolution in Economics and Technology* and Danah Zohar's *The Quantum Self: Human Nature and Consciousness Defined by the New Physics*). The quantum paradigm offers a set of assumptions that provide a more complete and appropriate understanding of leadership. For example, quantum physics explains that at the deepest levels, reality is a field, an interaction that cannot be understood, in terms of separate parts.

The nine natural laws of leadership are based on these and other assumptions derived from the quantum worldview. These assumptions suggest a new mind-set, the Quantum Leadership paradigm, that offers a more compelling description of leadership.

To illustrate, Quantum Leadership explains that leadership is best understood in terms of leaders and followers *together*. Through the lens of Quantum Leadership we recognize that leadership is a field, an interaction, an interdependence of leaders and followers. Quantum Leadership defines the power of leadership as the connection between leaders and followers who together play a role in generating leadership power. The Quantum Leadership paradigm expands the part everyone can play in guiding an organization.

Quantum Leadership also offers guidance for leaders in today's competitive environment. Successful businesses cannot compete using a fragmented approach. The global competitive environment is best understood as a total field. Quantum Leadership shows leaders how to be "field conscious" so they can apply a broad perspective about the larger competitive field while maintaining a sharp focus on localized interactions.

This book describes the Quantum Leadership paradigm and offers a model for guiding leadership action. The model explains how leaders recognize solutions to problems and take advantage of opportunities. The model defines how leaders perform actions that enlighten followers to join the leader. At the foundation of the model is the key to reinforcing and developing more enlightened, life-supporting leaders. Quantum Leadership recognizes that consciousness, how people process information, creates leadership. Quantum Leadership directs people to expand their consciousness so that they can overcome the limitations and destructive biases that result in life-damaging or mistake-ridden leadership action. With greater self-awareness, Quantum Leaders can harness the full power of leadership and use that power in a more enlightened way.

Practical Action Ideas

The Natural Laws of Leadership offers more than 200 practical action ideas to guide leaders. These action ideas are not absolutes that guarantee specific results in a particular circumstance. Newton's cause-and-effect determinism does not fit the reality of leading. The action ideas reflect the quantum assumption that probabilities, nonlinearity, and uncertainty characterize the leader's arena of action. They provide possibilities to consider and experiment with as part of the application of leadership.

The action ideas provide choices designed to increase your arsenal of potential ways to succeed. Some may not appeal to you. Ignore them in favor of those you do like. There will be situations when it is not possible to try certain action ideas. Focus on those you can use and do not get mired in what cannot be done. Some action ideas may be easier to apply than others. Work on implementing a range of actions from easy to more difficult so that you stretch your capacity. Some action ideas will work in one circumstance and not in another. Avoid becoming robotic and assuming that what worked once will always work in the future. A key to success in action is to learn from the implementation of every action idea and incorporate that learning into decisions about subsequent action ideas.

◆◆◆

Overview of Chapters

- Chapter 1 provides a brief case study to illustrate how we typically think about leadership and to show the limitations of traditional views.
- Chapter 2 spells out the nine natural laws of leadership.
- Chapter 3 describes the Quantum Leadership paradigm by contrasting the five assumptions of the traditional classical physics leadership mind-set with the five assumptions of the quantum view. The chapter also describes how Quantum Leadership is more appropriate for modern organizations than classical leadership.
- Chapter 4 presents the Quantum Leadership model and describes how it more accurately fits today's competitive conditions. It also details how the model offers a practical guide for more enlightened leadership.
- Chapter 5 describes the Quantum Leader within or our capacity to use our mind or consciousness. The chapter defines the four quantum powers of consciousness.
- Chapter 6 details how Quantum Leaders identify problems and possibilities and define courses of action to solve problems and exploit opportunities. Quantum Leaders perceive what others don't. They recognize events and process information that others overlook, ignore, or to which others simply do not know how to respond.
- Chapter 7 explains how Quantum Leaders go into The G.A.P., the place where they gain another perspective. G.A.P. thinking enables Quantum Leaders to break the boundaries that limit, bias, or distort perception. It opens leaders to new ways of observing, interpreting, and evaluating information so they can chart more useful courses of action.
- Chapter 8 describes how Quantum Leaders gain commitment from followers. It details the influence tactics leaders use to enlighten followers so that they perceive the merit of the leader and the leader's course of action.

- Chapter 9 presents how Quantum Leaders create shared meaning, the connection that attracts followers. Quantum Leaders match the follower's values and reframe information so that followers can understand and accept the leader's message.
- Chapter 10 offers ways Quantum Leaders influence others and explains how this process occurs at the subtlest levels of information processing. Quantum Leaders speak the language of the listener to influence action. People have internal codes or a private mental language they use to create meaning. Quantum Leaders speak this language to influence followers.
- Chapter 11 explains how Quantum Leaders cultivate relationships with others so that they are more likely to follow.
- Chapter 12 differentiates leaders from managers by explaining how leaders are better understood through a quantum approach and how managers are more clearly perceived through the lens of classical physics.
- Chapter 13 explains how to develop Quantum Leaders who have expanded consciousness, the fundamental source of leadership.
- Chapter 14 provides the insights we have gained and the lessons we have learned over our careers regarding the challenges and great opportunities that exist to develop Quantum Leaders.

◆◆◆

Our Personal Perspective

We believe that every person has the capacity to take the lead. Some people may lead on the global worldscape theater of business or international politics or in the arenas of world health or education. Others may lead in small groups or one-to-one interactions. In every case, the mechanics or science of leadership is the same. This book describes that science in terms of the nine natural laws and the Quantum Leadership paradigm.

We also know that leaders at all levels and in all arenas must be artful in their implementation of the science. This requires the expansion of consciousness. The Quantum Leadership paradigm describes the tools for being more "wakeful," or conscious about the artful reality of leading.

Consciousness is the one indispensable ingredient that establishes the basis for enlightened leadership. By expanding consciousness, the Quantum Leader's relationship to the world changes at the fundamental level of mind. With expanded consciousness the Quantum Leader has the solid intention to lead. Increased awareness enables the Quantum Leader to apply the highly focused attention needed to resolve problems and exploit opportunities. Heightened perception improves and refines the quality of discrimination so we can consider more choices and interpret choices in more constructive ways. Expanded consciousness forms the basis for effective initiative to take positive action.

The German philosopher Goethe wrote:

> *"If I accept you as you are, I will make you worse; however, if I treat you as though you are what you are capable of becoming, I help you become that."*

We hope this second edition of this book helps each reader enliven the consciousness within him or herself to become a life-supporting Quantum Leader.

1

In Search of Leadership

"Leadership, I'm not sure how to define it,
but I know it when I see it."
Dwight David Eisenhower, U.S. president and five-star general

Leadership. The word inspires multiple images. Think of the power leaders bring for positive change. Consider leaders whose force can misdirect. Recall how leader capacity can often be absent when we need it most. To fulfill the search for leadership we need to examine what we believe represents leadership and why.

Who Is the Leader?

Everyone sitting at the large conference table wonders what will happen now that Tom Hammonds, Chem-Labs' dynamic founder and vigorous, hands-on president, is in the hospital. He will survive the massive stroke suffered seventy-two hours ago, but he remains in a coma and it is unclear when or if he will regain his full faculties.

The stroke was completely unexpected. Hammonds had not even considered the need to mold a successor, thinking there would be plenty of time for that later.

Hushed, anxious comments pass among the twenty-three Chem-Labs managers, supervisors, and senior-level employees. Then Barry Sherman, the longest-tenured of Chem-Labs' four managers, stands and addresses the group. "This news is a severe blow," he states, "but we have to remain calm. We have to stay on track. We can work through this."

Barry stops as the president's secretary quickly enters the room and hands him an email. "This just came in from Beijing, the China group," she says in a quiet, nervous tone. "I had to show it to somebody immediately."

The words Beijing *and* China *create a stir. For nine months, Hammonds had worked to establish a market in China. The move was expected to more than double Chem-Labs' revenues over the next three years. It would serve as a springboard for international expansion into the entire Pacific Rim.*

"What does the email say?" Helen Gitler, Chem-Lab's newest manager asks.

"The consortium expresses their condolences and wishes Tom Hammonds a speedy recovery," Barry says. "They then state, 'Due to these unfortunate circumstances, we need to reevaluate our position regarding our joint business venture."

Several members of the group make comments at once. "This can't be!" "Damn! How can they do this now?" "First, Tom, now this. What else will go wrong?"

Barry waves a hand and says, "Okay. Let's remain calm. This isn't our only important deal."

"What does it mean?" one of the senior employees asks.

"Have we lost the deal completely?" another queries.

"No one can be sure," Helen declares. "We need more information."

Bud Parsons, one of Chem-Labs' long-time supervisors, nods in agreement and says, "I think you're right, Helen."

"We should reply to the Chinese immediately," Helen proposes. "Tell them we can still work out the deal. Ask them for more information. Let's draft an email back to them."

"Why don't we try to set up a meeting," Bud suggests. "Someone should go to their offices," he states, looking at Helen.

"That's a good idea, Bud," Helen replies. "Personal relationships mean a lot to the Chinese. I am willing to work on setting that up."

"Just hold on," Barry's says in a raised voice. "We should wait to see about Tom's condition. It will be risky to move ahead. I say we wait. Let's keep our energies focused on domestic operations for now. They offer more certainty than the China venture. We don't want to do anything rash." Barry looks directly at Helen. "No one here was directly involved in the negotiations with the Chinese. I say we wait."

Roger Klein, another of the company's managers, shrugs in apparent resignation. "Barry's in charge," he concedes. "We should comply with what Barry says."

"Look," Helen responds, her eyes narrowing, "1 know how the project unfolded. I say we can keep it going."

"Come on, Helen," Roger says, "you're new to the firm -"

Helen cuts him off and speaks with emphasis. "Roger, I know how much potential this deal holds for us. We should keep working on it."

Tony Franzini, another manager, looks toward Barry. and says, "1 agree with Helen. We should give her idea a try." He then turns to Helen. "Do you think the email really means they want to pull out?"

"We should reply to the Chinese quickly," Helen proposes. "Tell them we can still work out the deal. Ask them when we could meet to address their concerns. Let's contact them right away."

Bud nods in agreement. He knows that Helen was brought into the company because of her experience in the Pacific Rim. "How do we proceed, Helen?"

"It all depends," she says thoughtfully. "Naturally we have to be alert. Their email might be a negotiating ploy to gain some new advantage. Our Chinese friends might be relying on one of their maxims, 'When the enemy is thrown into disorder, crush him.' I say we contact Chen and ask him to suggest a meeting with them - the sooner the better. Their response will tell us

something about the strategy they're using and what else we have to do to rebuild a connection."

Roger speaks sternly: "Helen, Barry told us we have to hold off. He's the senior manager now. Barry said that -

Helen makes direct eye contact with Roger and says, "Roger, I know how the Chinese think. I say we can pull this off."

Roger turns toward Barry. "Who does she think she is?" he mutters.

"Listen Helen," Barry responds, "I'm the firm's negotiation expert, not you. And I've been with the firm longer than anybody. You're outside your authority." He scans the faces of the other members of the group. "1 order you all to hold tight."

Tony Franzini leans toward Barry. "Barry, can't you see the logic? Helen's proactive approach gives us much more leverage than just waiting. I support her."

Barry retorts, "1 say we have to wait. We have to regroup. The important thing is..."

Helen speaks to the entire group: "Holding back could kill the China deal. Our schedule calls for action within two days. If we take steps now, we might still pull it off. We've invested a lot in the China venture. We should move forward. It's a chance. It's something to try."

Barry looks around the room. "Don't listen to her!" he demands. "I say we hold off!"

One of the supervisors murmurs, "Well, Barry's in charge." One of the senior-level employees states, "Yeah, we have to do what he says, don't we?" Several other employees nod.

Bud counters these comments. "Helen's idea is a good one. We should contact Chen and work with him to set up the meeting. I'm willing to support her." Another supervisor says, "Okay, me too." Two employees state in unison, "We're behind Helen."

When we ask members of both private and public organizations, "Who is the leader in this story?" almost everyone picks Helen Gitler. We agree. However, when we ask them what makes her the leader, the responses we get reveal a problem in the way people think about leadership.

People typically choose Helen because they perceive her as:.

- Decisive
- The one with a vision
- Positive and enthusiastic
- Self-confident
- Willing to listen
- Interested in learning
- The one with expertise, credibility
- Action-oriented
- Encouraging to others

These are admirable qualities and behaviors. However, are they valid reasons for labeling Helen the "leader" in this story? Do they really explain what it means to be a leader?

Consider Barry Sherman. His actions and attributes are actually very similar to Helen's. Barry also has a "vision." He wants to focus on domestic operations. He is also very decisive about the action the company should take. He behaves with a positive confidence about his view. Yet, very few select Barry as the leader.

On the other hand, Barry tries to shut Helen out, which suggests he is a poor listener. However, Helen is an equally selective listener. She interrupts Barry and responds curtly to Roger Klein. Barry can also be criticized because he did not appear receptive to learning. Yet, Helen did not display any interest in learning more about Barry's position either. Helen, it appears, does not consistently display some of the "leadership" qualities people ascribe to her.

Consider expertise. Helen's expertise about Chinese culture is used to explain her leadership abilities. Yet Barry also has substantial expertise based on his longer tenure with the organization and his specialty as the company's negotiator. His background would be important for any organization in such a chaotic situation.

The most frequently mentioned difference between Helen and Barry is that she is "action-oriented" while Barry advocates waiting. Suppose for the sake of discussion that Helen's action results in disaster. Imagine that following her advice causes even greater chaos, upsetting the organization's already unbalanced equilibrium. Furthermore, suppose that Barry's "action" (deciding to wait is a type of action) turns out to help the company dramatically. In such a scenario, Barry would be the hero and Helen the goat.

Our point in making this last distinction is that the common "bias for action" label associated with leadership is actually a bias for *successful* action. Unfortunately, the outcome of any action is never completely certain. Attributing leadership to those with an "action-orientation" does not seem to be a categorically valid descriptor of a leader.

We are, of course, playing devil's advocate regarding this story and the labels used to describe its two main characters. We do believe that Helen is a leader, and we do not believe that Barry is a leader in this situation. We will return to a discussion of Helen and Barry in Chapter 2 and offer an explanation of their roles in this story. Our real purpose in comparing Helen and Barry is to demonstrate that what makes Helen a leader is not, essentially, a function of the qualities and behaviors people usually ascribe to her.

Critical Questions

What, then, makes Helen, or anyone else, a leader? What is leadership? When and how does leadership occur? And what enables some people to become leaders?

Answers to these questions are central to understanding leadership and to describing how to lead. Today's competitive realities make those answers more important than ever. Rapid, accelerating, unrelenting change has altered the foundation of corporate enterprise and government bureaucracy. Organizations and government agencies are under tremendous pressure since they have been RRRECQD (pronounced "wrecked"). That is, *r*einventing, *r*ightsizing, *r*eengineering, *e*mpowerment, *c*ustomer- and *q*uality-*d*riven efforts have transformed the way they operate. In addition, the many forms of threat from terrorist acts - explosives, biological agents, kidnaping - cannot be effectively addressed without competent, confident, and capable leadership.

More and better leaders are essential to guide organizations in today's changing, unpredictable environment.

Efforts to understand leaders and leadership have not been completely satisfactory. The shelves of local bookstores and libraries bulge with thousands of leadership texts. Almost every one of them provides a different model or theory. Unfortunately, many leadership models contradict each other. None has achieved universal acceptance among those who aspire to lead.

We have learned a lot about leadership. However, the most fundamental order, patterns, and practices that define leadership and how to lead are still not clearly defined. No integrated explanation has been provided. To fulfill the search for leadership requires defining the valid, reliable, and generalizable "natural laws" that describe all leaders and clarify the real power of leadership.

2

The Nine Natural Laws of Leadership

"I ask, how would nature solve this? I try to think like nature to find the right questions. You don't invent the answers, you reveal the answers from nature. In nature the answers to our problems already exist."
Dr. Jonas Salk, inventor of Salk vaccine

Imagine you could simultaneously view all of the interactions within your organization. You would notice obvious patterns. Many of these patterns would be predictably consistent, occurring in the same way day after day. People arrive and leave work; they hold meetings and communicate; they produce products and provide services in recognizably repeatable ways. Some patterns occur less frequently, but they are never the less fairly stable.

Patterns of Nature

The regular patterns in any discipline represent the "laws of nature" for that field. Natural law describes the intelligence or order that occurs in the universe. Picture the motion of the planets. Think of the growth of plants. Visualize the intertwined structure of DNA. Consider nature's most primary transformations of matter into energy and energy back into matter. All these actions and events occur based on laws of nature that govern the action and direction of these processes.

The definable patterns of human interaction that occur in organizations represent their laws of nature. Understanding those laws and being able to operate in accordance with them provides greater individual and organizational effectiveness.

Of course, not all organizational activity fits into predictable formations. Some events appear chaotic. Irregularity and unpredictability infect organizational life. New competitive opportunities create uncertainty. Small changes in certain conditions can trigger wild fluctuations in activity. Consider the following examples. One person leaves a work group and suddenly the group cannot function effectively. Two senior managers with different goals initiate a battle of wills against each other which creates destructive conflict throughout the entire organization. A technological breakthrough opens up a lucrative market niche. A change in trade laws creates new possibilities for unlimited commerce.

The locus of leadership lies in the randomness, uncertainty, and opportunity inherent in these situations. Leaders provide direction and guidance through chaos. They take advantage of uncharted opportunities. Leaders help entire organizations grapple with competitive survival and pursue strategies into unknown arenas. Leaders become important when divisions or individual departments struggle to be effective and pursue dramatic improvements. Even localized irregularities require individuals to step up and take the risk of leadership. For example, when a work group goes off track or when a team is focused on meeting a new product quality initiative, someone has to step up and guide the group.

The Elusive Mystery: The Leadership Pattern

The complexity inherent in leadership has created difficulty in defining it and in describing how to lead effectively. A recognizable leadership pattern remains elusive because of the vast variety of leaders.

Consider the differences between several well-known leaders

- Lincoln's compassion versus the coldness of Lenin
- Martin Luther King, Jr.'s lofty and poetic rhetoric versus the word wrangling and sentence mangling of George W. Bush
- Mary Kay Ash's supportive, cheerleading approach as the founder of Mary Kay Cosmetics versus the tongue lashing, impatience of hotelier Leona Helmsly, known as the "Queen of Scream."

Leadership practice appears even messier because of its paradoxical reality. The same leadership approach can work in very different contexts. Yet, a leadership strategy that works in one particular situation may not work again at another time under the same conditions.

Exploring Leadership's Deeper Realities

Science resolves nature's mysteries by delving into its primary patterns. The most fundamental natural laws exist as intelligence waiting to be discovered. For example, as late as the 1920s, even Nobel Prize winners in physics firmly held that the atom was indivisible. Further investigation revealed deeper truths that allowed us to split the atom.

The discovery of more fundamental natural laws reveals more accurate descriptions of the primary sources of nature's energy and creativity. The atom is more fundamental and has greater power than the molecule, and the subatomic level is more basic and powerful than the atomic tier.

To understand and gain mastery of leadership requires uncovering its most fundamental natural laws. We must drill down to recognize the most basic and universal aspects of leadership to comprehend and apply its power most effectively.

Such natural laws of leadership add value when they meet four criteria:

1. They precisely define what it means to be a leader across the complexity and range of leadership in all contexts. The pattern represented by the laws would apply as much to a single leader and follower as to a leader of a group, organization, nation, or society.
2. They clearly differentiate leaders from non-leaders and from other organizational roles.
3. They effectively identify the common source of all leadership capability.
4. They suggest practical action ideas that provide useful choices for those who take the lead in their organizations.

The Nine Natural Laws of Leadership that we posit meet these four standards. These laws draw from the most compelling insights of many thoughtful practitioners and scholars. The laws offer a new focus regarding the meaning and practice of leadership. They build on and reinforce each other to provide an integrated portrait of leadership. Each law suggests practical ways to guide leaders in the field of action. The Field Guide section at the end of each chapter provides these practical suggestions as "action ideas." The Guide enables leaders to align themselves with each of the nine laws and increase their leadership power. The action ideas in the Field Guide do not represent absolute "right" or guaranteed ways to predict a specific result in a particular circumstance; rather they represent choices for the artful application of leadership.

The Nine Natural Laws of Leadership

The Nine Natural Laws of Leadership are:

1. A leader has willing followers.
2. "Leadership" is a field of interaction, a relationship between leaders and followers.

3. Leadership occurs as an event.
4. Leaders use influence beyond formal authority.
5. Leaders provide direction outside the boundaries of organizationally defined procedures.
6. Leadership involves risk and uncertainty.
7. Not everyone will follow a leader's initiative.
8. Consciousness - information processing capacity - creates leadership.
9. Leadership is a self-referral process. Leaders and followers process information from their own subjective, internal frame of reference.

Natural Law of Leadership 1: A Leader Has Willing Followers

What does it mean to be a leader? The first natural law of leadership answers this fundamental question: A leader has willing followers. No one can be a leader without gaining the support of others. Yet this core element of what it means to be a leader is typically overlooked.

Traditional views define a person as a "leader" because he or she has certain traits, qualities, habits, or based on the person's behaviors. However, as the comparison between Helen and Barry outlined in Chapter 1 shows, individual qualities and behaviors do not clearly differentiate leaders from non-leaders. Helen and Barry display similar attributes, yet Helen is the leader because Bud, Tony, and others willingly follow her direction. She has their commitment. Those who go along with Barry comply. They do what he says because he is "in charge" and is the "one with authority." They have to listen to him.

Having good traits, qualities, habits and behaviors makes one a "good person." Everyone should strive to be a good person. Yet, being a good person does not mean people will follow you. Followers are the underlying element that defines all leaders in all situations. The well-known individuals noted above - Lincoln, Lenin, King, Bush, Ash, and Wachner - were leaders when they gained followers as opposed to they were leaders because they had positive attributes.

Understanding the follower as a necessary ally is central to explain the complexity of leading. In 1993, both Gerald Levin and N. J. "Nick" Nicholas sought to lead Time-Warner, the company Steve Ross created by merging the publishing and film production companies. Levin prevailed because he had the willing support of Ross and the company's board of directors. Nicholas was an accomplished executive. He had talent, drive, a good track record, and many other fine qualities. But Nicholas could not get the key players at Time-Warner to follow or align themselves with him. Gaining and keeping followers-allies is the basic requirement to be a leader's.

Natural Law 2: "Leadership" is a Field of Interaction

Leaders and leadership are not the same. When people say, "We need better leadership," they typically mean, "We need a different leader." However, "leadership" represents something more than the leader alone. Leadership encompasses the leader and the follower *together*.

The second natural law of leadership reveals that the power we call "leadership" refers to the interaction of leader and follower. Followers are allies who join the leader, and together they create the energy that drives organizations. In Chapter 1, leadership occurred when Bud, Tony, and others aligned with Helen's proposed direction.

The mistaken idea that leadership power resides within a single person most frequently occurs in the case of heroic, highly visible leaders. Consider how Lee Iacocca is credited with the dramatic turnaround of Chrysler. Recall how Steve Jobs is acclaimed as the creator of Apple Computer. Think about how Gloria Steinem is hailed for the emergence of the women's movement. These individuals had dramatic impact. Yet they were only able to do so in relationship with their followers.

Typically, all glory and grandeur goes to the leader. Being a follower is usually thought of as a second-class or low status role. The second natural law of leadership changes our view of followers. It recognizes the collegial, partnering role followers play with leaders. Followers are allies who represent the necessary opposite side of the leadership coin.

Leadership is not a person, a position, or a program. Leadership is a relationship or field of interaction that occurs when the leader and the follower connect. The leadership field is an undivided wholeness that resembles a dance. Watch Fred Astaire and Ginger Rogers dance in one of their exquisite routines. The symmetry of the dance does not unfold from Fred's graceful lead alone, from Ginger's flawless following, or from the dance's spellbinding choreography. The wonder of the dance emanates from the totality of Fred-Ginger-music-movement-floor. The dance is a field - a pattern of relationship that connects all the diverse parts simultaneously.

Leadership is also a dance, the interacting ebb and flow between leader and follower. To understand the leadership field we must, as Gary Zukav advised in *The Dancing Wu Li Masters* regarding all of nature, "observe the dance." Pay attention to the interaction between leader and follower, and consider their relationship.

Natural Law 3: Leadership Occurs as an Event

People usually view leadership as continuous. They perceive it is an ongoing characteristic of a powerful person defined by a set of enduring habits, values, or standards. The common phrase "natural-born leader" reinforces the belief that leadership is a durable quality. This approach fails to appreciate that leadership exists as the leader-follower field and that these alliances are transitory.

Anyone who has struggled with the challenge of leading knows how tenuous it can be. People can lose interest in a leader's particular path. In the early 1990s, the General Motors board deposed Robert Stempel because they believed he could not steer the organization onto the right track. In 1992, Americans abandoned George H.W. Bush because they wanted change. In 2000, Al Gore got 500,000 more votes for President than George W. Bush but lost the Electoral College vote. Gore then disappeared and had virtually no impact on the political scene for years. In 2004, Howard Dean was running far in front of others who sought the Democratic nomination for President. He lost the Iowa primary and his bid for the Presidency was over. In each of these cases, followers lost interest in their former leader.

Leaders also know that their initiatives require capturing, and then recapturing, followers' commitment. Bill Clinton's 1992 election as America's political leader was followed by a repeated struggle to maintain support for his legislative efforts.

The third natural law of leadership reveals that leadership occurs as an "event." Leader-follower fields begin, have a middle, and an end. They occur as discrete interactions each time a leader and follower join (for a comprehensive description, see *The Leadership Event: The Moments of True Leadership that Transform Organizations*, Warren Blank and Aaron Brown, The Leadership Group Press, 2nd edition, 2006). Helen's leadership event described in Chapter 1 originated when Bud followed her suggestion to contact the Chinese. That specific event enlarged when Helen gained Tony as a follower. It expanded again when one of the supervisors and two of the employees joined with her. Her leadership event will exist as long as others follow Helen's lead for this particular venture.

Leadership can appear continuous if a leader manifests multiple leadership events. Some followers remain loyal to a particular leader over long periods of time and support that leader throughout a variety of circumstances. For example, Margaret Thatcher maintained a core of willing followers throughout her twelve-year tenure as British prime minister. Her political leadership ended in 1992 when John Majors gained a greater number of followers. The bulk of leadership events, however, have a shorter shelf life. They occur as brief leader-follower interactions in specific circumstances. Gaps exist between gaining followers in one circumstance and attracting them or others in another situation.

The concept of leadership as an event explains that leadership occurs throughout organizations. Numerous leaders at all levels gain followers in a variety of situations. In small group meetings that get off track, a leadership event occurs when someone gains support to redirect the group on its agenda. A leadership event happens when one person offers direction that another willingly accepts. When someone inspires an entire organization or community to support a particular direction, a leadership event occurs. When people gain followers up or down the corporate and governmental ladder, energy surges in the organization as discrete events of leadership power.

Natural Law 4: Leaders Use Influence Beyond Formal Authority

Leaders gain followers through influence; however, managers also rely on influence to get things done. The difference between the two is the *source* of the leader's influence. Consider how Helen influenced Bud and Tony to follow in Chapter 1. Helen did not force Bud to join her. She had no formal authority over Tony since they were peers in the organizational hierarchy. Bud and Tony voluntarily committed to follow Helen. In contrast, those who supported Barry clarified that his influence was based on his being "in charge."

A common belief is that being the boss makes a person a leader. Managerial influence and leadership influence are quite different. A leader's influence arises from followers' interactions with the leader. A manager's influence stems from position in the hierarchy. Leadership is person-to-person influence. Management is position-to-position (superior to subordinate) influence. Management authority is defined by the rigid lines on the organizational chart. Leadership influence occurs as a spider web of interactions that link people who want to join together. Leader-follower interactions are based on commitment. Manager-subordinate associations rely on command. The leader inspires others to want to follow or align with him or her. A manager can require staff to comply with organizationally defined demands that the manager has formal authority to rule.

Of course, managers can also don the leader's hat. Helen was a manager. Those who supported her were not obeying her formal role. Her followers willingly responded rather than merely submitted to a boss's directives. Being a leader, someone others follow, can result in selection to managerial position. This is what happens in a true democratic election. The candidate whom the public votes into office then obtains formal position power. Your candidate may not win, which means you do not want to follow the person who is duly elected. But you have to comply with the election winner because of the authority of the office.

We like to ask a simple question to determine if "the boss" is a leader: Would you *willingly* do what your boss said IF your boss did NOT have a position of formal authority and the right to command and demand compliance? Those who answer "yes" reveal how their boss is a "leader-manager." Such bosses know how to develop leader-quality relationships. Those who answer, "no," disclose that their boss has a title and position of power but does not effectively establish the kind of interaction that creates followership.

Natural Law 5: Leaders Provide Direction Outside the Boundaries of Organizationally Defined Procedures

When people and organizations need direction, they can look to a manager or person in formal power. Or, someone can step up and offer direction - take the lead - that gains willing followers. While both provide direction, leaders chart direction in a different domain than managers.

In Chapter 1, both Barry and Helen outlined a path of action for their company. Barry's approach was to "stay the course." He wanted people to stay within the established, organizationally defined plan. Helen pointed in a direction beyond the path prescribed by existing procedures. Barry's direction represents traveling along the institutionally structured track already laid down by the organization. Helen stepped forth into unstructured territory.

The fifth natural law clarifies that leaders direct action outside the prescribed lines created by organizational rules, regulations, policies, and procedures. The leader steps up when no defined path exists. A "leadership arena" exists when the institutional structure does not offer certain guidance on how to proceed. Eventually in every organization, the established path can become blocked. People might get stuck in a rut. A leader must emerge to overcome such unplanned problems. The leadership arena also defines new possibilities that may emerge that are not on the existing course. Consider Clay Chandler's report in *Fortune* about Liu Chuanzhi, Chairman of Chinese computer maker Lenovo. Chuanzhi's $3 billion dollar company had a 27% market share in China. In December 2004 Lenovo purchased IBM's PC division. Chuanzhi's goal was to take a new path and make Lenovo global so it could exploit the worldwide $200 billion dollar PC market.

A popular idea today is that "managers do things right" and "leaders do the right things." It is a catchy distinction. But how do we know the right thing except in retrospect? Since 1998, DaimlerChrysler lost $60 billion in stock market value under the direction of Chairman Jüürgen Schrempp as reported in *Fortune* by Alex Taylor III. It does not appear Schrempp has done the "right things" One thing he has been able to do is maintain his core cadre of followers. The DaimlerChrysler board remains unwavering in its support of the embattled Chairman. They even renewed his contract. Can anyone prescribe the elusive "right thing" he has to do now to lead his struggling company?

Both leaders and managers must do the right thing, and both have to do things right. They simply operate in different domains. The fifth natural law reveals that leaders emerge when people and organizations face unknown arenas that require someone to step up, take the lead, and gain willing followers. As Sun Tzu said in The Art of War, "Don't follow where the pathway goes, lead instead where there is no path and leave a trail."

Natural Law 6: Leadership Involves Risk and Uncertainty

Leaders live without a safety net. The unchartered leadership arena is fraught with ambiguity and chaos. The leader's task always involves risk and uncertainty. Operating in the nonprescribed, unstructured leadership arena demands performing action in unstable circumstances. In Chapter 1, Barry sought to avoid risk. Helen was willing to embrace it.

The practical reality of leading requires accepting that risk and uncertainty are part of the leadership territory. Taking risks may not result in success. No one can completely control the results of action. Leaders recognize that they cannot ensure specific results. They nevertheless accept risk as part of the challenge of leading. Michael Dell criticized Liu Chuanzhi's purchase of IBM. As cited in *Fortune*, Dell claims efforts to bring together large computer companies have had "ruinous results." Chuanzhi recognizes the risks. He commented, "We're determined to make possible things he (Dell) thinks are impossible." Chuanzhi goes on to note that most people thought Michael Dell's company would never be successful either.

Natural Law 7: Not Everyone Will Follow a Leader's Initiative

Leaders face limits. Perhaps the most critical limit is that not everyone will follow a leader. In the late 1940s, W. Edwards Deming recognized the need for a new approach to manufacturing. No one in America was interested in his ideas at that time. In the 1960s, the heads of IBM rejected Ross Perot's suggestion that IBM should service the software it sold. In 2005, Carly Fiorina was ousted as head of HP because the board no longer wanted to follow her lead.

No leader, not even the so-called great leaders, such as Ghandi or Lincoln, has everyone's support. Gaining followers is unpredictable. Allies can be hard to come by. Some people reject the leader's initiative. Others stall when the leader suggests a course of action. In Chapter 1, Helen did not have the support of all the people in the meeting.

Efforts to prescribe a "correct" leadership style and directives that attempt to ensure leader effectiveness have limited utility. No one has a crystal ball to foretell the future. Uncertainty is always present, especially in the uncharted leadership arena. Some people do not trust that a leader can guide them effectively. Others will not step into the risk-filled arena with anyone. To succeed requires focusing on those who will follow, gaining their support, and then moving forward.

Natural Law 8: Consciousness - Information Processing Capacity - Creates Leadership

Leadership begins with an idea that might resolve a problem or exploit an opportunity. A leader gains followers when he or she performs action that influences followers so they willingly accept the leader's direction. In effect, leader and followers become of one mind. Consciousness - the capacity to process information - is the underlying source of leadership power. The leadership dance occurs in the theater of consciousness.

Consciousness defines how people receive, interpret, and evaluate information to create meaning from it. Through consciousness, leaders turn what Margaret Wheatley, in *Leadership and the New Science*, calls the environment's raw "information-energy" into a useful direction. Leaders gain followers when both parties process information in similar ways. The mechanics of the process begin within the leader.

The leader's consciousness perceives the non-prescribed, uncharted leadership arena. Leaders recognize opportunities and become aware of obstacles that others do not or cannot perceive. For example, in 1977 Larry Ellison, CEO and cofounder of the software company Oracle, was intrigued by an IBM research publication on relational database management that allowed users to analyze information in any way they wanted rather than along rigidly defined, predetermined lines. Recognizing the boon provided by this flexibility, Ellison and Oracle cofounder Bob Miner wrote and marketed a relational database program three years ahead of IBM. Ellison also adapted the Oracle version to run on mainframes and smaller computers made by any manufacturer. IBM's version ran only on its more costly equipment. Oracle became an attractive alternative for those seeking lower-cost data management. By 1994, Oracle had $1.6 billion in annual sales, making it the top corporate database producer. According to Alan Deutschman in *Fortune*, Oracle held a 34 percent to 26 percent market share edge over IBM,

Simply stated, leaders think differently from non-leaders. Leaders integrate information that is sometimes unrelated into new, more useful combinations that offer solutions and provide direction. In Chapter 1, Helen interpreted her company's chaotic situation as a time to move ahead. Barry processed information in terms of the prescribed boundaries of the organization's existing course of action. His direction gave expression to a path already defined by the organization. His idea was not necessarily wrong. Rather, it did not represent a leader's path: an insight into the non-prescribed leadership arena.

A leader must influence followers to recognize his or her direction as useful. Leaders connect with followers when followers go "on-line" with the leader's level of consciousness. Helen's interpretation resonated with Tony and Bud. So they supported her lead. Their consciousness moved with hers. The leader-follower field is a bond or interaction of consciousness. The shared field represents collective consciousness in action awareness, united by an idea about how to solve a problem or exploit a possibility.

Consider the importance of consciousness in terms of Kenneth Labich's conclusions regarding the most common reasons companies fail. Labich reveals that companies blunder because of the limited consciousness of those who should be providing direction. He explains in *Fortune* that companies fail because:

- People do not effectively process information regarding the fundamentals of an industry or business managers do not understand key profitability drivers.
- People do not ask key questions about an organization's core expertise - managers are clueless about what made their organizations successful in the first place.
- People do not perceive and overcome potential obstacles - managers suffer from short attention spans.
- People rely on established premises that do not match current reality - managers cannot see the need to move beyond what worked in the past.
- Organizations fail because people do not understand their most important customer needs, nor do they understand why their customers defect to competitors -managers fail to install a formal system for distilling and interpreting information from the field.

Take Sears, once America's retail giant, which has fallen far behind Wal-Mart as the top retailer. Sears stumbled because its managers ignored important and obvious signals from its environment. Well into the 1980s, Sears's competitive strategic analyses did not even include mention of Wal-Mart as a competitive threat despite Wal-Mart's huge success. The unwillingness or inability to process that information strangled Sears's market competitiveness.

Leaders also misfire when they cannot change their followers' consciousness and gain their commitment to the leader's direction. The leader's source of power, influence beyond authority, occurs on the level of consciousness. In the early 1990s, John Akers was deposed as head of IBM. He could not convince others that the solution to Big Blue's problems was to break it up into several "Baby Blues." IBM's board of directors did not buy it. The breakup plan was scrapped soon after Akers was replaced. Akers could not enlighten the board to his way of thinking. They pushed Akers aside.

In a larger sense, leaders either shape the followers' consciousness or leaders can do no more than mirror the people's consciousness. Typically, we view leaders in the driver's seat, steering their organizations with a sure and steady hand. But leaders can attract only followers who are on a similar wavelength of awareness. Leaders must meet the follower at the follower's level of consciousness before they can lead the follower to a new level.

The leader as one who shapes and mirrors consciousness clarifies the paradoxes inherent in leadership. People want leaders to guide them forward toward new and better results. They also expect leaders to take them where the people want to go. People look to leaders for direction. And, some people are unwilling to follow leaders because the leader does not meet the people's needs. In essence, a leader's course of action stretches people beyond boundaries. Yet, leaders must also calibrate their actions to fit the people's consciousness. In the final analysis, leaders reflect their followers, and followers get the leaders they deserve.

The failure to address the role of consciousness in leadership is perhaps the most glaring weakness in existing leadership theory and prescription. Typically, books on leadership explore only the outward manifestation of consciousness, such as the actions and the attributes the leader displays. Only a few include a discussion of consciousness or even a reference to consciousness. Among these books are Peter Vaill's *Managing as a Performing Art*, Peter Senge's *The Fifth Discipline*, and Margaret Wheatley's *Leadership and the New Science*. In Renesch's edited collection, *New Traditions in Business*, the chapter by Michael Ray explains the importance of consciousness. A full understanding of leadership requires awareness of how information processing creates the leadership field. This brings us to the last leadership law.

Natural Law 9: Leadership Is a Self-Referral Process

Consciousness is how people process information. Self-referral defines the "who" that processes the information. Leaders and followers process information from their own subjective, internal "self-referral identity," or frame of reference

Knowledge, intelligence, experience, judgment, and wisdom are structured in the subjective state of one's consciousness, just as the structure of a computer software program defines how it processes information. But human consciousness transcends computing. It is knowing you are computing. The "knower" is the self, the inner identity who does the computing. The "self" that processes information determines our reality.

Self-referral explains that the world is as we are. Our subjective state of consciousness creates our reality. Leaders interpret and respond to problems and possibilities in a manner consistent with their states of consciousness. For example, consider the differences in the massive social programs of Lyndon Baines Johnson's Great Society and Ronald Reagan's anti-big government agenda. Compare the nonviolence of Ghandi with the cruelty of Hitler. And recall Alice Paul's fight for women's voting rights versus turn-of-the-century President Grover Cleveland's statement, "Sensible and responsible women do not want to vote." Every leader sees the world through his or her specific lenses. Similarly, followers identify with the leader because the leader fits the followers' self-referral image of what a leader should be. Followers accept a leader's course of action because they have self-referral with the direction.

In Chapter 1, Helen had self-referral with the China venture. Her inner self, the structure of her subjective consciousness, interpreted the situation in a way that urged her to take action to maintain the deal. Bud's comment, "I think you're right, Helen," and Tony's remark, "I agree with Helen," demonstrated their self-referral with Helen and her ideas. From their level of consciousness, Helen made sense. Barry, in contrast, had little self-referral with the China operation. He could not identify with Helen or with her direction. When challenged by Tony, Barry could not "see the logic" behind Helen's idea.

Leaders fail to gain followers when they do not meet the followers at their level of consciousness. For example, a manager for a wholesale food distributor proposed several customer service and team development efforts to improve her work group's lagging effectiveness. Members of the group commented, "This isn't of any value to us," "The problem lies elsewhere," and "She doesn't understand what's going on." The manager had not established the connection with their level of consciousness that was necessary for her to influence them to follow.

The self-referral concept is central to understanding and practicing leadership. Most leadership models attempt to define objective determinants to describe leaders. Such models imply that leadership exists as an entity separate from the leader and the followers' subjective point of view. Self-referral clarifies that leadership exists within the consciousness of the leader and the followers.

Self-referral also explains why divisive and destructive leadership fields occur. Some leaders function from a less evolved, restricted, or even violent state of consciousness. The horrors wrought by Adolph Hitler, Joseph Stalin, Jim Jones, David Koresh, and Osama bin Laden reveal their self-referral interpretation of reality. Followers who support destructive leaders operate from a similar state of consciousness. Negative fields of collective consciousness exist because of a narrowly defined self. Harmful actions reveal a self-referral identity structured in terms of harmful beliefs, values, and judgments.

Self-referral reveals the first and foremost directive to develop proactive, positive, life-supporting leadership power. Leaders have to expand their consciousness. What else but a lack of consciousness can explain the behavior of FEMA Chief

Michael Brown after hurricane Katrina ravaged the Gulf Coast in 2005. Two days after the Katrina left her destructive wake, Brown, in response to a message from a FEMA employee located in New Orleans, said, "Thanks for the update. Anything I need to do or tweak?"

Limited awareness results in ineffective perception of even obvious problems. Effective leaders operate from a more unified, enlightened state. They transcend the boundaries that limit or prejudicially distort perception. The expansion of consciousness shifts leaders from seeing themselves in the world to seeing the world in themselves.

The laws of nature are not necessarily benevolent; hurricanes, floods, earthquakes, and disease are part of natural law, and they can be destructive. Similarly, the nine natural laws describe both life-supporting leaders and destructive ones. To realize benefit from aligning with and mastering the natural laws of leadership requires creating more and better life-supporting leaders and limiting the emergence of harmful leaders. The Nine Natural Laws of Leadership provide a means to achieve this end because they are based on a paradigm that allows us to prescribe more enlightened leadership practice.

FIELD GUIDE 1

Action Idea 1.1: Focus on gaining followers.

When you choose to take initiative on a particular task, ask yourself, "Who do I need to follow me or align themselves with me?" or "Whose support is necessary?" Then concentrate on gaining the backing of these people by using Action Idea 1.2.

Action Idea 1.2: Build solid work relationships with others.

The quality of relationships you have with others is central to leadership. Others are more likely to follow when you step forward to lead if they know you and trust you. Building solid work relationships is an ongoing activity. Chapter 11 provides more information and action ideas on how to build leader-quality relationships.

Action Idea 1.3: Concentrate on the leadership event.

Accept the variable duration and scope of your ability to gain followers. Take initiative when action is needed to gain followers-allies. Create the field when necessary. Share leadership power by reinforcing others as willing followers-allies.

Action Idea 1.4: Develop influence beyond authority.

Take on tasks relevant to the organization's core mission. Gain access to critical information networks (knowledge is power) and mentor other people; develop task expertise, attend training or formal education programs, and support others' work projects. All of these actions will increase your ability to influence people. Chapters 8, 9, and 10 provide more information and action ideas on how to enhance influence beyond authority.

Action Idea 1.5: Fix your sights on nonprescribed areas.

Look for opportunities and seek ways to resolve problems beyond your job description and outside the prescribed organizational boundaries set by rules, regulations, policies, and procedures. Pay attention to projects or responsibilities that are not fully defined and have few established requirements. Focus on what is not working. Ask questions to identify possibilities and challenge assumptions. Ask yourself each day: "What more can I do to move the organization forward?"

Action Idea 1.6: Embrace risk and uncertainty as a challenge.

Risk is an interpretation. View risk as a challenge, just as you might be energized to solve a knotty mathematical problem, succeed in a difficult negotiation, or perform well in a tough tennis match. Transform the tension created by uncertainty into the productive energy needed to take action. Use the adrenaline that typically flows during risky times as power that transforms anxiety into action. Then enjoy the action without being attached to the unpredictable fruits of action.

Action Idea 1.7: Attend to those who will follow.

Since not everyone will always follow, focus on those who will support your lead. Pay attention to those who acknowledge your lead as useful. Give consideration to anyone who offers you positive support. Align with the critical followers by asking yourself, "Who must I get to follow me to achieve this initiative?" A few key allies can bring success to your initiative. Seek them out, but remember that sometimes no one will follow. The reasons are explained by leadership laws 8 and 9. Apply Action Ideas 1.8 and 1.9 to minimize not gaining followers.

Action Idea 1.8 : Clarify expectations.

Expectations reveal one filter people use to interpret reality. What we expect is what we get. To lead requires continually exploring what matters to others, how they interpret events, and the meaning they assign to a situation. To discover the self-referral identity people use to define their world, hold meetings in which expectations are clarified. Ask participants, "What do you expect from. . . ? "What is important to you about. . . ?"The answers will help you meet the followers at their level of consciousness. Clarify your expectations to make it easier for others to understand and accept your position. The potential to manifest the leadership field increases when leaders understand the follower's self-referral frame of reference.

Action Idea 1.9: Develop greater self-awareness.

Greater self-awareness means knowing the strengths and limitations of your consciousness. Become aware of how you restrict or overload your information reception process. Explore the assumptions and judgments you make when you interpret information. Are your assumptions based on information or derived from what you suppose exists? Do your judgments represent old mental programs, or are they formed through a dialectic learning process of thesis-antithesis-synthesis? Think about how you respond to information. Are you overly cautious and unwilling to commit to action? Do you move to the other extreme and act without thinking? Do you balance analytical analysis with intuitive insight? Continually update your information base. Explore alternate ways to interpret data. Use different models to evaluate ideas.

3

The Quantum Leadership Paradigm

"A paradigm shift is like a boat, you don't want to miss it."
John Huey, Fortune magazine writer

I boarded the plane at Washington National Airport, took a book out of my briefcase, and began to read. The woman in the seat next to me glanced at the book and asked, "Are you a physicist?"

"No," I answered.

"But that's a physics book, isn't it?" she persisted.

"Yes," I began to explain, but she immediately broke in, "Do you work in an R&D lab?"

"No," I replied."

Then you must be helping one of your kids with a science project," she said.

I paused for a moment to get her attention and said, "Actually, I provide leadership consulting and training programs. I'm reading this book to help me understand the laws of leadership."

Her inquisitive expression turned into a puzzled look. "What," she asked incredulously, "does physics have to do with leadership?"

The Physics of Leadership

Most people do not recognize a connection between physics and leadership. The knowledge of physics seems far removed from the challenges and demands of organizational life. Stories of leaders - both the heroes who satisfy and the villains who disappoint - fascinate us. Yet, images of atoms and Einstein often just bewilder us.

Leadership and physics do share a common focus. Physics explains the energy, matter, and motion that define how the universe works. In the same way, leadership is the power that galvanizes human energy and translates it into action. So the exercise of leadership can be viewed as the practice of human physics.

Leadership today is typically understood in terms of the seventeenth century physics paradigm developed by Sir Isaac Newton and known as classical physics. Newton physics proposed laws that he believed were the "ironclad" descriptors of nature. His assumption, which the world accepted as true, was that classical physics was the final and complete word about how certain elements of the universe worked. Newton's paradigm was revolutionary for its time. It stood for over 200 years as a complete model of the universe.

At the beginning of the twentieth century, a new paradigm, known as quantum physics, revealed a more fundamental reality of nature. Quantum physics revealed that the classical physics paradigm offers only a partial view of nature's order. Quantum physics shattered the idea that the Newtonian worldview was the final word on natural law. Quantum physics revealed a more primary power of nature. It explained events that were beyond the scope of Newton's paradigm. Classical physics still offers a "correct" view of certain aspects of nature. Quantum physics describes deeper layers of natural law.

The assumptions that define Newton's paradigm of reality are the basis for most leadership definitions, theories, and models. Furthermore, the classical physics assumptions have limited a full and complete understanding of leadership. Quantum physics is based on a set of assumptions that provide a platform to explain the meaning of leadership more clearly and to more effectively describe how to lead. A shift to a quantum view of leadership also offers a way to develop more life-supporting, enlightened leadership.

The Shift to Quantum Leadership

Toward the end of our flight, my inquisitive seat mate again asked if she really had to understand physics to grasp the full meaning of leadership. I explained that from one point of view, she did not. We do not have to understand the force of gravity to avoid spinning off the planet. We do not need to know about DNA in order to get to work each day.

Yet, by understanding the basic assumptions of physics that underlie our view of leadership, we will have a clearer insight into the leader's complex task. By embracing a quantum view, people can harness more leadership power and direct that power in more positive directions.

The Nine Natural Laws of Leadership are based on the quantum physics paradigm assumptions. They reveal that leadership is better understood and practiced as a quantum phenomenon. The nine laws provide a new view of leadership, the Quantum Leadership paradigm. Quantum Leadership expands the potentiality for more and better leadership at all levels.

Two Views of Leadership

The Quantum Leadership paradigm differs from the classical physics view in terms of five critical assumptions, as shown in Table 3. 1. The Quantum Paradigm provides a language and a framework for more clearly understanding and more fully describing leadership practice than the approach offered through Newton's world view. The rest of this chapter presents the Quantum Leadership paradigm by describing these five assumptions. The chapter explains how the quantum view of leadership enables us to harness the full power of leadership and use that power in a more enlightened way.

Table 3.1
Classical Physics vs. Quantum Physics Views of Leadership

Classical Physics View of Leadership	Quantum Physics View of Leadership
1. Leadership is its parts. 2. Leadership is a continuous attribute of a person. 3. Leadership influence is based on force. 4. Leadership conforms to cause-and-effect logic. 5. Leadership is an objective phenomenon.	1. Leadership is a field. 2. Leadership is a discontinuous event. 3. Leadership influence is an interaction. 4. Leadership is unstructured and unpredictable. 5. Leadership is a subjective phenomenon

Leadership Parts vs. the Leadership Field

Several years ago, a middle manager from a large petroleum company asked me if I had read Ken Follett's *On the Wings of Eagles*. The book offers a crackling account of the rescue in 1978 of two EDS executives from a heavily guarded fortress in Iran by a group of hand-picked EDS volunteers trained by a retired Green Beret lieutenant colonel. The petroleum manager reverently recounted Follett's description of Ross Perot, the head of EDS. He cited Perot's exceptional character traits such as boldness, active response to crisis, and strength of will. The manager then shook his head knowingly and proclaimed, "Now that's leadership!"

Such views reflect a widespread, but inaccurate, assumption about leadership derived from the classical physics paradigm. I agreed that Perot's actions were admirable. I also explained that individual attributes or behaviors do not provide an accurate definition of a "true leader."

Leadership is Not the Parts

The traditional assumption about leadership is that it can be explained by describing the parts: the habits, characteristics, and behaviors of single individuals. According to this perspective, leadership becomes the decisive force of GE's CEO Jack Welch, the intuitive genius of Microsoft's Bill Gates, the commanding presence of General Norman Schwarzkopf, or the compassionate patience of Mother Teresa.

The parts view stems from the impact of Newton's paradigm on our leadership mind-set. Newton described reality as made up of separate, solid bits of matter. He proclaimed that, to understand reality, you must examine its distinct, visible building blocks.

Through this lens, it makes sense to examine individual attributes or qualities of certain leaders and then develop lists of specific "leadership" traits or habits. Taking Newton's view that the parts define reality, a leader is defined based on a composite of an individual's personal qualities. Similarly, the notion of "leadership" is represented by a single individual.

This approach does not fit a fundamental reality: **Leaders do not exist without followers**. Individual characteristics or habits are relevant only as part of the leader-follower field of interaction. The leader alone does not fully describe the dynamics of leadership.

Leadership is a Field

Leadership is better understood as a field of interaction. It is not so much personal as it is interpersonal. Quantum physics asserts that to know nature, you must view it as a set of interconnected fields. At the deeper layers of natural law, no separate parts exist. From the quantum view, nothing that resembles visible, solid matter can be seen. The field is the fundamental reality, an undivided wholeness of information-energy.

Through the quantum lens it appears that you are looking through a porthole that frames only the ocean. You cannot distinguish any waves or droplets of water as separate and distinct from the ocean. You see only the homogeneous oneness of the field. As Danah Zohar explains in *The Quantum Self*, the integral reality of a quantum field compares to the many voices of a choir that merge into one.

Through the quantum lens we recognize leadership as a field. Those who initiate an action become “true leaders” only when someone follows (the first natural law of leadership). A person’s individual characteristics and behaviors have meaning only in relationship with others. For example, Jack Welch transformed GE partly through his hard-nosed decisions such as massive employee layoffs and the sale of several of GE’s business units. These actions earned him the label “neutron Jack.” But tough-mindedness did not make him a leader. Rather, it was that people followed him. Welch’s rigorous standard setting could have been rejected by personnel at GE and his actions stymied. He would not have been labeled “manager of the decade” by *Fortune* without support - willing followers - for his decisions.

The field reality of leadership may seem abstract and distant from our ordinary experience. However, we do recognize the field reality of organizations. Walk into any organization and notice the pervasive “look and feel” of the place. Observe the purposeful and ordered interactions between the workers and their tasks. You are witness to an organization’s “culture:” the nonmaterial, invisible field of shared beliefs and assumptions that define “the way it is” within a company. The patterns of behavior, the physical layout, the artifacts on the walls, and the configuration of materials on desks make up the culture’s observable effect. The culture exists as a nonmaterial field of regularities that underlie surface appearances.

Quantum Leadership focuses attention on the interaction, not the separate parts, as the key to understanding leadership. A central interaction is the leader-follower relationship (the second natural law of leadership). Thus, “leadership” at Microsoft is not Bill Gates’s innovativeness but the unity or connection between Gates and his people.

Field-conscious Quantum Leaders seek ways to draw the creative intelligence of individuals together. They strive to unite it and increase its power to play out success in their organizations. Reverend Jesse Jackson offered a succinct description of the leadership field reality when he commented that leaders do not choose sides but rather bring sides together.

Field-conscious Quantum Leaders continually build bridges and establish common ground so that others become more receptive to their leadership initiatives. These leaders focus on the allies they need in specific circumstances. They "lead" when they gain support for a department-level project, acquire commitment for a citywide initiative, get backing for an organization-wide restructuring effort from key constituents, or secure sponsorship for a three-person committee. Support, commitment, backing, sponsorship describe the quality of interaction that is the leadership fields. Quantum Leaders draw followers to them and align them in a coherent direction.

Ronald Reagan proved to be a master of this process. Upon assuming the presidency in 1980, he and his wife held small, intimate dinner parties in the White House. He invited members of Congress, the press, and various other powerful people. These dinners were not about politics or the global, national, or even local issues of the day. Reagan did not direct the table talk to economic, social, or political matters. Rather, he and Nancy Reagan told stories of their life together. They charmed their guests with revealing personal details about what they thought and how they felt. The Reagans eagerly inquired about their guests, attended closely to their disclosures, and cheered and encouraged their stories. Reagan used these dinner parties to build a base of relationships, labeled by some as "networking" and by others as "bonding." Quantum Leaders realize they must establish the mutual trust and confidence that enhances the possibility of gaining willing followers.

Failure to comprehend the importance of the field can restrict business success. Consider the Fortune magazine story about Steve Job's bumpy ride with his touch-feely iPhone. According to the article's author Brent Schlender, over 1.5 million iPhones sold in the first five months after its introduction into the marketplace. This number far exceeded Job's initial sales goals. Yet, a lack of attention to various "field" realities have inhibited the iPhone ringing in greater revenues. Schlender attributes this to a lack of understanding of the complexities involved in selling phones as compared to selling PC's. For example, Jobs formed an exclusive link with AT&T wireless network. However, AT&T's wireless coverage is sluggish and spotty. That drove about 20% of iPhone customers to hack into another network. Apple's revenues suffer because it is estimated that they get a sizeable cut of AT&T's monthly service charge. Similarly, Jobs disallowed outsiders from writing programs for use on the iPhone when it first came out. This irked customers who commonly use third-party applications on handheld devices. Jobs also offered a 33% price reduction on the gadget just two months after it came to market. Many initial higher paying customers wanted to hang up the iPhone because of this abrupt price change. Schlender acknowledges that the iPhone is a fantastic device. Jobs' initial success might have been even greater had more attention been given to the larger field of issues that impact this very smart phone.

Quantum Leadership recognizes that the leader and the follower contribute to leadership. Both are necessary participants. Organizations that reward leaders and followers reinforce and expand the role both play in creating the power that drives organizations. The field view expands leadership power.

Quantum Leadership truly empowers people. A leader is empowered by recognizing that he or she influences the quality of interaction with followers. Willing followers are not second-class citizens. They are not passive like sheep who flock to the shepherd's call. Rather, they are empowered by the recognition that they fuel the leader's fire. Followers enable leaders when they support the leader's initiative.

Thinking of leadership as a field provides everyone with a mind-set to respond effectively to the ever-increasing diversity within organizations. Quantum Leadership acknowledges that leaders cannot perceive themselves as separate from others. Rather than dismiss the diverse needs and interests of others, field-conscious leaders recognize the need to build a common ground to unite with needed followers.

Leadership Continuity vs. Leadership Discontinuity

Consider the stories about several well-known individuals. Lee Iacocca led Chrysler out of debt. Gloria Steinem guided the modern women's movement to prominence. Steve Jobs harvested Apple into a golden business. Bill Gore fashioned Gore-Tex into a billion-dollar products company. Frances Hesselbein revitalized the Girl Scouts of America. Meg Whitman energized e-bay into an on-line powerhouse.

I label these people "high-visibility media leaders" because of the frequent portrayals of their larger-than-life personas in news stories, books, and on television. Certainly these individuals deserve credit for their numerous, impactful leadership actions. Their stories also fuel a mistaken belief about leadership as a continuous attribute or action.

Leadership is Not a Continuous Attribute

Newton's paradigm suggests that leadership is a continuous phenomenon. Newton's laws describe action as a seamless flow. For example, when a ball rolls down a hill, you can observe the ball at every point. This continuous model describes the reality of solid matter quite well, but it fails to describe leadership.

Consider how some people gain followers only for a short time and only once in a while. Recall some recent meetings in your own organization. Can you remember how one person emerged to gain willing followers for a specific idea, and then another person stepped forward to further that initiative or take a different tack? Did perhaps then a third person step up and take the lead? A meeting chairperson's position might remain continuous, but several different people often rise to take the lead. The leadership mantle frequently moves around the room as different leaders gain followers.

Thinking of leadership as a continuous attribute masks the reality that all leaders, even the so-called great leaders, do not permanently maintain followers. Consider the roller-coaster leadership career of Lee Iacocca. Iacocca ascended to the presidency of Ford, was fired abruptly, and then reemerged to guide Chrysler to success. Recall how Steve Jobs blossomed with Apple and then bombed with NeXT. Remember how Cisco CEO John Chambers was dubbed "best manager in America" by *Fortune* in 1999. In 2001, Cisco stock dropped 65% and many felt the CEO was headed for the chamber of horrors. By July 2004, Chambers had come roaring back. Cisco was the best-performing major high-tech stock for the next two years. Iacocca, Jobs, Chambers and all other prominent leaders have periods when they cannot continue to attract followers.

Leadership is a Discontinuous Event

Leadership is better understood as a discontinuous reality. Leaders and followers connect as an event (the third natural law of leadership). The connection can manifest itself over various time spans.

Discontinuity is a quantum phenomenon. Quantum physics explains that discrete units of energy (the word quanta means "packets of energy") pop up in one place and then in another without going through the space in between. To grasp this rather illogical reality, picture a "quantum ball" about to fall from the top step of a stairway. The unique action of the quantum ball, says Amit Goswami in *The Self-Aware Universe*, has it on one step, then appearing on the next step without traversing the space in between. Such "quantum jumps" sound fantastic, but such activity precisely describes reality in the quantum realm.

Leadership is discontinuous. The field exists only as long as leaders have followers. Breaks exist between leadership events just as a motion picture is made up of separate frames and just as spaces exist between the letters in words such as:

l | e | a | d | e | r | s | h | i | p

A leader who frequently and consistently attracts followers gives the appearance of leadership continuity. However, as the up-and-down experience of Iacocca, Jobs, Chambers, and many others shows, leadership fields are tenuous. Followers join with a leader and then break off. Perhaps they rejoin the leader later. Or, they may never commit to the leader again.

Because leadership is discontinuous, anyone can manifest a leadership event in the everyday activity of organizational life. Quantum discontinuity clarifies that leadership is not restricted to a select few high-visibility types. The leadership mantle can jump from one person to another as various leader-follower connections occur in the day-to-day, hour-to-hour, and minute-to-minute activities that form the foundation of most people's experience throughout organizations.

Focusing on the few high-profile individuals who continuously gain followers limits the concept of leadership. The assumption that high-visibility leaders represent the primary domain of leadership action intimidates people. Few can imitate the grand feats accomplished by those who function at the highest levels of government, business, or social systems. Their experience is out of reach for most people. After all, how many people become president of a major corporation, serve at the head of a national government, lead a massive social or religious movement, direct armies in significant battles, or ascend to other highly visible positions?

The concept of discontinuous leadership action helps today's streamlined organizations that focus on empowerment. Multiple leadership events need to occur in the deep fabric of organizational life. Consider one-on-one interactions on the shop floor, conversations held in open office spaces, small-group conferences. When there is a need, people must take the lead at this level as well as in department-wide meetings, top-floor sessions of corporate boards, and high-level meetings of heads of state. Whether people toil on the loading dock or spend their time in the boardroom, knowing they can create a leadership event if only for a day, an hour, or a moment empowers them, and it adds to the organization's sum total of leadership (see *The Leadership Event: The Moments of True Leadership that Transform Organizations*, 2nd edition, for a more thorough description).

Leadership Influence as a Force vs. an Interaction

Leadership creates the energy that moves an organization. The philosopher Bertrand Russell noted that "the fundamental concept in social science is power, in the same sense in which energy is the fundamental concept in physics." Power, as the capacity to influence, is the currency leaders use to influence others.

Leadership Influence in Not Based on Force

Leaders are typically portrayed as captains of industry and heads of state who can wield the power of the purse or enforce their will through military might or command people to carry out their dictates. In organizations, people commonly view their bosses or managers as leaders because of the formal authority of the position. Being a boss or a manager does not make someone a leader. We have all known bosses who could not lead us to the water fountain even if we needed a drink.

Influence as force derives from the classical physics perspective of a world made of visible, measurable matter. Classical physics describes nature's forces as propelling things through space by overcoming other inhibiting forces, such as inertia and friction. This kind of influence is an energy-exhausting process. Matter wears out. It gets tired and loses its structure. In the same way, managers who rely on the force of formal authority experience a physical and emotional drain. Force-driven managers constantly work against the drag of opposing forces in the form of political battles over "turf." They struggle with complaints from subordinates that "it's not my job." Force-guided actions result in blocking tactics such as "we've never done it that way before."

Leadership Influence is an Interaction

Leadership fields occur through shared commitment, not force. Shared commitment occurs because of the quality of the interaction between leaders and followers.

At the quantum level, influence results from interactions. The mere association of information-energy transforms the energy and creates unlimited possibilities. The self-interacting dynamics of the quantum field translate potentialities into actualities. As a medium of interaction, the power of the field resides in its relational qualities, its interconnectedness.

Quantum Leadership indicates that a leader's influence does not depend upon force. Leader influence dwells in what Margaret Wheatley, in her book *Leadership and the New Science*, calls a "medium of connection." Leaders gain followers through influence based on interactions beyond formal authority (the fourth natural law of leadership). They foster trust, care, concern, and mutual respect, so they attract followers. No one can force others to follow willingly.

Leadership fields represent an interaction of human information-energy: an invisible reality or spatial geometry of motivation to work together. Leadership influence resembles laser light. Such light occurs when separate light beams are transformed into a coherent interaction pattern of multiple light waves. Coherent laser light can cut through the hardest materials. The extraordinary impact of leadership occurs because leadership influence represents a powerful bond of human interaction.

The fact that we do not always look at leadership influence as interaction provides one explanation why we lack leaders. Many presume they need formal authority to lead. We often hear comments such as, "I don't have the authority to do that," or, "I have to get approval before I can do anything." Quantum Leadership directs people to go beyond formal authority. It guides them to create the real power of leadership by developing the necessary quality of interaction that attracts others to follow.

Influence as interaction also shows us how to lead in the era of the revolutionary change we face today. Consider the simultaneous dramatic impact of economic globalization, organizational reengineering, information technology, and workforce diversification. These actions strain the utility of formal authority as the way to get things done. Frequent, rapid change destroys the legitimacy of prescribed stations of power. As people cut across national borders and create new processes to accomplish work, position-to-position influence impedes progress. When anyone can access information instantly and almost everyone works with diverse others, dictates like "Do it my way or else!" have little weight. Person-to-person influence, the basis of Quantum Leader impact, becomes paramount as traditional hierarchies of authority break down.

The rise of self-directed work teams also limits the validity of formal authority as a source of success. The key question of who leads when no one is in charge can be answered by recognizing that "being in charge" does not confer leadership. Those who succeed in transformational times will develop influence beyond authority as the basis of their impact on organizations.

Leadership influence as interaction also defines how leaders master the locus of their power. Quantum Leaders interact with their environment to determine a course of action. They interact with followers to attract their support. They interact with their consciousness, their "inner selves," to define their intentions, focus of attention, choices, and the direction of their initiative.

Leadership as Cause and Effect vs. Unpredictability

In 1994, the American Management Association found that 66 percent of companies that downsized reported no increases in productivity, and 55 percent of downsized companies had no gains in operating profits. Furthermore, 80 percent of the downsized companies surveyed admitted that the employees who remained were suffering from low morale.

I imagine that in each case, someone in these rightsized organizations used cause-and-effect logic to demonstrate how personnel cutbacks would boost profits and productivity. Predictability and certainty create a sense of stability and security. Most efforts to rationalize work, to define procedures, and to "get organized" are based on the belief that these actions will bring about successful results.

Cause-and-Effect Logic Does Not Describe Leadership

Newton perceived reality as a great ticking clock set in unceasing, predictable motion and propelled by deterministic forces. Central to his worldview is the assumption that events occur because of cause and effect. Newton saw the world as guided by predictable, deterministic forces that govern the action of matter. For example, if you roll a billiard ball to your left, it moves in a predictable line. If it collides with other billiard balls, specific and measurable forces determine their paths and the speed of all resulting motion. However, cause-and-effect thinking restricts people's ability to change. It creates the belief that an approach or strategy that worked well in the past will work again. To operate successfully in the leadership arena, we must transcend the limits of the clockworks, linear cause-and-effect reality.

Leadership Involves Unpredictability

Leaders operate in a messy world. The Quantum Leadership paradigm accounts for the unpredictable, uncertain, nondeterministic reality of leadership. In the quantum world, packets of energy or quanta fluctuate in odd ways. They leap from one place to another with no certainty about where or when they will make the jump. They do not obey the linear logic of Newton's reality.

Quantum fields are not subject to deterministic laws of force or pressure. You cannot predict a field's specific behavior, regardless of how much you know about it. Yet the quantum domain is not random chaos. Interactions occur in globally recognizable patterns. Although localized action does not repeat along exactly the same paths, a degree of coherence exists. As in a gambling casino, probabilities govern the patterns of quantum action.

Quantum Leadership shows us that leaders operate in an uncharted arena outside the predictable lines defined by deterministic rules and standard operating procedures (the fifth natural law of leadership). Leaders offer direction when people do not know how to solve problems. Leaders plot action steps when people fail to recognize or do not know how to exploit opportunities. The leadership arena is, by definition, an unstructured theater of uncertainties.

The unpredictability of the quantum casino means that risk is ever-present in life. Likewise, leadership always involves taking a "risk of initiative" (the sixth natural law of leadership). The "correctness" of any voyage into the risk and uncertainty of the leadership arena is always unclear. The probability that the leader will identify a successful path depends on his or her interaction with the environment. The probability that he or she can influence and gain the commitment of followers depends on their interaction. Some may follow, and others may not (the seventh natural law of leadership).

The unpredictability and risk that attach to leadership explains why some organizations experience a leadership vacuum. A desire for certainty creates a focus on establishing fail-safe mechanisms such as rigid rules and regulations and manuals full of fixed procedures and policies. Since the leadership arena cannot be controlled using this approach, people shy away. Simply put, most people are unwilling to take reasonable risks.

But in an era of change, uncertainty abounds. No one can escape the perilous impact of revolutionary change. Leaders accept risk and uncertainty as part of the territory. They adopt a mind-set of paying careful attention to their surroundings. They continuously fine-tune their discrimination about choices. And then leaders act. Their intention to lead drives them to take reasonable risks.

Quantum Leadership transcends a fail-safe approach in favor of the belief that it is safe to fail. Quantum Leadership accepts the unpredictability of leadership and shuns cookbook suggestions about how to lead. Quantum Leadership provides choices for action, not prescriptions, and follows through with a clear strategy and actionable tasks.

Leadership as Objective vs. Subjective

Leadership unpredictability does not mean that you throw the dice or spin the roulette wheel and simply hope. In the quantum casino, leaders have an ace up their sleeve. The ace has a subjective face. The structure of that face is based in consciousness or how information is processed.

Leadership is Not Objective

Most approaches to leadership emerge from the assumption of an objective reality where the observer stands separate from the observed. Newton's physics suggests that the predictable world of matter exists "out there." He believed that the world was independent of interference by your scrutiny. He perceived humans as passive witnesses to an objective and material reality acted upon by propelling and restraining forces.

The belief that leadership is an objective reality results in efforts to define traits, behaviors, habits, and attributes as supposed indicators of a "real leader." Prescriptions for "effective" leadership attempt to define impartial standards that are supposed to exist. However, the objective approach does not apply to leadership. Consider how two politicians can explain the same situation in totally different ways, and how two voters can respond to the same politician in completely opposite ways. Note how two business managers might use the same data to evaluate a problem and come up with diametrically opposed solutions.

Leadership is Subjective

Leadership is a subjective reality based in the consciousness of the leader and his or her followers. For example, an air force base was experiencing the shock waves of change caused by its uncertain role after the end of the cold war, the impending reductions in forces, and the tightening squeeze of funding cutbacks. In one meeting, the participants got into a heated argument about whether the base general was a "leader." One colonel argued in favor of the general. The colonel cited three of the general's "leadership" characteristics. He listed the general's sense of the big picture, good communication skills, and a high level of self-esteem. The civilians at the meeting strongly disagreed in this assessment about the general. They felt the general lacked empathy and did not display a deep concern for those who were facing difficult changes.

It was clear that both the colonel and the civilians were stuck in the assumption that leadership was an objective reality based on visible parts. They failed to recognize that their subjective consciousness, their self-referral information processing, defined leadership. Had they understood this fundamental aspect of leadership, they could have explained their interactions with the general. They would have realized why the general gained some people as followers but not others.

The Quantum Leadership paradigm explains that reality is subjective. Consciousness, or how people process information, creates meaning. Consciousness translates potentiality, which refers to what could be, into probabilities for action, which explain what we decide "is." Quantum physics shows that the interaction of your consciousness with your surroundings makes you an active participant-creator of your reality. You affect what you observe. What you observe depends upon what you choose to observe. And your interpretation depends on your subjective information processing. Your act of observation and interpretation alters the world.

This notion goes against most of our education. We learned during formal schooling the "correct labels" for things, people, and events. We were programmed to believe in certain "objective truths" that were "proven" by the scientific method or verified by our religious traditions. Our belief in objectivity exists by virtue of the "correctness," "truths," and "proofs" we were taught.

Yet "proven" truths can be invalid hoaxes. For thirty years science fully accepted that the bone fragments of a supposed prehistoric human, labeled Piltdown Man, represented the missing link between apes and humans. Later investigation found that the remains were merely carefully doctored evidence planted to promote a hoax. Supposedly proven truths can also be dangerously wrong. Thalidomide was supposed to be a boon for pregnant women. The drug turned out to cause severe birth defects in the fetus. DDT was supposed to save food crops from insects at no danger to humans. Subsequent study uncovered the damaging impact of the pesticide on human health. The expansion of human awareness changed these "realities."

Consciousness creates leadership (the eighth natural law of leadership) because leaders and followers unite according to how they process information in any situation. When consciousness connects, a shared reality exists. Followers accept the leader, and the leadership field manifests itself. The field is a self-referential identity with the leader's and followers' consciousness (the ninth natural law of leadership).

For example, Wal-Mart employees loved Sam Walton. The Green Bay Packer players were devoted to coach Vince Lombardi. The Wal-Mart employees and Green Bay players, respectively, identified with their leaders. Self-referral explains that the leader and follower are reflections of each other.

Quantum physics indicates that consciousness serves as the creative element and causal agent of the universe. This makes consciousness infinitely more important than matter. Our consciousness subjectively filters how we receive information. It defines how we interpret that information. Consciousness also structures how we respond to it. In terms of leadership, the quantum mechanics of this self-referral leadership process begin when a spark of the leader's consciousness perceives the need for action in a particular direction.

For example, in 1991, Louis Katopodis, president of Fiesta Mart, a Houston-based grocery chain, saw an opportunity to expand the organization into other cities in Texas. His subjective interpretation of the environment energized him to propose a direction. When this happens, the leader in effect says, "Follow me this way." For Katopodis that meant convincing the board of directors and the senior management group to open new stores in three cities: Austin, Beaumont, and Dallas. The meaning of the leader's direction exists within the leader.

A similar spark of consciousness must occur within the followers-allies. They subjectively evaluate the leader and the leader's direction and respond, "Yes, I will follow." They signal an acceptance of and connection with the leader. The sparks of leader- and follower-consciousness ignite to form the leadership field. Leader and followers perceive the situation from a similar perspective. They unify their consciousness and become one mind. They form an alliance of awareness, mutually committed to a direction. In this connection the power of leadership bursts forth.

The connection of leader-follower consciousness is analogous to tuning the dial on a radio. When listeners turn the dial to the proper frequency, they make a connection and the sound comes in clearly. When they miss the channel, only static comes through.

Leadership influence occurs when the leader and follower tune in on a similar wavelength of awareness. The connection is nonmaterial. Quantum Leadership influence is consciousness connecting in an invisible spatial geometry that binds people together. In his book *Microcosm*, George Gilder explains this quantum reality of life: "Physicists now agree that matter derives from waves, fields, and probabilities. To comprehend nature, we have to stop thinking of the world as basically material and begin imagining it as a manifestation of consciousness."

We observe the quantum connection of subjective consciousness at all organizational levels and throughout all organizational areas. People make a commitment to follow or align with someone in a wide range of circumstances. This occurs at the large-scale, organization-wide strategic level. It happens at very the specific project level which only affects small groups. And, the connection happens when just a few people at a particular workstation commit to one person's subjective consciousness. The subjective consciousness of others interprets the leader's path. When they recognize its utility, they follow.

The quantum connection was evident at Fiesta Mart when Katopodis gained the necessary commitment of followers to his direction. One top manager remarked to me, "Louis really knows what he's doing." When I asked what that meant, he replied, "Well, Louis made a lot of sense because I thought there were good opportunities in each of the three cities Louis wanted to move into. I thought Louis was on the right track. I felt comfortable with his plan of action." The manager's statements reveal that the self-referral, subjective consciousness of the follower creates the leadership connection.

A universe without objectivity does not mean that standards do not exist. Through the lens of the Quantum Leadership paradigm, we see that leaders reflect the standards of both their self-referral consciousness and the collective, self-referential consciousness of their followers. People do not follow or align with those whom they perceive as alien to themselves. When a person gives expression to a direction, it reveals the quality of the person's intentions and range of discrimination. If the direction resonates in some consistent way with another's self-referral awareness, they will follow.

The meaning of the direction exists within the leader. The meaning of the leader exists within the follower. By referring back to themselves, leaders determine a direction in their own image. By referring back to themselves, followers create the leader in their own image. Thus, leadership standards exist within the leader's and followers' consciousness.

This does not mean that all leaders are benevolent. Leaders who operate from a less evolved state of consciousness can chart a course that is divisive or destructive. They attract followers who have self-referral with such action. The Nine Natural Laws of Leadership are descriptive. The laws define what leaders are rather than what they should be. Yet we want leaders who have high standards. We want to follow those who are truly compassionate, competent, and life supporting. The Quantum Leadership paradigm provides a means of prescribing how to lead in a more enlightened manner. The key is the expansion of consciousness.

Specific expressions of consciousness such as thoughts are manifestations of an underlying source of awareness. Thoughts define what we are conscious of. For example, you are conscious of the words on this page. Those thoughts indicate that you have the capacity to be conscious. That is, a source of awareness or ground state of pure consciousness exists within. The source of consciousness is like a well from which water can be drawn. A specific expression of consciousness is like a bucket of water drawn from the well. If the flow of well water is cut off or blocked in some way, we cannot receive the water. If the flow of awareness from pure consciousness is blocked, the leader's energy, creativity, and intelligence cannot be fully expressed. Furthermore, if expressions of consciousness are programmed along narrow, divisive, or negative lines, the leader's thinking and action can be restricted, divisive, or destructive. The hope for more enlightened leaders lies in expanding the access and increasing the flow from the source of consciousness within us.

The expansion of consciousness means enhancing the flow of pure consciousness, which is accomplished in two ways. First, the capacity to process information must be increased by improving the conductor or circuitry of consciousness. This circuitry exists as the level of mind-body fitness or our neurophysiological efficiency. When one's mind and body are dull, tired, or undernourished, consciousness does not move very well. Such a person lacks the energy, creativity, and intelligence to operate in the challenging leadership arena. The second way to expand the flow of pure consciousness is to transcend the limits of programmed and conditioned thinking and action. Awareness of opportunities becomes restricted when limited frames of reference and prejudicial bias filter awareness. Recognition of alternatives to overcome obstacles is reduced when alternate interpretations of reality are discarded or unnoticed. Leaders then fail to map the territory to identify possibilities and problems, and they do not chart courses of action that lead to success.

As consciousness expands, our relationship to the world changes because our self-referral identity expands. Expanded consciousness enhances our sense of unity. We recognize the unifying interdependencies that underlie apparent diversity. Expanded consciousness increases our sense of responsibility. We are more able to respond. Expanded consciousness changes our reference point. We no longer see ourselves in the world but see the world in ourselves. Pasteur noted that "chance favors those who are prepared for it." Quantum leadership offers an understanding and methodology to prepare for the future and put chance on our side.

◆◆◆

FIELD GUIDE 2

Action Idea 2.1: Ask the right leadership questions.

Most people who aspire to lead ask the wrong initial questions. "How do I lead?" or, "What do I have to do to be a leader?" reveal a mistaken belief that leadership is made up of parts. The correct questions are, "How do I get others to follow me?" "What are the needs of others?" and "How do I gain allies?"

Action Idea 2.2: Unmask "Lone Ranger leadership."

"Lone Ranger leadership" reflects the assumption that leadership can be found in the habits and behaviors of one person. The fabled masked man was perceived as the sole author of law, order, and success. Personal sketches of bold and daring lone individuals and vivid descriptions of their style and flair fill leadership folklore. To clarify the reality of leadership as a field, unmask Lone Ranger leadership. Define leadership in your organization in terms of the field of leader-follower interaction. Each time someone claims that leadership is one person, challenge that assumption. Demonstrate how the leader and follower work together to create the power of leadership. Provide others with examples from specific work experiences showing that the focus on the leader alone masks leadership's essential reality. Clarify to others that leadership lies in the unity of leaders and followers.

Action Idea 2.3: Expand your field into different parts of the organization.

Most of us interact with the same people each day based on the places we typically visit over the course of the workday. This is our Personal Traffic Pattern (PTP). Sometimes the pattern becomes so fixed that we fail to realize we have limited our interactions with others. In fact, sometimes we shy away from certain work areas because we are unfamiliar with the people in them.

Alter and expand your PTP to establish better relationships with a wider network of people and to expand the scope of your interactions field. Spend time getting to know others in areas you typically do not visit. Expand your radar screen of awareness to tune in with people who work in areas related to your job. Patricia Grysavage, Director of Executive Management and Communications for the Department of Veterans Affairs, used this action idea by spending fifteen minutes a week in areas of her organization she rarely visits. Joe Frick, Director of the Management Services Division in the U.S. Department of Agriculture, spent one day a month talking to employees in various divisions about important work efforts. Like Pat and Joe, seek ways to expand your field of interactions. Time spent in "new" areas will also increase your capacity to establish the leadership relationship foundation since you can use the time to get to know people better.

Action Idea 2.4: Multiply leadership events.

Multiply the quanta of leadership power that pop up throughout your organization by recognizing every leadership event regardless of its scope or duration. Make it clear to others that many diverse occurrences of leader-follower fields demonstrate leadership. Show people that being a leader is not a continuous reality owned by a select few. Encourage others to gain followers-allies in small-group meetings and in other day-to-day events. Read, *The Leadership Event: The Moments of True Leadership that Transform Organization*, 2nd edition, to understand this more fully.

Action Idea 2.5: Pass the ball.

Leadership power expands when it is shared. Pass your support to others by becoming a willing follower when their initiatives prove worthy. Relinquish your lead when someone else steps up with an idea that has merit. Reward others for their stints as leaders even if the event is very brief. Honor the discontinuous nature of leadership as not only acceptable but highly valued especially if your organization has flattened its hierarchy. This effort will encourage more people to take the kind of initiative that becomes essential when companies restructure.

Action Idea 2.6: Get past high-visibility media leadership mania.

The preoccupation with high-visibility media leaders limits an organization's ability to take advantage of the full potential of its people. Recognize that those who make the front pages and are featured on the nightly news represent only a small portion of total leadership potential. Educate those in your organization that the select few who frequently and consistently take action are aligning with the same natural laws of leadership that govern any initiative. This means everyone can take a leadership role.

Action Idea 2.7: Distinguish between managerial and leadership roles.

Explain to others that the role of leader is distinct from the role of manager. The manager's role is to guide people to do what the organization defines as a job requirement. The leader's role is to enter into the non-prescribed arena beyond rules and regulations. Reinforce mangers who have this role. Acknowledge them for fulfilling required responsibilities. Enhance managerial action. Clarify the need for managers to take initiative in the leadership arena. Increase leadership at all organizational levels. Support and encourage non-managers who take the lead. Acknowledge such efforts. Congratulate such action when it results in making a positive difference.

Action Idea 2.8: Double your face-to-face contact frequency.

The interaction that joins followers and leaders in a leadership event depends on the quality of interaction that already exists between them. Doubling face-to-face contact provides a structured way to develop positive interactions with others. Set aside time each week for such contact with each person in your area to improve the quantity and quality of interaction.

Action Idea 2.9: Analyze your interactions with the environment and with yourself.

Quantum Leadership defines interaction as the key to leadership influence. Consider how you typically interpret and respond to information about problems and opportunities. Are you proactive or reactive? Do you engage in situations, or do you tend to analyze from a distance? After considering your typical pattern of interaction, ask yourself, "How does my approach serve me?" If you realize you can do better by changing your interaction with the environment, try a different approach.

Conduct the same analysis for your interactions with yourself, your inner world of thoughts and feelings, the internal sense of "I" from which you view the world. How clear are you regarding your intentions? What can you do to be clearer? What do you typically pay attention to and why? How can you improve your focus of attention? How do you decide what events mean? What could you do to refine your discrimination? How could you create more choices?

Finding the answers to these questions will take some reflection. Spend a few minutes each day analyzing your interactions. Keep a personal journal to track your ideas. Over time you will improve the quality of your interaction with the environment and with yourself, which will propel you to greater leadership power.

Learn stress management techniques such as Transcendental Meditation. Take a yoga class. Attend a health and fitness seminar. All of these methods will enable you to be more focused, relaxed, and internally coherent. You will be able to know yourself and interact with your environment more effectively from this state of awareness.

Action Idea 2.10: Let go of cause-and-effect thinking...once in awhile.

To let go of cause-and-effect thinking means to suspend the belief in a cause-and-effect sequence of actions. Use information as a springboard to explore nonlinear leaps of logic. For example, instead of assuming that Plan A will result in Outcome B, play with the idea that Plan A will create outcome Not-B, Outcome X, and/or Outcome Z. By using this thinking, you may become aware of new possibilities that are more appropriate to discern behavior in the Quantum Leadership arena. Letting go of cause-and-effect thinking helps us continually learn and adapt to information rather than force information into predetermined logic.

Action Idea 2.11: Look for global patterns.

Accepting the idea of uncertainty does not mean adopting the view that there is nothing but hopeless chaos. Global patterns do exist in the quantum realm, and leaders can use them as a guide to action. Look for global patterns, but do not be fooled into thinking they will duplicate in exactly the same, deterministic manner every time. Rather, look for the global nonlinear patterns-those that repeat, but rarely (in any specific case) along exactly the same lines.

For example, in the process redesign work we do for organizations, we observe the following global pattern of behavior. People first recognize the value in outlining the process used to accomplish a task. They then experience a backlash against the procedure. They complain that there are too many steps. They resist the process redesign work because they feel it is impossible to figure out all the steps. The causes behind this global pattern vary. Some people simply lack an understanding of how work gets done. Others are unwilling to make the time to think the process through. Still others desire to keep work habits secret to maintain personal control.

The results of this global pattern vary as well. People act out a variety of conflicts. They fail to complete the assignment. They go off on a tangent about “other problems” that they believe are more serious. We are never certain what will happen in any specific process redesign effort because even small changes in certain conditions can create major changes. However, the underlying global pattern remains clear. People recognize the value, they experience backlash, they complain, and they resist. The pattern plays out differently each time, and it is a very obvious pattern. Armed with awareness of this "aperiodic" pattern, we are able to respond to clients in more effective ways. We understand order exists in chaos, but we are not fooled into thinking the order unfolds in a routine way. We are able to respond to the organization's need because we recognize the global pattern.

Action Idea 2.12: Cultivate greater mind-body coherence.

Our state of consciousness depends on our mental and physical states. We think more clearly when the brain works in a more orderly way. We respond with more energy when the physical body operates in a more fluid fashion. Our self-referral consciousness reflects our mind-body coherence. We are more open to possibilities. We can more effectively to adapt to change. We are more capable of overcoming obstacles when mind-body coherence is greater. Diet, exercise, rest, sleep, and lifestyle all affect this coherence. Consider what and how you eat. Analyze the extent and frequency of exercise you do. Assess the quality and quantity of rest and sleep you get. Evaluate, and your lifestyle habits. Do your actions enable you to be more or less conscious? Does your behavior promote more or less capacity to process information? By improving mind-body coherence, you increase your capacity to contact and draw from pure consciousness, your underlying power source, to be more conscious. This strengthens your ability to take the leader role.

4

Enlightened Leaders for a Quantum Age

"The quantum era is still unfolding. . .
in a transformation of the world."
George Gilder, author of Microcosm

Quantum Leadership represents a more complete approach to leading than the perspective based on Newtonian assumptions. It meets the realities of a competitive business environment and adds value to leadership practice because it offers a model that guides leaders to function in a more enlightened and life-supporting manner.

Competitive Business Realities

We live in a quantum era. Today's organizations must compete using an integrated, field view of the environment. "Go global or die" is heard throughout all major industries as companies face an interconnected worldscape, a global field-of business markets. Companies operating in this marketplace need a switchboard like network of linkages. They must create fields of interaction that consolidate local areas and then unify the organization into a whole within larger fields. The economic globalization and unification of previously fragmented markets requires today's leaders to operate with a "whole world mind."

Organizations recognize they can no longer operate as independent parts. Team-based structures are essential as organizations partner, rightsize, restructure, and reinvent themselves. Quality, service, and organizational process problems and opportunities are now viewed as systemic, not as localized issues. Flattened hierarchies and worker empowerment demand multiple leaders at all levels rather than reliance on formal authority and prescribed, deterministic modes of operating. Cross-functional work teams represent human consciousness unified into fields of coherent action.

In *Managing on the Edge*, Richard T. Pascali recounts key decision rules of Don Peterson, Ford Motor Company's President during the 1980s. Peterson recognized that if he were to lead Ford to build world-class cars, he needed to unite all aspects of the company into a unified field. Peterson understood that Ford's "manufacturing problem" was not a manufacturing problem alone. For manufacturing to work effectively, it had to be tied closely to the other organizational functions. What was necessary was a thorough transformation of virtually all aspects of the company. This included a greater involvement of sales, marketing, design, engineering, and finance. It required a rebalancing of power between the line and staff functions. It involved increased levels of participation by individual workers and their unions. It consisted of the redesign of central control systems, communication networks, corporate values, and strategy. Ford regarded these shifts as requiring discontinuous change.

Peterson saw the fundamental power of a unified approach over a separate parts approach. His efforts paid off. Ford's share of the U.S. auto market increased from 16 percent in 1980 to 22 percent in 1987. New quality standards in Ford's manufacturing processes steered it from poorest to number one among the Big Three automakers.

Peterson's focus on discontinuous change strikes a familiar chord that reverberates throughout today's competitive arena.

The rapid pace of environmental and technological change means that incremental, one-foot-following-the-other goals and action plans do not work during periods of abrupt transformation. A key standard for success is "stretch targets." Such gigantic, seemingly unreachable milestones drive leaders to take dramatic leaps forward and reinvent how they do business.

Command-and-control tactics are now being replaced by reliance on commitment as the basis for effective influence. Self-directed work teams rely on the interaction of their members to guide the group's activity. Increased workforce diversity means that organizations can no longer simply demand that people assimilate and fit themselves into a "traditional" ethnic/gender mold. Successful organizations must carefully cultivate commitment through coaching and development of employee skills and potentialities. Partnering with suppliers, customers, and producers has become commonplace as organizations rely on positive interaction as a means to competitive success.

Traditional notions of predictability and stability have been shattered. Thirty percent of companies in the 2000 *Fortune 100* were not on that list by 2007. The percentage of executives who stay with a company for life dropped from 53% in 1980 to 45% in 2001. By 1991, only fourteen of the original fifty-two companies rated as "excellent" in a 1982 study by Tom Peters and Bob Waterman could still be categorized in this way. No company has an ensured lock on market success. No company holds an industry position so dominant that it can buffer dynamic change. In the late 1980's, that impregnable fortress IBM swooned under the heat of intense competition from smaller companies. By 1992, "Big Blue" proved to be too sluggish and inflexible for the rapidly changing information processing marketplace. The dot com bust of 2001 blasted notions of certainty regarding many business models.

The quantum, nonmaterial, and invisible reality of human information processing capacity determines competitive success. People are not separate observers of an objective world. Subjective perception is reality. Quality products and services are defined by the customer's point of view. Intellectual capital, which is structured in the individual and collective consciousness of the workforce, is today's new competitive advantage. The invisible power of the mind takes precedence over matter.

The true wealth of nations is in creative brain power. Material resources such as buildings and balance sheets are supplanted by information-energy. Solid matter has become a lesser power source.

Successful organizations in this interconnected, discontinuously changing, unpredictable world driven by subjective perception require Quantum Leaders. Such men and women embrace the uncertainty of the leadership arena and rely on the development of consciousness as the real power of leadership.

The Quantum Leadership Model

Quantum Leadership offers a practical model for guiding all leaders. It provides enlightened, life-supporting solutions to overcome problems and exploit opportunities. Quantum Leadership practice compares to a game set on a broadly defined playing field in which the game changes as it unfolds and the players interact. The Quantum Leadership model guides leadership practice. It defines a set of underlying, stable interactions that occur when leaders lead. The model offers choices to create these interactions.

Figure 4-1 depicts the Quantum Leadership model.

Figure 4-1. The Quantum Leadership Model

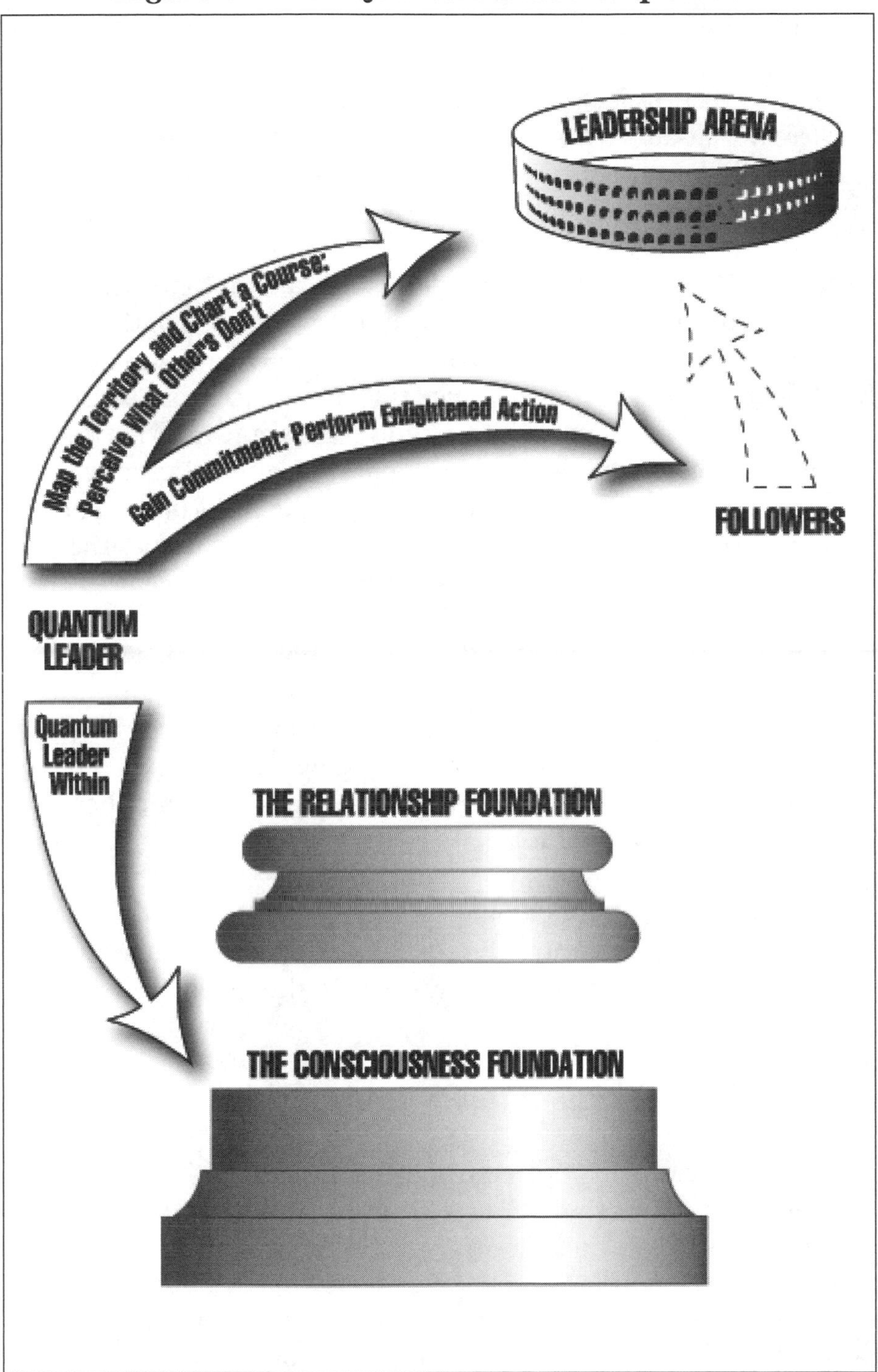

The model defines three essential interactions that make up the Quantum Leadership process.

1. *The Quantum Leader-leadership arena interaction.* The arrow that arcs from the Quantum Leader up to the leadership arena designates this interaction. Quantum Leaders create this interaction. They map the territory to perceive possibilities or identify problems in the leadership arena. They chart a course to establish a path that exploits opportunities or resolves problems. To accomplish this process, Quantum Leaders perceive what others do not.
2. *The Quantum Leader-follower interaction.* The arrow that connects the Quantum Leader and followers specifies this interaction. Quantum Leaders create this connection when they perform enlightened action to gain commitment. The quality of relationship forms the foundation that underlies the Quantum Leader-follower interaction.
3. *The Quantum Leader-consciousness interaction.* The arrow between the Quantum Leader and the consciousness foundation indicates this interaction. Quantum Leaders self-refer to their consciousness, their information processing source to know themselves better. They express the particular structure of their consciousness to define the Quantum Leader within.

The dotted arrow that connects the follower with the leadership arena illustrates the result of the three interactions. Followers join the leader and venture into the leadership arena.

Mapping the Territory and Charting a Course: Perceiving What Others Don't

Note the arrow in Figure 4-1. It arcs up from the Quantum Leader to the leadership arena. This indicates how Quantum Leaders direct their consciousness to interact with the vague, uncertain territory of the leadership arena. Quantum Leaders map the territory and then chart a course. These processes define how Quantum Leaders operate outside prescribed boundaries (the fifth natural law of leadership).

Quantum Leaders perceive what others don't when they map the territory and chart a course. That means that their awareness has the distinctive quality of a more insightful level of consciousness. People typically do not need direction when they know what to do or when they know how to do it. Whether they are right or wrong, if they firmly believe they are on the correct course, they usually do not seek guidance. Nor will they heed it if offered. Quantum Leaders become important when uncertainty clouds people's awareness and people do not know what to do. Anyone can recognize a blazing forest fire. The real skill lies in sniffing out the first smoke. Quantum Leaders also add value when they can demonstrate a superior course of action that others do not recognize.

Consider a story about Martha Hahn who was the Associate State Director for the Bureau of Land Management (BLM) in Colorado in 1993. She mapped the territory and charted a course during a BLM Field Committee meeting. This group is made up of BLM managers from all parts of the United States. The meeting's purpose was to identify issues critical to the bureau's mission. Hahn's concern was the growing diversity of the public that the bureau served. She recognized the increased numbers of women, Hispanics, and other minorities who used BLM services at federal parks and in federal recreation areas. Yet the BLM was traditionally weak in its ability to recruit, maintain, and then promote women into its upper ranks. Hahn believed the BLM had to revamp its practices. She charted a course to resolve the problem. Her direction was to audit the bureau's culture. She wanted to identify exactly what the BLM needed to do differently regarding its practices with women employees.

Hahn raised the diversity issue during a brainstorming activity in the BLM meeting. She explained her concern about inclusion of women. "We need to look at our procedures for responding to women within BLM, and then we need to improve them." "That's pretty straightforward," one committee member retorted. "We know how to do that." Many of the field committee members gave tacit agreement to this comment. Someone else raised a point on a different topic, and the group began discussing that. Hahn challenged the group. "I think that's part of the problem," she stated easily but firmly. "We have approached this as a simple issue, but it isn't. Complex cultural forces and deeply rooted biases have limited our ability to deal with the issue effectively."

Hahn's comments reveal how perceiving what others don't might provide a new, innovative insight for others. Her perception was unique. She clarified that existing BLM approaches had not met the organization's need and had also masked the need for a new direction.

Perceiving what others don't might be an idea that was lost, forgotten, or not timely in a previous circumstance. Ronald Reagan's successful run for the presidency in 1980 was based on ideas that were almost identical to the approach to government he had first extolled in 1964 and had maintained throughout his political career. In 1980, Reagan mapped the territory and charted a course to reintroduce possibilities that had been dormant, forgotten, or unacceptable to the majority of Americans.

In business, perceiving what others don't may also mean simply reintroducing lost or forgotten ideas in response to business cycles. Consider an organization in which someone takes initiative and gets support to expand operations, such as adding a new production line. Then, over time, someone gains backing to trim expenses or reduce labor costs. Developing new production lines and instituting labor cutbacks are not new or radical innovations. Yet they become fodder for leadership because the person who perceives them does so at a time when the directives are relevant to the organization and no one else has recognized the need for such action.

Quantum Leaders perceive what others don't when they step ahead of the pack to guide people forward. Quantum Leadership describes the choices available for doing this (see Chapter 6). These processes involve the leader's capacity to gain another perspective of awareness. We refer to this process as "going into the G.A.P." or Gaining Another Perspective.

Quantum Leaders think differently from others. They direct their awareness along channels of information processing that go beyond heavy reliance on Newtonian logic. Quantum Leadership explains how leaders break the boundaries that limit and misdirect perception of the leadership arena. By gaining another perspective, Quantum Leaders open themselves to new ways of observing, interpreting, and evaluating information. This allows their awareness to recognize patterns of intelligence, order, and possibility that provide new approaches to action. Gaining another perspective equips Quantum Leaders to interact with the leadership arena beyond the confines created by restricted attention and by conditioned, limited perception.

Operating from the G.A.P. illustrates how the leader's consciousness creates leadership (the eighth natural law of leadership). Martha Hahn was in the G.A.P. She identified the impact of BLM's cultural roots. She recognized the need to audit current practices. Quantum Leadership describes specific techniques to guide awareness into the G.A.P. (see Chapter 7).

The Quantum Leader-Follower Interaction

Gaining Commitment: Performing Enlightened Action

Once Quantum Leaders identify a course of action, they need to gain willing followers (the first natural law of leadership). To gain follower commitment, they perform enlightened action. They inspire followers to recognize and accept their course of action. Performing enlightened action is analogous to turning on a light to show the way in a pitch-dark room. The leader's message enlightens followers to support and venture forth with the leader.

Recall that Martha Hahn's comments about issues regarding women in the BLM were initially passed over by the group. Hahn had to challenge the field committee to recognize that diversity and the gender issue were in fact problems. Her comments rang true with Bill Calkins, then Associate State Director of Alaska, who chimed in, "Martha's right." Calkins' comment got others talking about the issue. Yet some still interpreted the problem in ways that Hahn recognized as misunderstanding the real issue. She challenged the group. "I need to make a point," she stated. "We're just rehashing what we already know. We need to act now and launch a new direction, not simply talk and retalk issues. We don't need more talk. We need action."

"Well, what should we do?" Calkins asked Hahn. Everyone looked directly at her. She spoke clearly. "We need to assess the hiring and recruitment process that we now use. I suggest we form a quality team to outline our process. Then we can find ways to improve it. We also need to clearly identify the specific needs of women already in BLM to help us determine the actions that will better serve them. I suggest we develop and administer a survey of the staff as soon as possible." These statements catalyzed the group. "Let's do it," Calkins replied, and the entire committee nodded their agreement.

Martha Hahn effectively communicated her ideas because she had adapted her message to meet the needs of the situation. Quantum Leadership provides choices that increase communication flexibility. This is the capacity to use multiple channels to clarify the message. Quantum Leadership offers ways to improve communication congruence. It defines the capacity to present a message with consistency. Ultimately, Hahn gained the field committee's commitment because the meaning of her ideas resonated with the committee members. She created a connection of consciousness. Hahn met the field committee at their self-referral level of consciousness (the ninth natural law of leadership). She connected with them at the source of meaning creation.

Quantum Leadership describes how performing enlightened action involves communication that creates shared meaning and influences followers at the level of consciousness. Meaning is created through values and the frames of reference people use. Quantum Leaders create shared meaning when they perform action that resonates with the followers' values. They connect with followers when they frame or reframe information from a reference point that followers understand and accept as worth supporting.

Prior to the BLM meeting, Calkins already shared Hahn's interpretation of the BLM practices in dealing with minorities. Her statements gave clear expression to thoughts he already had. That made it easy to establish a shared sense of meaning with him. Hahn won over the rest of the group because her ideas resonated with key values of the field committee members. The BLM tradition included meeting individual needs. The field committee members valued an action orientation. Hahn framed her leadership direction as a set of specific steps. This helped others understand her ideas and believe they were appropriate. She also created shared meaning by suggesting the use of quality teams, an accepted and valued approach in the BLM for resolving problems. Quantum Leadership offers techniques for creating shared meaning (see Chapter 9).

Values are important reflections of information processing. Values indicate the emotional level of meaning. Values reflect what we care about. Frames of reference are important reflections of information processing in terms of the content and context of our information perspective. Enlightened action also involves a subtler form of influence that is beyond authority (the fourth natural law of leadership). Quantum Leader influence occurs on the level of consciousness where people actually code raw data into meaningful information. Leaders match the specific internal information processing codes followers use to represent reality in their mind. Quantum Leaders speak the followers' "private mental language" (PML). Our PML determines the structure of information processing.

Martha Hahn matched the private mental language of many of the field committee members. She provided specific details on how to approach the diversity problem, instead of giving only a general overview. Her ideas made sense because most of these field committee members code information in terms of details. That is, they accept and understand information more readily when it is provided in terms of particulars. Reliance on either details or generalities is one of the internal codes that make up a person's private mental language. Hahn connected with the field committee on their wavelength of consciousness because she tapped into the actual structure they used to code information. The Quantum Leadership model explains how to access the private mental language people use and how to influence others on this level (see Chapter 10).

The Relationship Foundation

Followers do not provide support without a requisite quality of relationship. Leadership is the relationship (the second natural law of leadership). During the BLM meeting, Bill Calkins was initially the strongest supporter of Martha Hahn's ideas. This was no accident. Long before the meeting, he had come to believe that diversity was a key issue for BLM. He also held Martha Hahn in high professional regard. Hahn and Calkins had an established, positive relationship. This made it easier for him to commit to her lead.

When would-be followers have no prior relationship with a potential leader, gaining commitment depends solely on the action the leader performs on the spot. It is difficult to develop high levels of trust and a strong sense of shared common ground in such circumstances. This reality partly explains why networking plays such an important role in today's organizations. It illustrates why name recognition is so important in politics.

Leaders lose followers when the quality of relationship cracks. A breakdown occurs when the leader loses the followers' trust. The leadership event ends. Quantum Leadership defines how to continually build and reinforce relationships with others. It explains how to establish a common ground, provide valued resources, and develop trust and credibility (see Chapter 11).

The Quantum Leader-Consciousness Interaction

The Consciousness Foundation

Quantum Leadership is structured in consciousness. The entire process emerges from the way leaders and followers process information. Consciousness forms a foundation that underlies the entire Quantum Leadership model. Quantum Leaders cannot directly control a follower's consciousness (although they can influence it by performing enlightened action). Quantum Leaders *can* control their own consciousness. They can refer back to their own source of awareness, their pure consciousness. They direct their thinking and action along the lines they choose. As Jack Welch, former CEO of General Electric, declares, "Quantum thinking has to become a way of life."

The Quantum Leader Within

Through self-referral, Quantum Leaders contact the leader within. They get in touch with their internal "architecture of awareness" that guides thinking and action. The Quantum Leader within has four components: intention, attention, judgment, and initiative.

The Quantum Leader within Martha Hahn was intent on taking the lead at the BLM Field Committee meeting. She focused her attention on a key issue she believed was critical to the bureau's future. Her capacities to judgment defined the problem. They enabled her to identify practical choices for resolving it. She took initiative when she felt it was necessary to gain followers.

Quantum Leaders know they have 100 percent control over the four components of awareness that define their leadership efforts. Quantum Leadership provides practical guidance about how to take control and restructure the internal architecture of the leader within. It helps leaders to become more conscious and enhance leadership (see Chapter 5). It offers a new motto for leaders:

I am conscious; therefore I can lead.

◆◆◆

FIELD GUIDE 3

Action Idea 3. 1: Become "field conscious."

Awareness must be focused on the full spectrum of interaction in the Quantum Leadership Model. Leaders must attend to how they map the territory to chart a course and simultaneously gain the commitment of willing followers. Quantum Leadership cannot be understood by looking at it piecemeal and by isolating its parts. You cannot simply add up the elements to understand it. That type of consciousness might work for a V-8 engine or a clock radio. It does not apply to leadership.

To become field conscious, pay attention to the connections that link the personal, social, political, economic, legal, and technical factors that affect the leadership arena. Recognize the myriad factors that have an impact on your interactions with followers. At times the field might encompass only the members of a small-group meeting and their issues. At other times, the field might encompass a more global sphere. Continually challenge yourself to be aware of the field - the interactions - not just the parts.

Action Idea 3.2: Meet followers at their level.

Interact with followers at their level of consciousness to gain their commitment. Consider how followers interpret the leadership arena. Find out how others typically take in, translate, and respond to information. Then present your leadership initiative in a message that matches their mode of information processing.

Martha Hahn knew that the field committee was an action-oriented group that understood information in terms of details. She specified the precise actions they should take. She met the group at their level and reinforced their level of consciousness. Armed with a clear direction, they were more willing to tackle the diversity issue.

Action Idea 3.3: Make it personal.

Relationships lie at the heart of the interpersonal connection within the leader-follower field. Spend time every day making personal contact with people. “Personal” does not mean you have to develop non-work related or social friendships. You can build quality relationships with others by focusing only on work if that makes others more comfortable. For many people, work consumes a good portion of who they are. It offers a lot of material to get to know them.

Find ways to personalize your contact with others by asking them what matters to them about work. Consider Bob Crawford, CEO of fast-growing Brook Furniture Rental. He recognizes the importance of the interpersonal connection. He finds time to accompany members of his 150-person sales force when they call on accounts. Customer reaction to his visits is powerful and positive. They tell him he is the first company president to give them a personal touch.

Action Idea 3.4: Become aware of pure consciousness.

Can you think of a time when you seemed to witness your thoughts from a quiet place within? Have you ever had the experience of not actually thinking about anything but being exquisitely alert? Perhaps you have had such experiences, even if they were only momentary. For some, such incidents sound like New Age claptrap. However, many people recognize the need to find a source of internal stability amid the chaos and complexity of modern life. Introspection and time for reflection are now accepted among forward-thinking members of organizations.

Many people believe being aware means constantly thinking *about something*. Yet behind our thoughts exists a state of mind that is pure awareness.

Thinking typically means being conscious of something. Being conscious or wakeful depends on the capacity to be conscious. This capacity derives from the existence of pure consciousness or awareness itself. By contacting and experiencing the state of pure consciousness, your quality of information processing expands.

Pure awareness represents the internal source or reservoir of information processing potential. It can be compared to an ocean. Thoughts represent only the surface and localized waves or even more localized drops of water. The ocean represents the source of awareness. By contacting the source, we can take action from an expanded platform of awareness. Or as Lao-Tzu, the sixth century B.C. Chinese philosopher stated, "The way to do is to be."

Stanford University professors Michael Ray and Rochelle Myers, in their book *Creativity in Business*, recommend a specific set of yoga exercises known as Surya Namaskar to contact the inner resource of pure awareness. These simple bending and stretching postures relax the body so that the mind can also settle down to its source.

Meditation techniques are another effective way to experience pure consciousness. Several hundred scientific research studies on the Transcendental Meditation (TM) technique, taught by Maharishi Mahesh Yogi, have shown very positive and dramatic results. Regular practice of the TM technique improves practical indicators of information processing capacity. Among these are faster reaction time, improved perceptual motor performance, enhanced learning ability, better memory, more creativity, and greater cognitive flexibility. Scientific research on the TM technique also shows it improves brain wave coherence and the stability of the nervous system. The Transcendental Meditation technique is the simplest and most powerful tool available to connect to that pure consciousness level. It offers a very practical way to expand the platform of awareness of the Quantum Leader within.

5

The Quantum Leader Within

"What lies behind us and what lies before us are small matters compared to what lies within us."
Ralph Waldo Emerson

Dick Frazar runs five miles every day. The positive impact of his daily regimen is obvious. Approaching fifty, Dick's face shines with youthful vigor. His firm, well-proportioned physique moves with the fluid grace of a trained athlete. Yet the purpose of Dick's run extends beyond his desire for physical fitness. He uses the time to focus in on his consciousness. He defines the architecture of the Quantum Leader within him.

Dick was a mid-level manager in a large southwestern utility company. He had a lot to think about during his daily run. His company had just completed a major downsizing effort and internal reorganization. He had been assigned the additional responsibility to direct a division that served as a liaison between outside customers and several company departments. His new division had been hit particularly hard by the downsizing. It had lost more than 20 percent of its staff, including all but one of its administrative support people. The disgruntled reaction by division members alone would have been enough to occupy Dick's thinking. His challenge was compounded by complaints from other departments that the group was a surly, hard-to-work-with crew that was not meeting company needs.

Dick's work to improve his new division began in his consciousness - his capacity to process information. The Quantum Leadership model defines the Quantum Leader - consciousness interaction as the starting place for leadership. Quantum Leadership is based in our awareness, sense of self, or consciousness. The Quantum Leader's tasks - map the territory, chart a course and gain the commitment of willing followers - are the overt, resultant activities that reflect the invisible content and character of the inner world of mind. During his daily run, Dick systematically configured and reconfigured the form and function of his awareness regarding how to lead his new division. He consciously established the foundation for taking a leadership role in the situation he faced.

The Source of the Quantum Leader Within

Consciousness creates leadership (the eighth natural law of leadership). The Quantum Leadership model indicates that Quantum Leaders refer to their consciousness to contact their source of leadership (Figure 5-1). The leader's capacity to map the territory and chart a course in the uncertain leadership arena requires lively consciousness.

Quantum Leaders express their consciousness through the structure of awareness. This structure has four components:

1. Intention
2. Attention
3. Judgment
4. Initiative

Figure 5.1. The Quantum Leadership model: The consciousness foundation.

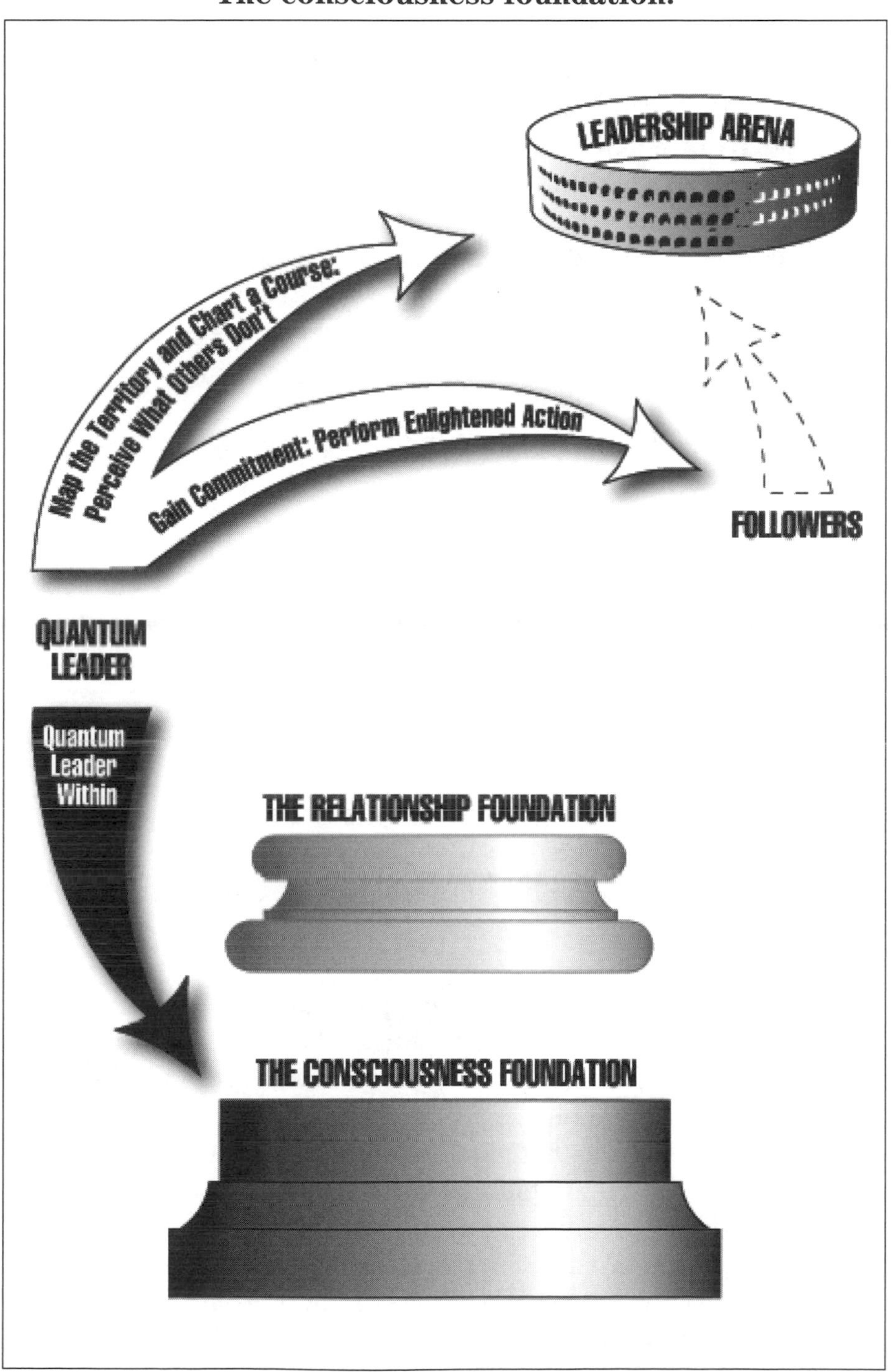

The interaction among these four components creates the unique, subjective reality of the Quantum Leader's information processing method. This reality is the leader's self-referral identity defined in the ninth natural law of leadership. The four components typically unfold sequentially. Intention guides attention. Attention drives judgment. Judgment directs initiative. Yet each component interacts with and reinforces the others as an interconnected network. The Quantum Leader within emerges from the sequential and simultaneous self-interacting dynamics of these four components.

Quantum Leader Intention

Leading begins with a *conscious intention.* Intention forms the foundation for the energy allocated to any endeavor. It defines the innermost core of the leader's purpose, desire, motivation, and values. As Charles de Gaulle once said, "Nothing great will ever be achieved without great men, and men are great only if they are determined to be so."

Quantum Leaders distinguish themselves because, first and foremost, they have the intention to lead. They enter situations with the desire to step into the risk zone of uncertainty and influence others to follow. The dynamics are the same whether the leader operates in one-on-one interactions, small-group tasks, or organization-wide efforts. The process is the same from short to long-term ventures.

Intention has organizing power. It defines the platform of consciousness on which all other thinking and action rest. Quantum Leaders consciously clarify their intention in each circumstance they encounter. They reaffirm their desire to lead and refine the purpose that guides them. When intention is foggy or uncertain, doubt inhibits the desire to lead.

Don Williams, president of Trammell Crow, explained the need for clarity of intention in the changing global economy. He stated, "Life today is fired at us point blank. People don't have time to refer to the Bible or to the company handbook. You've got to have all of that internalized."

Establish the Intention to Lead

Dick Frazar was clear about his intention: immediate action. He recognized that he had to deal with the unhappiness created by the downsizing. He knew he needed to address the dysfunctional conflict between members of the division caused by what some perceived as inequities in the distribution of work assignments. A history of poor communication practices among division members made it hard even to talk about these issues. In addition, the frequent complaints from other departments revealed that his division was creating company-wide performance problems. His people were not serving their internal customers. His intent was to resolve this problem.

Dick's intention may seem obvious. It could be argued that anyone else in his position would have had a similar purpose. However, two other managers at his company provide an interesting contrast. Both had worked with the division for several years before Dick arrived. Both were well aware of the division's behavior and its poor relationship with other departments. Nevertheless, neither felt a need to address the issue. One manager even criticized Dick for his efforts, saying they were not necessary.

Dick's example reveals the conscious intent necessary to make a positive difference rather than accept anything less. Robert Nelson, a store manager at Fiesta Mart, the Houston-based grocer, also displayed this quality of intention. Fiesta established a new performance development system for its store and department managers. The first phase of the program required managers to work with their employees in a comprehensive program of goal setting, feedback, coaching, and appraisal sessions. A week after the system was rolled out, Nelson took action that extended beyond the prescribed implementation boundaries. He explained his intention:

> *This system offers a powerful tool. I can reward excellent individual performance and root out the cause of problems in my store. I know that the system will help me if I know how I am doing. I asked my department managers to give me feedback as part of the overall*

process. Their input will help me improve my approach to evaluating and developing others.

The second stage of the performance development process included a process in which personnel receive feedback from their supervisor, peers, and subordinates. Nelson's intention spurred him to take that step right away, despite the fact that he had to put additional effort into an already time-consuming process.

Quantum Leader intention does not require years of soul searching. It does not involve magical powers. You only have to look within yourself and ask, "What is my intention now?" Your immediate answer will tell all. If your clear intention is to lead, you will ignite the first sparks to direct your consciousness into the leadership arena and gain willing followers.

The First Failure of Leadership

The first failure is the lack of conscious intention to lead. Movement stalls without the propelling force of intention. Motivation evaporates. The leader cannot overcome obstacles or take advantage of opportunities.

A 1992 *USA Today* survey by Marcia Staimer asked executives from five industries, "Is your company committed to quality?" The percentage of executives in each industry who said yes was:

Consumer products:	35 percent
Pharmaceuticals:	23 percent
Retailing:	20 percent
Banking:	15 percent
Computers:	15 percent

These low percentages are appalling given the emphasis placed on quality as a competitive necessity. They illustrate part of the reason Japanese manufacturing and service industries outstripped American firms in the 1980's.

The First Quantum Power of Consciousness: Control Over Intention

We have 100 percent control over our intention. We can intend to lead, or not. We can intend to figure out how to resolve problems and exploit opportunities or not. We can intend to create the necessary commitment to action in followers or not. Regardless of anything outside us, we own our intention without restriction, because intention resides in our consciousness. The full mastery of intention provides the initial spark of Quantum Leadership power.

Traditional science places power in forces and pressures that operate on nature from the outside. Think of the pushing, pulling, lifting, and restraining-forces needed to move matter. Picture the effort involved in material crushing against material to change its form.

Quantum physics reveals an inner power: the nonmaterial information-energy of consciousness. Intention is the first spark of consciousness that defines the Quantum Leader within. Intention indicates our seed of desire and the quality of our regard. Quantum Leaders create their intention. They have complete control over it. They consciously and willfully direct their intention to lead.

Not only do we have control over our intention, we are the only ones who know what it is. In work with members of industry and government, we often hear people question other's intentions. Complaints about negative intentions are expressed with comments such as, "My boss is only in it for himself," "The people at the top don't care," or, "None of the political appointees want to listen." This frustration is understandable especially when problems accumulate and an organization's forward momentum stalls.

Some people do have negative intentions. Some people are bullies, tyrants, crooks, and liars. Some betray us. Yet no one really knows the intention of another. We evaluate intention by action, but intention is always hidden within.

Instead of speculating about the intentions of others, we suggest that people clarify their own intention. Looking within will better serve ourselves, our company, and our country. Each of us can decide at any moment what motivates us and what matters to us. We can consciously define our inner purpose and direct it toward progress. As American lawyer and writer Robert G. Ingersoll noted, "It is a blessed thing that in every age someone has had the individuality enough and courage enough to stand by his own convictions." Quantum Leaders spend their energy establishing their intention to lead. They direct their awareness toward attracting others to join them.

Quantum Leader Attention

Attention reflects the design of intention. What you intend guides how you attend. Attention is the Quantum Leader's beam of consciousness directed outward toward the arena of possibilities and problems.

The Quantum Paradigm explains that consciousness illuminates and creates reality. People move toward what they focus on. Thus, attention creates. What you put your attention on grows stronger in your life. What you pay significant attention to becomes your life.

Attention is generative. It creates information for the future. Attention is adaptive. It relies on information for the moment. Kenneth W Butterworth, Chairman of Loctite Corporation from 1980 to 1995, directed his attention to the 95 percent of the world that does not live in the United States. As early as 1960, he began searching the globe for markets for Loctite's industrial adhesives and sealants. He continued to establish contacts and to set up future markets. In the summer of 1991, he traveled to Russia for ten days. His attention was guided by a "go-and-see" attitude. Butterworth was aware that many shied away from the politically tumultuous and economically unstable countries of the former Soviet Union. But, he kept his attention open to it and created successful markets in the region.

Bill Gates of Microsoft illustrates the power of attention turned way up high. Part of Gates's successful lead in the information processing industry is his in-depth knowledge of his company's products and the industry itself. Gates reads voraciously and devours detailed information. He recalls minor points from meetings held six months earlier, which even his product team often cannot remember. At Microsoft, this high-powered attention to detail has its own label in the company's lexicon: granularity.

Mastering the Quantum Leader within means paying attention to what is relevant. Quantum Leaders direct their beam of consciousness like an x-ray. They peer into a situation's inner workings and focus their consciousness like a probe. They investigate and explore for opportunities and ways to overcome problems. Quantum Leaders tune their senses to find and figure out the facts. They snoop and search for signals to understand what is going on.

Motivated by his intention to lead, Dick Frazar turned the beam of his attention onto his new division. He spent several days at the division's offices. He personally watched what was going on. He talked to division members about their work. He commissioned a task force to investigate the group's operation and how it served its customers. He had an external consultant conduct in-depth, one-on-one interviews to explore issues with each division member. And he met with members of other divisions to determine their concerns. His attention power searched for possibilities and solutions to problems.

In the same way, the power of attention guided Sam Walton's now legendary practice of constantly traveling around the country and visiting each of his stores. Walton often drove his own car or piloted his private plane from one small town to the next. He quizzed his employees for ideas. He walked the aisles to assess the merchandise. He talked to customers about their likes and suggestions. Every Saturday starting at 3 A.M., he pored over weekly sales printouts searching for opportunities or trouble spots. He viewed these actions as the most important things he did.

Attention plays a vital role in today's economy. High-tech industries hope for dramatic productivity gains from artificial intelligence. AI, as it is known, defines computerized equipment that mirrors human mental aptitudes and performs human tasks with lightning speed and complete efficiency. Quantum Leaders recognize that a similar kind of productivity can also increase through the power mastered through IA or increased attention.

Attention overcomes obstacles. During 1987 and 1988, John Lainhart, an inspector general for the U.S. government, focused his attention on improving security and operating system software for ten federal agency computer centers. These software packages disburse more than $273 billion annually to support primary federal agency missions. Lainhart's government-wide audit team was directed to assess the integrity of the federal computer system. They were tasked to develop recommendations for improvements that affected computer system integrity. The inspector general (IG) community traditionally avoided complicated system software assessments. The IG believed that the technical complexities were too great. The IG thought the necessary computer-assisted audit technologies were not available. But Lainhart never accepted this viewpoint. His intention was strong. Take the lead, tackle the problem, and make some progress.

Lainhart focused on how to do the job, not on why it could not be done. Several years earlier, he had developed a specialized software audit tool for the Department of Transportation. He thought that the same software could be modified and applied to other federal agencies. Lainhart also directed his attention to overcome the specific causes for hesitation in the inspector general community. He focused on several key issues. These issues included showing how to use the software in a well-planned manner, providing technical assistance on using the software, and demonstrating that the audit would result in significant dollar savings. Lainhart's attention paid off. All ten inspectors general signed on to the project. The audit produced under Lainhart's leadership was hailed by the Computer Systems Security and Privacy Advisory Board. This panel of eminent public and private sector representatives proclaimed that Lainhart's program was one of the best pieces of computer security work ever done in the federal government.

The Second Quantum Power of Consciousness: Control Over Attention

Quantum Leaders understand that they also control 100 percent of their attention power. They can focus their attention in any direction or on any level of reality no matter where they are and regardless of the circumstances.

Classical physics confines attention to material reality. It gives power to what can be observed and measured with the five senses alone. The classical physics mind-set isolates us. It separates us from the "objective" world of matter.

Quantum physics shows us that attention is not dependent on matter. Rather, the power of consciousness serves as the creative element of the universe. We design the world and alter it by virtue of our attention.

The range of our attention power is defined by limits we impose on ourselves. If our limits are narrow, the seeds for trouble are sown. For example, during the late 1980's, General Motors ignored the efforts of Japanese car makers. Instead GM focused all of its attention on one of its key American competitors, Ford. The lack of attention to Japan's automobile actions resulted in an increase in Japan's share of the U.S. car market of 10 percent from 1985 to 1991. GM's market share decreased 7 percent during that same period. Similar problems plagued GM during the 2005-2006 time frame. The company focused on big trucks and SUV's instead of more fuel-efficient vehicles. GM's market share of vehicles sold in the United States is expected to fall below Toyota as a result of GM's focus of attention.

In the same way, CBS directed its attention to NBC and ABC and disregarded CNN. Xerox used its attentional resources to worry about IBM and Kodak while Canon walked away with the copier business.

Failures of attention can be avoided. Everyone has access to attention power and anyone can increase that power. Quantum Leaders consider: "What do I focus on during the day, and what do I let slip by?" "Who do I talk to or ignore?" "Where do I go each day, and what areas do I rarely visit?" "What do I read carefully, and what sources do I ignore?" "Who do I listen to or shut out?" Answers to these questions reveal one's attention patterns. Quantum Leaders alter their patterns to increase their effectiveness. They open themselves up to new avenues of information. In an exquisite state of heightened attention reinforced by the intention to lead, the Quantum Leader within can map the territory, chart a course in the leadership arena, and gain followers.

Quantum Leader Judgment

Judgment is the capacity to make distinctions. It penetrates and differentiates to discern what is more important and what is not. Judgment maximizes available alternatives and determines how we interpret events.

Quantum Leaders know that judgment is essential in the risk-filled leadership arena. Judgment is paramount when no clear model or rule is available. A choice must be made in response to existing policies and procedures when they no longer support effective action. Judicious analysis is essential when information is incomplete. Judgment is also vital when attempting to influence diverse individuals to become willing followers.

A manager once remarked to us with no small amount of frustration in his voice, "Yeah, I know leadership requires judgment, but how do I make the right choices?" We understood how he felt. We also recognized that his question reflected the classical physics world view. The belief that the "right" choice can be known beforehand stems from the Newtonian paradigm that reality is deterministic and objective.

Quantum Leadership embraces the Heisenberg Uncertainty Principle. Werner Heisenberg, a pioneer in quantum physics, posited that it is impossible to simultaneously know both the position and the momentum of quantum particles. Heisenberg found that the wavelike motion of a particle was suspended when we observed the particle's position. This meant the particle's speed could not be known. When the particle's wavelike momentum was observed, it became a blur and its position was lost. This paradoxical finding revealed that we alter reality when we observe it.

Heisenberg's finding was supposed to be meaningful only on the level of quantum particles. The Uncertainty Principle was not supposed to apply to large objects or ordinary events such as getting to work or directing a work group. However, it turns out that it does have relevance to the practical reality of leading.

Anyone who has grappled with leading realizes that there are no markers sprinkled along the path of action that absolutely define the road to certain success. Totally correct action in the leadership wilderness cannot be completely "known" in a way that eliminates all doubt. Rather uncertainty of outcomes dominates the leadership arena. Leaders are expected to guide. Paradoxically, they can never be sure where they will end up.

Quantum Leaders map the territory to *discover* possibilities and obstacles. They chart a course to *figure out* where to go and how to gain followers. These efforts are always fraught with uncertainty. Quantum physics reveals that leadership uncertainty extends beyond the problem of not knowing the outcome of a course of action. It includes the uncertainty that any action can have objective meaning. Quantum Leadership accepts that the act of observation creates either the particle or the wave. Quantum Leadership also embraces that the meaning the leader assigns to events depends on the leader's consciousness. Intention and attention guide what the leader chooses to observe. Judgment directs how the leader chooses to interpret the environment. The Quantum Leader's judgment, based in consciousness, creates meaning. A lack of consciousness creates nothing or worse yet, chaos!

Judgment, as it is defined here, goes beyond the findings of psychological studies of perception. This research suggests that people often distort what they see. People use selective perception to notice only certain events. They rely on stereotypes to evaluate people and situations. Implicit within such studies is the belief that we *mistakenly* interpret events. That is, it is assumed that an objective reality exists but we simply do not recognize it or else fail to understand it accurately. Quantum physics shows that reality depends on the observer's consciousness. Quantum Leaders recognize that consciousness unfolds through intention and attention. Consciousness makes a judgment that creates the meaning of reality for the observer.

Dick Frazar's judgment clarified his approach to the problematic division. As a result of his highly focused attention, Dick discovered several possibilities for action: (1) The division could be eliminated and the work outsourced. (2) Massive changes in the division's personnel could be made such as firing or transferring certain people in an effort to modify the group's disruptive behavior patterns. (3) Dick could challenge the group to reinvent itself and he would provide his support for this effort. Each choice had its pluses and minuses.

Dick chose the third option. He decided to work with the group to bring about needed changes. He attributed the group's problems to a lack of support from previous management. He also believed that several individuals within the group truly wanted to change. Dick felt that his support would show the group that he wanted to empower them. He felt his choice would also send a powerful and positive message to other managers about how to maximize the organization's human capital.

All these choices occurred in Dick's consciousness at his locus of judgment. Others in the company preferred to disband the division or fire certain personnel. They assigned different meanings to information about the division.

Dick commissioned an external consultant to conduct a two-day team-building retreat in a well-appointed resort hotel. He wanted to send a message to the group that they deserved a positive environment in which to work on issues. Dick personally answered the busy telephones to cover the group's work activity while they attended the team-building session. This let them know he would support them in every way he could. After the team-building retreat, Dick contracted for a one-day conflict management training program to help the group overcome problems handling differences. He wanted them to know that he believed in collaboration over destructive competition as the approach to resolve problems. Dick also convinced the other divisions to participate in a customer service audit of his division. He believed his division members needed to understand how others viewed them. He was convinced that they would assist their internal customers better if they were given specific suggestions for change.

These particular choices reveal Dick's clarity of judgment. His choices reflected the meaning he assigned to his reality. Despite the positive impact of the actions Dick took, another manager criticized Dick for his choices.

The Quantum Leader within creates the path while also traveling along it by consciously making choices. Quantum Leaders maximize and assign meaning to choices that provide opportunities for overcoming obstacles. Sam Walton continually looked for ways to attract more customer loyalty and help his employees organize for greater success. Therefore, he spent hours visiting his stores. He gathered as much information as he could and was as aware as possible. In contrast, former RJR Nabisco CEO Lou Gerstner admitted that the company blundered in 1992 because it ignored choices about consumer product demand for low-priced, generic cigarettes. RJR Nabisco had pumped most of its $2.5 billion marketing budget into its high-priced cigarette brands. Phillip Morris and England's BAT Industries' flooded the market with cheap alternatives. Industry volume for plain-wrapped cigarettes ballooned to 10 percent. RJR failed to interpret this information as meaningful.

The Third Quantum Power of Consciousness: Control Over Judgment

Quantum Leaders know that they have 100 percent control over their quality of judgment. They accept responsibility for what happens to them because they determine the meaning of what happens. Quantum Leaders know that all potentialities exist. They understand that they can choose what to observe. They can create alternative possibilities to interpret what they observe.

Quantum Leaders continually generate choices. They create multiple options to uncover as many possibilities as they can. This requires having the intention to do so and keeping attention power focused. You have probably heard statements such as, "That's it! I don't want to talk about it any more!" or, "No, there's no use considering this any further!" Such declarations reveal that consciousness has shut down. They signal that the process of judgment has halted.

Quantum Leaders keep consciousness flexible. This supports the need to interpret every possibility in the most useful manner. Nordstrom, the highly successful, Seattle-based retailer with sales of $8.5 billion in 2006, has formalized this notion for its employees. Its employee policy manual consists of one sentence: *"Use your best judgment at all times."* Keeping consciousness flexible means being aware of the framework or meaning assigned to choices. It involves consciously reframing the choices to create meanings that inspire action and motivate others to follow. This also demands that one's intention be flexible. It involves adapting attention to take in new data.

Quantum Leaders use the components of the Quantum Leadership model to keep consciousness moving and flexible. They map the territory and chart a course to perceive what others don't. They go into the G.A.P. with 100 percent control over judgment, Quantum Leaders know that it is better not to decide until they have to. They seek additional information and evaluate possibilities. They do not *make up their minds*, which usually means closing the mind down, until they are required to make a choice.

Ultimately, of course, a choice for action must be made. Time and space boundaries ultimately limit the range of choices that can be developed. Deadlines must be met. Resources are limited. Important information may not be available. Intention, attention, and judgment guide the Quantum Leader within to take initiative.

Quantum Leader Initiative

Initiative means action. As Napoleon said, "Take time to deliberate, but when the time for action has arrived, stop thinking and go in." And as Ralph Waldo Emerson said, "Good thoughts are no better than good dreams unless they are expressed."

Yasutsugu Takeda's initiative helped create Hitachi's flourishing optoelectronics business because he took action by working with semiconductor lasers. When Takeda first arrived at the company's research labs in 1970, he could not interest any

Hitachi factory in commercializing semiconductor lasers. The lasers were hard to fabricate. General Electric had invented lasers. They backed out of the area precisely because of these fabrication problems. Takeda was unwilling to be derailed by others' disappointments. He created a catalog of semiconductor lasers he could custom-produce at his workbench. He mailed copies to IBM, Bell Telephone, Xerox, and Canon, who placed orders to begin manufacturing the lasers. Armed with the orders, Takeda persuaded the head of one of the Hitachi chip production plants to begin manufacture. By 1992, Hitachi had cornered 60 percent of the world's market for the special laser devices now used by AT&T and others in their transcontinental fiber optic telephone networks.

Initiative has its opposite. It involves thinking about what to do without taking action. Inaction, despite the best intentions, attention, and judgment, foretells failure for those who would otherwise lead. Or as the saying goes, "He who hesitates is lunch!"

In a July 1990, political consultant David Gergan noted that the public would never forget George H.W. Bush's comment as a candidate. "Read my lips." After Bush approved a tax hike, Gergan also argued that the American people would forgive Bush if he acted courageously. In a column written for *U.S. News and World Report*, Gergan suggested that Bush would be exonerated if he would take the necessary steps to wrap up an agreement and solve the budget problem once and for all. Gergan called it "a defining moment" for the President. Yet Bush failed to take action in response to that moment. Instead, he blamed Congress as an unwilling player in the budget morass. Inaction on the domestic economic front plagued Bush throughout the remainder of his presidency. On November 3, 1992, the voters refused to follow him for four more years.

Initiative is the product of intention, attention, and judgment. Initiative results in Quantum Leaders mapping the territory and charting a course. It drives leaders to perceive what others don't. It motivates leaders to perform enlightened action to gain follower commitment. The Quantum Leader within formulates action based on these other three components of consciousness. Initiative curves back through consciousness and motivates the leader within to recommit the intention to lead. Initiative refocuses attention on possibilities and solutions. It refines judgment to develop more choices and to assign meanings that inspire and motivate.

The internal work Dick Frazar did during his daily run paid off for his new division. His intention to make a difference, the hours of attention he devoted to understanding the situation, and his judgments translated into successful action. The team-building and conflict-management interventions he instituted caused key changes within his division. Division members restructured job assignments to even out the workload. A weekly staff discussion meeting was initiated to improve internal communication. Differences could surface more easily. Problem resolution moved towards win-win solutions. The customer service audit resulted in more open and positive lines of communication between the division and its internal customers. Cross-functional learning was introduced so that all groups could better understand others' procedures. This helped everyone be more responsive to each other's work demands. The division members' surly attitudes softened as they came to understand and appreciate the needs and expectations of other departments. Work efficiency increased and staff morale improved.

The Fourth Quantum Power of Consciousness: The Nike Effect

Quantum Leaders recognize that life has limits. They know that action always involves risk. They accept that they cannot do everything. But they also embrace the idea that they can always do *something.* They know they have 100 percent control over their initiative.

The science fiction film *Aliens* depicts a commando group sent into space to investigate a strange alien found during an initial mission. In one scene, the character Ripley and an inexperienced officer in charge of the group observe the commandos on special video equipment as the group reconnoiters the deserted facility in which the alien creature lives. When the commandoes come under a brutal attack by the alien, chaos reigns. Under severe threat, they need direction from their young officer. He becomes paralyzed by fear and confusion. He is incapable of offering meaningful guidance. Ripley shouts at the officer, "Do something, do something," but he remains frozen. Finally, Ripley leaps forward and drives into the facility, rescuing the besieged commandoes.

Ripley's dramatic action illustrates that the Quantum Leader within wears Nike running shoes. The leader is willing to "Just Do It!" The Quantum Leader's consciousness is outfitted with mental Nikes that help him or her take the necessary leap of leadership.

Neuharth's Newspaper: A Feature Story on the Leader Within

It took The Wall Street Journal seventy-seven years to reach a circulation of 1 million readers. USA Today did it in just one year. In just seven years after its inception, with almost 4.8 million readers, "McPaper," as *USA Today* has been labeled, became the number one daily in the United States. As of 2007, *USA Today* still remains number one.

The dramatic impact of *USA Today* originated in the consciousness of Al Neuharth, its founder and father. Neuharth carried in his mind the idea of a national daily newspaper from the time he joined the newspaper business in the 1950's in South Dakota. His intention stayed with him throughout his climb to the top of the Gannett publishing empire.

Neuharth's purpose, says Peter Pritchard in *The Making of McPaper*, was to create a different kind of news daily. Not only would it be national in scope, it would be, in Neuharth's words, "enlightening and enjoyable to the nation's readers; informative and impelling to the nation's leaders; challenging and competitive to the nation's journalists; refreshing and rewarding to the nation's advertisers." He wanted *USA Today* to "serve as a forum for better understanding and unity to make the USA truly one nation."

Once the paper was launched, Neuharth focused his attention on creating the unique format that jumps out from its TV look-alike racks. Neuharth had the paper on his mind when he jogged each day, during meeting breaks, and as he crisscrossed the country in the corporate jet. He spent hours personally checking *USA Today* paper racks in different cities. As he jogged past racks, he would check to make sure that they were filled with papers. Obsessed with quality, he sometimes drove from rack to rack in a limo. His pockets bulged with quarters so he could drop coins in the paper rack slots and check to make sure the racks were stocked with papers. He assessed each issue's color, format, and "feel." In the October 15, 1982, Rochester, New York, edition, Neuharth noticed that the sky on the weather map was purple. He wrote a note to *USA Today* President Phil Gialanella: "Skies are basically blue. What happened?"

Thousands of choices were considered as the paper developed. Sometimes Neuharth's judgments were winners. The use of color photos, especially the full-page color weather maps, the state-by-state news briefs, and the extensive sports statistics were big hits. Some judgments resulted in major mistakes. He ignored the mail delivery and home subscription market. Why? Neuharth's judgment told him to think single-copy sales. This limited the meaningful possibilities of other distribution channels. He purchased a computer system that turned out to be too small to handle the paper's changing and expanding needs, including the huge volume of home subscriptions the paper eventually had.

USA Today has had its critics. It has been denounced as "junk-food journalism, tasty but without substance." The paper lost money for several years. Neuharth expected this and was willing to accept a period of losses. His intention included a long-term view rather than the typical limited sight that pursues short-term profits. Despite its detractors, no one can denounce the impact of Neuharth's newspaper. Nor can anyone deny that the paper has a loyal readership. Many have followed the lead that began and blossomed in Al Neuharth's consciousness. As of 2007, *USA Today* expanded to sell an international edition sold worldwide. Neuharth's news now exists as a consciousness expanding information source for the entire planet.

The Consequences of Consciousness

In his book, *America's Secret War*, George Friedman describes how and why America was caught completely off-guard on September 11, 2001. The entire process reflects the consciousness of key decision makers at the top levels of the U.S. government. Friedman recounts that the U.S. recognized Bin-Laden as an enemy to America. Yet, he explains that during the 1990's Bin-Laden was considered more of a "nuisance" than a serious physical threat to America's safety. Friedman contends that American foreign policy (intention) during that time was concerned with economic matters. He describes how intelligence experts spent almost all of their resources before 9/11 collecting data (attention) versus "connecting the dots" with analysis and interpretation. Friedman proposes that the Al Qaeda was born at the end of the Afghan war. He explains how America helped arm and train rebel fighters for war with the Soviet Union in the 1970's. Yet, he clarifies that the decision makers never considered (judgment) that those rebels would later turn directly against the United States. Given this state of consciousness, it is no wonder that actions (initiative) were not taken that could or would have stopped the attackers.

Experts might disagree with or totally discount Friedman's selection, analysis, interpretation, and conclusions about the facts. Yet alternate explanations about how 9/11 happened would still rely on the same mechanics of consciousness. They would merely propose different intentions, other directions of attention, and alternate judgments.

The key for those who choose to be Quantum Leaders is to self-refer. Clarify your intentions. Focus your attention. Refine your judgment. Then take initiative and learn from your results. This process needs to occur at the local level of small group action and one-on-one activity as well as on the global scale of international politics and business. The scope may be different, but the mechanics, or process of consciousness becoming more lively, expansive, and inclusive, are the same. Each of us makes a difference based on our individual consciousness and how we reflect and shape collective consciousness. It all comes down to choice and self-discipline.

FIELD GUIDE 4

Action Idea 4.1: Join Dick's run.

Make time each day, as Dick Frazar does on his daily run, to consider the structure of your intention. Determine what your intentions are, what they should be, and what they could be. This exercise requires exquisite sensitivity to the inner voice that defines who you are and what you can become. By making time to define your intention, you define the tenor and tone of that inner voice.

Action Idea 4.2: Clarify intention on the spot.

Define your specific intention before entering a situation. Ask yourself, "What is my intention in this situation?" You will know the answer once you reflect on it.

Action Idea 4.3: Focus your intention on leading.

Intend to take the lead. Map the territory and chart a course in the leadership arena. Determine to focus on gaining willing followers. Then be intent on making it happen. This simple act of establishing your intention to lead empowers you to find the means to take action. Do not wait for others to be better leaders. Develop the leader within yourself.

Action Idea 4.4: Adopt a daily opportunity/problem search.

This action idea uses the concept "seek and you shall find." Allocate time each day to search for opportunities or solutions to problems. Look for ways to save a few moments on a work task or determine how your organization can improve customer service, even if only in a small way.

Action Idea 4.5: Conduct an "attention analysis."

An "attention analysis" heightens awareness about a specific issue that requires some improvement. The analysis involves close scrutiny of a particular issue. For example, in the mid-1980s, Ray Alvord joined the Shell Oil Company's Organization Effectiveness and Training corporate office. Part of his mission was to upgrade the training programs offered to Shell managers. Alvord had a long history of adult education expertise in both the military and large corporations. He knew that video technology improved the presentation impact of training content and that it provided a powerful feedback tool for training participants engaged in role-plays. Alvord conducted an attention analysis of the use of videos in Shell's existing training programs by scrutinizing the content of each course. To his surprise he found that only a few instructors used them. When Alvord restructured several courses to include video technology, the instructors and participants reported improvements in the programs.

Action Idea 4.6: Join "AA" for 15 minutes a week.

This means that you "amble aimlessly" (AA) through your work place, keeping your attention open to new possibilities or previously unrecognized problems. Most people are extremely task focused at work, which can put blinders on their awareness. They rush from office to office and from meeting to meeting, or they move from one activity to another with their minds completely filled and unable to take in additional data. A high level of task focus can produce positive results (an attention analysis is an example of this type of behavior), but it can adversely narrow the scope of attention. By "ambling aimlessly" for a few minutes each week through your workplace, you take off the blinders of restricted attention and open your consciousness to new potentialities. Ambling aimlessly provides a time to stretch your mind so it can take in different configurations of information.

Action Idea 4.7: Invite options.

Over the next few weeks, give each person you work with the opportunity to develop at least one alternative option for a decision. More choices keep consciousness moving. The more choices there are, the more possibility there is for better choices. This enhances the capacity to make better judgements.

Action Idea 4.8: Generate five additional choices

When people find the "right answer," consciousness stops moving. During idea generation, most people limit their options by favoring a particular choice too quickly. Therefore, to keep consciousness lively, make it a practice to generate five (or more) additional choices after you believe you have made a really good one.

Action Idea 4.9: Change the meaning.

After you have thought through and interpreted a situation, spend a few minutes considering how the information you have could mean something different. Change the meaning to try and make it more productive, more inspiring, or more interesting.

Action Idea 4.10: Resolve to take the "risk of initiative" at least once a day.

Each day, resolve to take some initiative to overcome a problem, exploit a possibility, and take the lead. Move. Act. Your action will not always result in gaining willing followers, and even if it does, you might not always lead them toward a successful outcome. Initiative involves a risk, but do not be fearlessly foolish. Take reasonable risks. But take some action.

6

Map the Territory and Chart a Course: Perceive What Others Don't

"We all live under the same sky,
but we don't all have the same horizon."
Konrad Adenauer, West Germany's chancellor, 1949-1963

Ron Fisher walked out of the hotel into the blazing Dallas sunlight. He needed a break to think through all the information he had heard during the morning's meetings. It was March 1990. Fisher, a senior researcher at the U.S. Department of Transportation, was participating in a Federal Highway Administration national workshop. The gathered group of industry, government, and academic community experts, informally called Mobility 2000, focused on improving highway transportation through rapidly advancing electronics and communications technologies.

As Fisher walked, the sun's brilliance seemed to help him perceive that the meeting participants were overlooking a critical issue. The workshop had focused almost entirely on ways advanced information technologies could improve private automobile transportation. Fisher believed that more private auto usage would create serious problems. No matter how technologically sophisticated it might become, more cars meant increased pollution. Autos would continue to deplete energy resources. They would certainty create more highway congestion. He recognized that the proposed Mobility 2000 agenda needed to include an additional effort. He perceived the need to improve public transportation usage and increase the development of various ride-sharing choices.

When Fisher returned to Washington, he convinced Brian Clymer, his agency's head, that his vision was worth following. In May, Fisher got Clymer on the program at a national meeting that sought to review the Mobility 2000 effort. Clymer would promote the inclusion of public transportation on the Mobility 2000 agenda and gain a solid base of support. As a result of this summit, the Intelligent Vehicle Highway Society of America (IVHS) was formed. Fisher then built on the support Clymer had established. He convinced key leaders to add a new committee, the Advanced Public Transportation System, to the initial IVHS committee structure. Public transit is now fully integrated into the mainstream effort of the national IVHS program.

Moving Consciousness Into the Leadership Arena

The Quantum Leadership model indicates that Quantum Leaders interact with the leadership arena when they map the territory and chart a course. Mapping means recognizing possibilities and problems. Charting involves creating a direction that takes advantage of opportunities or overcomes obstacles (Figure 6-1). These are the processes Quantum Leaders execute when they operate beyond the boundaries of organizationally prescribed action (the fifth natural law of leadership).

Figure 6.1. The Quantum Leadership Model: The Leadership Arena

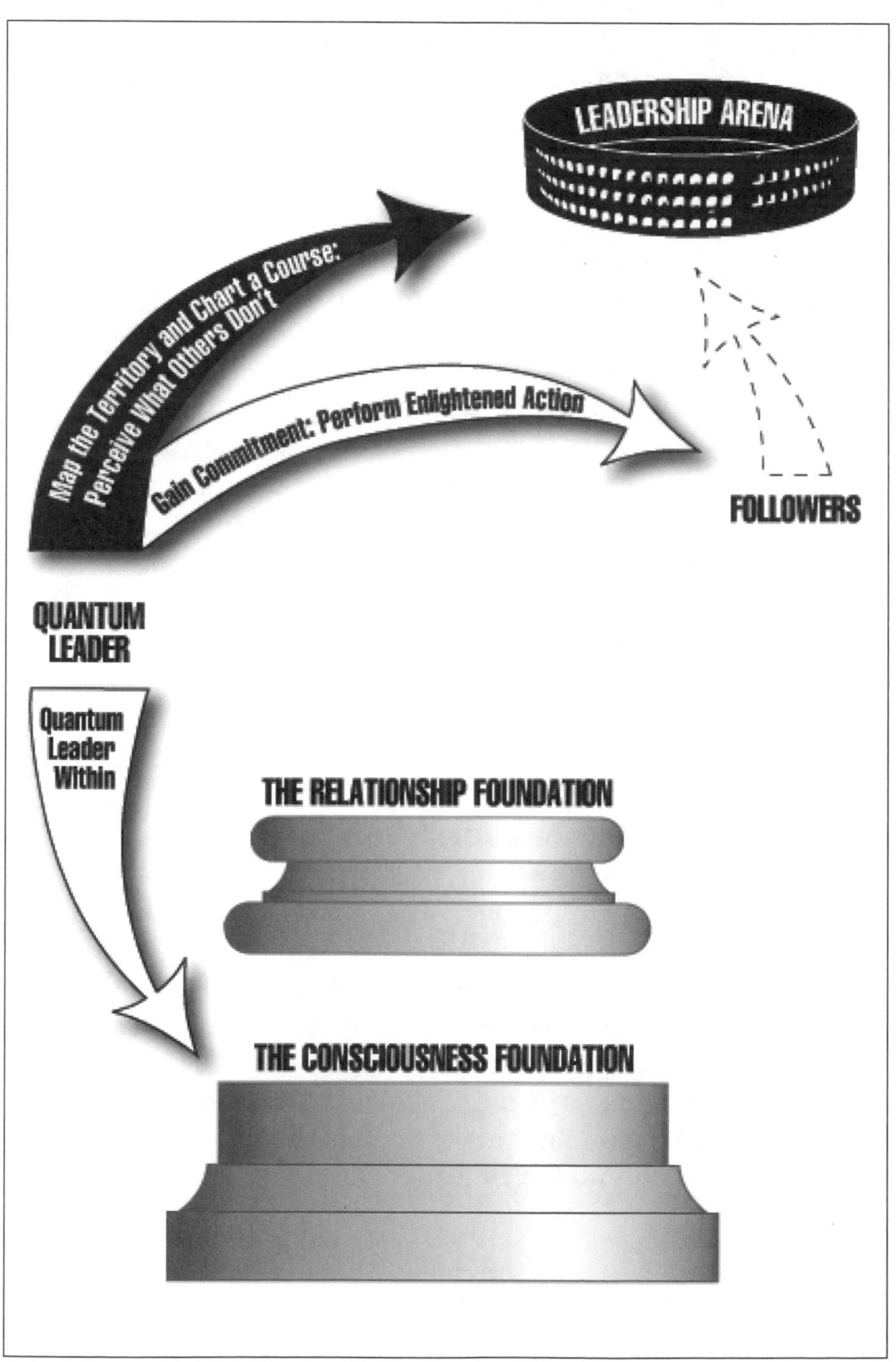

A Road Less Traveled

A simple metaphor explains the process of mapping the territory and charting a course. Picture a road. Imagine that it represents an organization's established pathway and the procedures prescribed to achieve goals or accomplish an agenda. For example, the road could represent the path established to achieve a corporation's strategy. It could symbolize the established procedures of a company's manufacturing procedures or employee benefits system. The road could even portray the prescribed guidelines that govern a small-group meeting, such as a voting system to make decisions. In all of these cases, the road defines the existing system. It is paved with strategies, plans, structures, rules, regulations, policies, and procedures (Figure 6-2).

Figure 6.2. Established organizational pathway

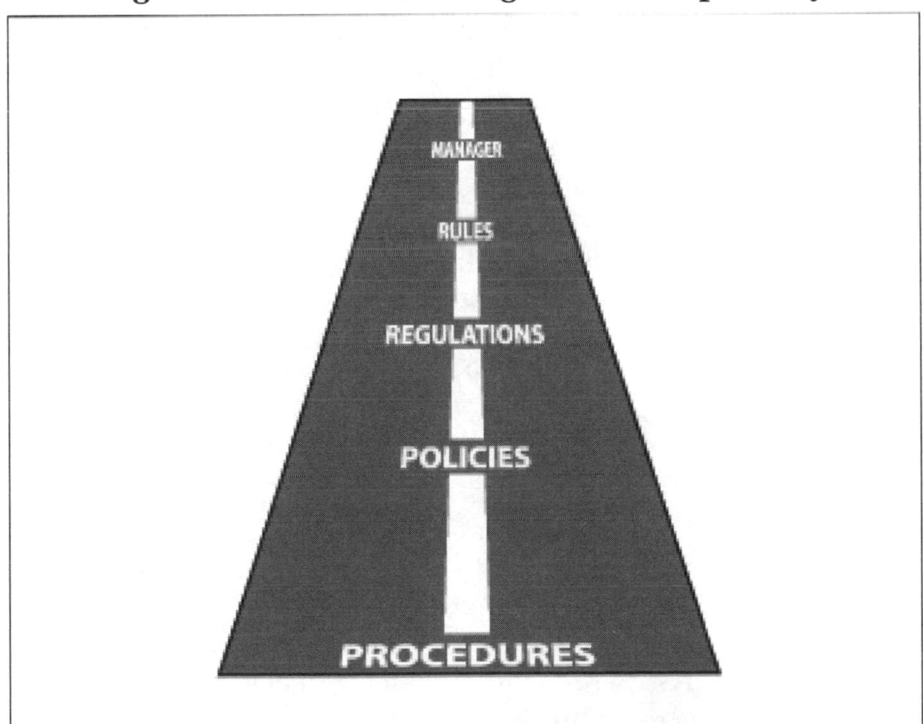

In the road metaphor, managers, or anyone else in positions of formal authority, are responsible for moving the organization or group along the road. They carry out the plan set by the system. They ensure that others comply with the rules, regulations, policies, and procedures. Managers who move straight down the center of the road in double-time are typically considered very successful. Such individuals, labeled the fast trackers, move ahead with unswerving energy. Yet even those who plod along, weaving their way ever so slowly forward, usually reap rewards as long as they continue to make progress along the pathway.

Managerial expertise and formal authority can effectively guide and direct work. It can enable the organization to successfully accomplish its goals if the road adequately enables people to get where they need to go. The prescribed path suffices when, people know what to do. Now imagine a deep rut in the road or an obstacle blocking the road (Figure 6-3). The rut causes people or an entire organization to get stuck. It could be a destructive flare-up between members of a diverse work group, which limits their ability to communicate. The rut could reflect a set of group norms that restrict an organization's ability to take risks. The rut might even be an organization-wide penchant for conducting endless rounds of meetings to make a single decision. If the established rules and regulations offer no method to get people out of the rut, they remain stuck. An obstacle is a barrier that blocks the way. For example, a competitor's unforeseen new product steals an organization's market share. An unexpected equipment breakdown halts a production line. No progress can be made if the established pathway provides no means to get past the unexpected obstacle represented by the roadblock.

There might also be an opportunity that exists off the established pathway. A new market segment or a new technology could create a positive possibility. A new method for designing work processes, or a new approach to evaluating employees could provide opportunities also. However, the means to exploit these opportunities do not exist if the established procedures provide no means to create a new path to them.

In each of these cases, Quantum Leaders are needed to identify the road less traveled. They map the territory to understand the ruts, identify the obstacles, and recognize available opportunities. Then they can chart a course to help people out of the ruts. They direct people around or through obstacles. Leaders also establish a new path to take advantage of opportunities.

Figure 6-3.
Obstacles, ruts, and opportunities along the road

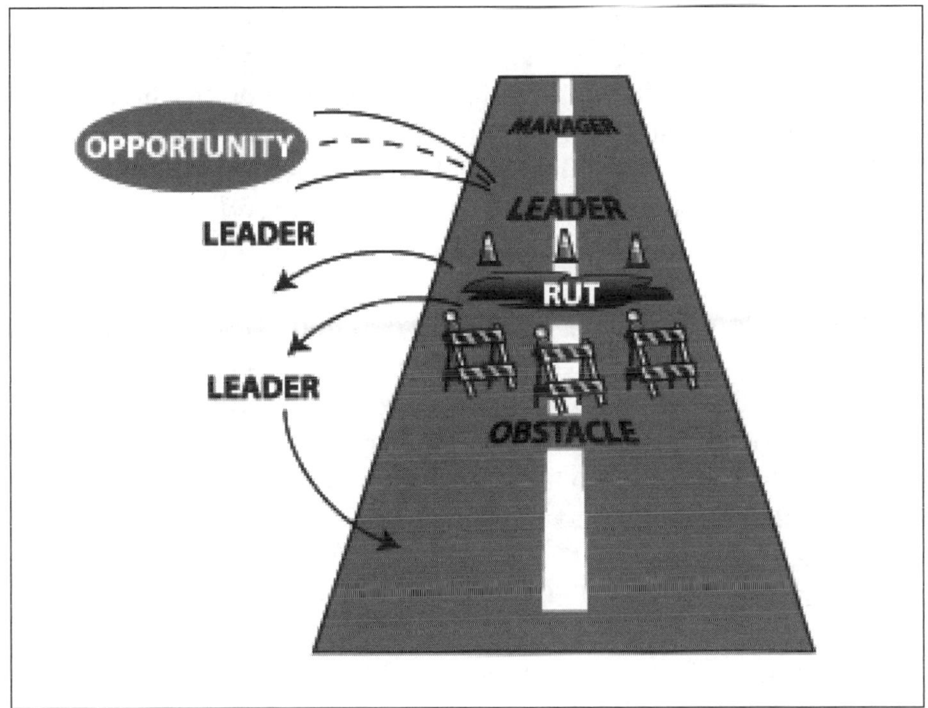

In 1990, Fortune magazine reported how Richard Miller, CEO of the computer company Wang, recognized how a leader helps a company get around a roadblock. One of his managers had discovered that customers had serious complaints about Wang's quality of service. The manager suggested a path to resolve the problem. He proposed giving customers who purchased certain computers a fax machine to gain easy access to Wang for service questions. Furthermore, the manager proposed that the free fax should include a number customers could use to fax messages directly to Miller's desk. Miller accepted the idea and commented, "In my book, that's leadership."

An example of getting out of a rut occurred during an organization's newly formed strategic planning task force meeting. The meeting stalled around the voting procedures the task force would use to make decisions. The organization was composed of three groups, which had always operated autonomously. The goal now was to integrate the organization into a more coherent whole. The task force had a proportionate number of members from each area. One area had five representatives, another had eight representatives, and eleven people represented the third.

Over the two days of its initial task force meeting, the group spent nearly four hours discussing the process it would use to make decisions. Sometimes the debate got heated. When members of one area proposed what it considered an ideal decision-making method, members of the two others balked. They feared that they were not fairly represented by that method. Various points of view were debated. Numerous pros and cons of different decision rules were suggested. But the rut kept getting deeper as the group seemed incapable of agreeing on how it would decide issues.

Finally, a woman who had been silent during these discussions explained that the group members from each of the three areas obviously did not trust members from the other two areas. She indicated that this was understandable since most of them had not worked together before. She thought that trust would come as they worked together. She also pointed out a key aspect of forming the task force. They needed to develop an integrated organizational strategy to blur the existing autonomous operating lines. Therefore, the task force members had to start thinking as representatives of the entire organization, not as delegates from their separate areas. Her comments catalyzed the group. They finally agreed on a decision-making method. The woman got the task force out of a rut and back on track.

Robert Epstein illustrated how leaders map the territory and chart a course to exploit opportunities. Epstein co-founded the computer company Sybase, one of Fortune magazine's 1992 fastest-growing companies. Epstein explained that "an established company's major goal is to defend what it did last year. That's the fatal flaw." Epstein broke that boundary with an opportunistic consciousness. He guided Sybase to create software for the new computer-networking trend. Bigger computer companies, entrenched in existing procedures, did not see the network trend coming.

Quantum Leaders also map the territory and chart a course to reengineer an organization's path. For example, Aetna Life & Casualty improved its process for serving customers whose cars were stolen. It reduced the claim time from a system that used to take between two and five days. The firm created an 800 number that provided all-in-one service. Customers could make one call and find out where to pick up a rental car, the name of the agent who would handle their claim, and an appointment date. Aetna CEO Ronald Compton told Fortune magazine that he expects to save $100 million annually from this reengineering effort.

The Beginner's Mind

Mapping the territory and charting a course occurs when the Quantum Leader's consciousness perceives what others don't. The leader has a unique insight into the uncertainty of the leadership arena. The importance of perceiving what others don't can be illustrated by picturing a group of people trapped in a burning room. Imagine that a pathway to safety is clearly evident to all. The people will not need someone to lead them. They will lead themselves. Now imagine that no visible way to safety is clear. Assume no one seems to know what to do. Someone has to take the lead or the group will perish. If one person then sees a way out and says, "Here, we can escape this way. Follow me!" and the group takes this directive, that person has perceived what others did not and gained followers.

Quantum Leaders have what Zen masters describe as the "beginner's mind." Such a mind is open to possibilities. It is not filled with limiting beliefs, restrictive biases, and faulty assumptions. The Quantum Leader's consciousness moves to identify deeper layers of order and possibilities where others observe only chaos or fail to recognize new choices.

Quantum Leaders know that to foresee something creates it. Ron Fisher foresaw the need for public transit to be part of a federal program to improve transportation. The Advanced Public Transit System was created as a result. The Wang manager perceived a unique method to provide customers with a means to ensure a high level of customer service. The woman in the strategic task force perceived that the group members would learn to trust each other and that they had to think as a unified organization. And Robert Epstein perceived the network trend while others did not.

Perceiving what others don't involves thinking the unthinkable to find and create the future. Observers marveled at Walt Disney's ability to "see beneath the surface." He could visualize possibilities. He pictured the magic and grandeur of Disneyworld in the undeveloped central Florida marshes.

Perceiving what others don't can have a dramatic impact. In *The Crisis Years*, historian Michael Bechloss describes an incident that occurred during the 1962 Cuban Missile crisis. At the height of tension, President Kennedy received a letter from Soviet Premier Khrushchev. It was an impassioned plea for peace worded in a conciliatory tone. Khrushchev seemed to be saying the Soviets would, without conditions, meet the president's demands to withdraw the offensive missiles that U.S. spy planes had discovered in Cuba. Kennedy was elated. The crisis seemed to be over. Then twelve hours later a second letter arrived from Khrushchev. Its tone sounded more belligerent. Khrushchev demanded concessions. In return for the removal of missiles from Cuba, the United States would have to dismantle its own missile sites in Turkey.

Kennedy was furious! He was also stumped. Why the second letter? What did it mean? He and his advisers considered a deeper, more distressing possibility. The language of the second communication did not sound like Khrushchev. What was going on in the halls of the Kremlin? Had the Soviet Central Committee ousted its premier? Was the military now in charge? How should the United States respond to the contradictory letters?

Kennedy gripped the two letters while he and his closest advisers anxiously considered their dilemma. McGeorge Bundy perceived a breathtakingly simple but ingenious solution. He proposed the president simply ignore the second letter. Bundy suggested Kennedy simply respond to the first one. Bundy reasoned that the first letter provided an offer the president could accept. Kennedy stopped in amazement. The idea was brilliant. It could work. He immediately directed Bundy, Attorney General Robert Kennedy, and Ted Sorenson, a key adviser, to draft a reply to the first letter.

The ploy worked. Khrushchev commanded the Soviet ships en route to Cuba to turn back. He ordered the dismantling of those missile sites already in place. He directed the removal of all offensive missile equipment from Cuba. The Cuban missile crisis was over.

Quantum Leadership begins when consciousness becomes alive, moves, and expands to meet a challenge. The classical physics mind-set created the belief that leadership begins with the visible, material reality of action. Quantum physics reveals that the actual starting point for leadership exists in consciousness.

The Components of the Quantum Leader's Consciousness

Mapping and charting have two components: vision and conscious observation. Quantum Leader consciousness perceives what others don't by moving in either or both of these directions to reveal possibilities or uncover problems.

Quantum Leader Vision

Vision is perhaps the most popular buzzword heard today in discussions of leadership and management. In our consulting work, when managers describe what it takes to be a leader, the statement, "The leader must have a vision," is frequently made.

Vision refers to the attractive and credible future state for an entire organization. Vision means attention to the future with a wide-angle and long-range lens of awareness. It involves comprehension of big picture possibilities.

Limited vision forecloses possibilities. In 1895, Lord Kelvin, president of the Royal Society, said, "Heavier than air flying machines are impossible." In 1927, Harry Warner, head of Warner Bros. Pictures, responding to the advent of talking pictures, snapped, "Who the hell wants to hear actors talk!"

A limited vision can foretell serious problems for a company. IBM could not see over the horizon when it chose to place an Intel Corp. microchip and use Microsoft Corp. operating software in its PCs. IBM's move allowed these two companies to become industry giants. It enabled anyone to get into the computer business and clone IBM machines. Had IBM executives perceived with a wider-angle, longer-term view, they might have purchased the technologies from these companies.

Perceptual blinders also stunned Digital Equipment. In 1975, Ken Olsen, Digital's dynamic and intelligent founder, argued, "Nobody is going to want a computer in their house." He ignored the burgeoning PC market in favor of mainframes. The outcome was a huge financial loss for Digital.

Failures of vision might explain a rash of CEO firings that swept across many organizations in the early 1990's: James Robinson III, discredited by American Express; Tom Barrett, wheeled out by Goodyear; James Ketelsen, drummed out by Tenneco; and Rod Canion, deleted by Compaq. In each case, the boards of directors sensed that a new eye was needed to perceive their company's future. Eastman Kodak moved CEO Kay R. Whitmore out of the picture in August 1993. The company's announcement that it would look for an outsider to replace him conveyed a clear message. Kodak wanted a fresh perspective. Only a new focus of consciousness could perceive ways to tackle the changing environment. With vision, Quantum Leaders map the territory to recognize the shape of the horizon and then chart a course to get there.

Map the Territory: Develop Vision

Quantum Leaders map the territory to create a vision of what their organization's future could be. Quantum Leaders focus their wide-angle, long-range lens of awareness on the organization's potential future.

The steps to create a vision include:

1. Identify an ideal future state.
2. Identify core competencies.
3. Consider how well existing strategies and competencies will take the organization to the future state - called a "Niagra Analysis."
4. Map your industry.
5. Map the global landscape.
6. Perform a stakeholder appraisal.

Field Guide 5, located at the end of this chapter, takes you through the specifics of each step. Ron Fisher's story offers a glimpse into how the Quantum Leader-as-perceiver uses the first three steps:

1. He perceived an ideal future: increased technological innovation and reduced pollution, reduced traffic congestion, and improved energy usage.
2. He identified the Department of Transportation's core competencies before he arrived in Dallas.
3. He conducted a Niagara analysis, which revealed a flaw that others did not recognize. He perceived the potential problems regarding an overemphasis on upgrading only private transportation methods. This prompted him to focus on integrating public transit into the overall effort.

In a 1993 article for *The New Yorker*, Ken Auletta describes how Barry Diller applied steps 4, 5, and 6. Diller had a vision for the shop-at-home TV network QVC. This company now has visitation rites in most living rooms today because of that vision. He helped build Fox into the fourth major TV power. In 1992, Diller quit Fox Inc. After leaving the network, he began looking into the world of global communications. He studied the key communications industries including TV networks, cable companies, telephone companies, computer companies, consumer electronics companies, and publishers.

For several months, Diller mapped the territory with focused attention on components of a world previously unknown to him.

He researched digital-compression technology, fiber optic cables, computer equipment, and computer services like Prodigy and interactive TV.

His mapping revealed many new insights. They made him think in new ways. He perceived a "communications enabler" that would sit next to a TV set. It would provide an interactive format to offer consumers any form of information or entertainment they wanted. The television would be transformed into an input-output device with a computer remote like a computer mouse. Diller perceived that TV cable systems would lead the way into the information future. He had learned that 63 percent of all American homes were already wired for cable. Furthermore, when Diller met with cable people, he was impressed by their lively, inquisitive nature and by the way they treated technology as an ally.

Diller hit upon QVC, the home shopping network, which he saw as a powerhouse for the future to realize his vision in the world of interactive media. In its first twenty months of operation, QVC earned nearly $56 million. By 2007, QVC sales were estimated at $1.6 billion. Diller perceived QVC as a vehicle-the springboard to a universe beyond the limited world of TV channels, an interactive information services medium. He became a partner and CEO of QVC.

The six steps clarify the forces you will face as you chart a course to move towards realizing your vision.

Chart a Course: Propose a Vision

Mapping the territory with vision provides a picture of the unknown future across a wide landscape. Quantum Leaders-as-perceivers then direct consciousness to chart a course to define or redefine how to get where they want to go.

The steps to propose a vision include:

1. Clarify what would make your company a success in the future - called a "future world screening."
2. Identify what must be done differently - called "produce your own movie."

Field Guide 5 also explains the specifics involved in these two steps.

Daniel Lubetzky demonstrated implementation of these steps in a 2004 *Fortune* story told by Elaine Pofeldt. In 1993, Lubetzky contacted Yoel Benesh just after Benesh's Israeli food factory was shut down. Lubetzky liked Benesh's sun-dried-tomato spread sold in non-descript jars. He was disappointed that the company had gone out of business. Benesh explained part of his difficulty. His Palestinian employees had to travel from the West Bank to the Gaza Strip where the factory was located. Terrorist violence frequently caused the Israeli government to shut the borders. Benesh's workers could not get to work on a regular basis so he had to shut down his factory.

Lubetzky proposed his vision. He clarified ways the company could succeed and several things he would do differently. Lubetzky would market the product in the U.S. He would highlight the Israeli-Palestinian cooperation with a brand name, Moshe & Ali. The label would include the slogan, *"Cooperation never tasted so good!"* and two cheery cartoon characters: Moshe, an Israeli chef and Ali, an Arab magician. Lubetzky pounded the pavement to market the product. He signed hundreds of stores within a year. Today, Moshe & Ali spreads sell in about 5,000 U.S. stores and yield a $10 million dollar profit.

Quantum Leader Conscious Observation

A friend once told me, "God is in the details." I heard from someone else that, "the devil is in the details." I am not sure which of these statements is true. Both do suggest that a conscious awareness of the details is important to some pretty powerful folks.

The second way Quantum Leaders map the territory and chart a course is through conscious observation. Conscious observers pay attention to the day-to-day, hour-to-hour, minute-to-minute realities that make up most people's daily work routine. They use a zoom lens focus on all the particulars. They map the specific possibilities and problems that affect the present and more immediate future to chart a course that addresses the detail surrounding opportunities and obstacles.

Conscious observers "look at the company, not at the paper," as Tom Watson, founder of IBM, described it. They go into the trenches to study, stare, and scrutinize what is going on. In 1970, Robert Townsend explained the value of conscious observation. He clarified the need to get out of the office and observe his company's operation. After one year as head of rental car company Avis, Townsend turned the company around from drowning in red ink to a highly profitable balance sheet. In *Up the Organization*, Townsend credits much of his success to the time he spent out of the executive suite and in the trenches with the employees and customers.

William Malec, chief financial officer of the Tennessee Valley Authority (TVA), practices conscious observation. One day each month he spends time doing the job of a TVA employee. Malec might scrub toilets at midnight. He could sort mail at 5:00 A.M. He might punch in data for the purchasing clerk. Or Malec could perform any one of the other jobs held by the 2,000 employees at the TVA facilities in Muscle Shoals, Alabama, Knoxville or Chattanooga, Tennessee. Malec explained his motivation to *Forbes* magazine: "When you get down into their jobs, they will tell you things you normally don't hear."

Henry Schinberg is president and chief operating officer of Johnston Coca-Cola Bottling Group of Chattanooga, Coke's number 2 bottler. Schinberg is also an astute conscious observer. Schinberg spends 80 percent of his time in the field. He meets with retailers and visits Johnston's sixty-five plants and distribution centers scattered throughout the Midwest. The computer terminal on his desk pumps out details that Schinberg drinks up ravenously. As he told *Fortune* writer Patricia Sellers, "I can tell you how much of each brand we sold yesterday in any city and the average discount and the profit margins."

King Henry V wandered from campfire to campfire, chatting with the soldiers on the eve of the Battle of Agincourt. Jack Welch, former CEO of General Electric, made time each month to go to Crotonville, GE's management development center. He met directly with managers attending courses and answered their questions.

Conscious observation is the quantum power of attention power turned up to high. It is a requirement of those at all organizational levels who have the intention to lead. Conscious observation may seem like a commonsense behavior. Yet, many organizations have suffered when consciousness failed to zoom in and respond to critical details.

Consider the Pinkerton Agency, America's first private detective firm. Pinkerton's logo is the unblinking eye. Its motto reads, "We never sleep." This focus helped Pinkerton become the largest, most revered security company in the country. Yet in 1988, Pinkerton's stellar reputation was severely tarnished. The company was bleeding money. It nuclear security division alone was losing $2 million a year. Some regional offices employed twenty people when only two were needed. Other branches were supposed to have entire fleets of automobiles, but no one could locate them. Still other branches had 120-day-old receivables with nobody out trying to collect them. It would not take Sherlock Holmes to recognize these elementary clues, described by S. Greengard in *American Way* magazine. Someone at Pinkerton must have been asleep to overlook such problems.

Here is a simple test to challenge your abilities as a conscious observer. Count the number of f's in the following:

Count The f's

The length of feature films
and the information they
contain cannot be found in
films of shorter duration.

How many did you get? Five, six, seven, eight? Count again if you did not find eight. Notice which ones you missed. People usually overlook the small details such as the f in the words "of." Or, they simply do not consider certain information such as the "f" in the title. Think of how this activity impacts your experience in meetings or while taking action on your own. Do you miss some small details because of lack of attention, failure to focus, or simply not being engaged?

Map the Territory: Develop Conscious Observation

Quantum Leaders map the territory with conscious observation to identify more immediate and localized opportunities and problems. They apply Lyndon B. Johnson's maxim, "Stop keeping your head below the grass." Johnson recognized the dangers in not looking around. He noted the failures that result from not minding what's going on. He realized the problems created when we do not observe, study, and scrutinize specific events. Johnson felt leaders needed to get their heads above the grass even if that put us at risk (the sixth natural law of leadership). Be a conscious observer. Lift your head up. Look at the events around you. There is safety below the grass. But you cannot perceive how to take the lead from that posture. Four specific actions will help you develop your conscious observer skills:

1. Devote time every day to the details - called "Watch the message board."
2. Pay constant attention - called "Place the Pala bird on your shoulder."
3. Consider your priorities before you ignore information - called "Remember the Challenger."
4. Practice "up periscope" on a daily basis.

Field Guide 5, located at the end of this chapter, describes how you apply these actions. Consider the following examples as illustrations of these three actions.

- A plant foreman walks through the site every day and reads equipment gauges, notes any employees who seem to be struggling, or observes how moving a pallet would allow carts to move more easily through narrow corridors.
- A software service supervisor peruses the daily call logs that specify types of problems customers frequently mention so that she can relay them back to the design group and eliminate the difficulties at their source.
- A security analyst challenges a group's dismissal of data about telephone inquiries related to the number of times her city's drawbridges open each day citing how such bridges would be easy targets for terrorist bombers.

Chart a Course: Propose a Conscious Observer's Direction

Mapping the territory with conscious observation provides a sharp focus of awareness. Quantum Leaders then direct their awareness to chart a course along a specific path for the more immediate and localized environment. The key here is to take action that addresses your conscious observer findings. For example, consider a retail manager who takes the time each day to notice a trend in customer traffic patterns in the store. This conscious observation suggests the value in moving certain merchandise so that customers notice it more easily and thus they might be more interested in purchasing it.

Abraham Lincoln illustrated this aspect of offering direction based on his conscious observation. He practically lived at the War Department during crucial Civil War battles. He slept on an office sofa so he could get information as soon as possible. He would peer over the telegrapher's shoulder and react instantly to breaking news. Lincoln took to the battlefield himself when he was dissatisfied with General McClellan's lack of aggressiveness in a battle for Norfolk, Virginia. Consciously observing, Lincoln traveled to a point near Norfolk where the Union troops were bogged down while McClellan stalled farther down the line. The president personally ordered an artillery assault. He then proceeded down the coast and walked ashore to scout the ideal spot for an amphibious landing. When Lincoln returned to the fort, he ordered an attack in which his troops quickly captured the city.

The same mechanics used to propose your vision are used to propose your conscious observer course of action except the focus is on localized specifics rather than long-term, big-picture issues. That means:

1. Clarify what would yield success for the specific issue.
2. Identify what must be done differently

Field Guide 5 describes a process to propose a conscious observer direction.

Quantum Perception: The Dual-Angle Lens

Futurist Alvin Toffler once said, "You have to think the big things while doing the small things so the small things go in the right direction." Quantum Leadership involves a combination of vision and conscious observation. Quantum Leaders use their long-range, wide-angle lens of awareness to perceive the extended path for their organization. They also zoom their consciousness in to uncover the day-to-day bumps and alternate routes along the way.

Bill Gates of Microsoft displays this dual-action Quantum Leader capability. He is as likely to check for mathematic errors in handouts and overhead slides as he is to critique fuzzy long-term marketing strategies.

Ray Kroc, McDonald's Restaurants founder, could see with both the long-term and close-up eye. On Kroc's numerous visits to McDonald's franchises around the world, he checked on every detail. He noted how hot the French fries were while also keeping in mind his overall vision: "Quality, Cleanliness, and Service."

Barry Diller supported his vision for QVC by conscious observation. He frequently interrupted what he was doing to watch QVC programming. He regularly attended to the actions of rival Home Shopping Network (HSN). If he noticed HSN selling lots of pillows, he might suggest that QVC offer them also.

The capacity to perceive simultaneously with a wide-angle, and a zoom lens might appear to require extraordinary perceptual ability. Yet we all have that capacity of consciousness. Think about driving a car. We can perceive both a changing traffic light several hundred yards away and observe the moving needle of the speedometer, less than two feet away. Consider your experience reading this book. One element of your awareness focuses on the words. You can also simultaneously be aware of how to apply what you read in your job. Consciousness is a quantum phenomenon. It is boundless and fluid information-energy, not hard and inflexible like solid matter. Field Guide 5 offers an action to practice dual-angle vision.

◆◆◆

FIELD GUIDE 5

Action Idea 5.1: Identify an ideal future state.

Focus your Quantum Leader-as-perceiver consciousness on what your organization could become in its industry or in related industries. JVC imagined a VCR sitting in every home; Motorola wants to place a hand-held personal communicator in your pocket. Defining what you want to become maps the territory of the uncreated future. Spend time each week imagining possible futures for your organization. Ask yourself, "If the organization could be anything it wanted to be, and do it well, what would we be?"

Action Idea 5.2: Identify core competencies.

What skills and technologies does your organization need to achieve your ideal future state? What will your organization have to do to provide customer benefits in unique ways that will distinguish it in the future? Federal Express founder Fred Smith had a vision of overnight package delivery. He foresaw the need to develop competencies in bar-code technology, wireless communication, and network management.

Action Idea 5.3: Conduct a "Niagara analysis."

If you found yourself in a boat heading for a plunge over Niagara Falls, you would have to make some fast decisions to change course. A Niagara analysis means you ask yourself: "Will the organization's existing strategy and competencies take it to the ideal future state, or will we plummet over the falls?" The previous two action ideas move your consciousness to perceive where you want to be and the resources you need to get there; the Niagara analysis brings the future and the present face to face to evaluate what you have to do to get where you want to go.

Action Idea 5.4: Map your industry.

Identify the key competitors you expect to face in the future based on your current industry rivals. Specify industry strengths and weaknesses in comparison to your organization. Be ruthless; this is not the time for wishful thinking or vain comparisons that diminish the capacities of your rivals. Your vision must not be blurred with overly optimistic forecasts.

Action Idea 5.5: Map the global landscape.

Specify factors from the larger global landscape that might have an impact on your organization. Think big. What technological trends could reshape or completely redefine your industry? Do not ignore industries or social/political forces that appear to be tangential. In a global competitive environment, everything can affect everything else. Negotiations between Denmark and other European nations regarding the formation of the European Community seemed far removed from store sales at Fiesta, a Houston-based grocery chain. Yet the European Community's bargaining activities led to a resolution regarding import restrictions on apples grown in Denmark. This affected Fiesta's produce offerings. Map the global landscape to increase your awareness of any second- or third-order influences on your organization's long-term behavior.

Action Idea 5.6: Perform a stakeholder appraisal.

List the key constituents your organization has to serve to survive today. Then list those whom you might serve in your desired future. Include any persons, groups, or institutions that can exert influence on your organization or that your organization strongly influences. Specify their interests, priorities, and expectations. Identify the potential opportunities and threats stakeholders pose to your company now and in the future. The three previous action ideas help clarify the forces you will face as you chart a course to move toward your vision.

Action Idea 5.7: Attend a future world screening.

Imagine that you have the chance to attend a unique cinema that shows films from the future. In the future world cinema, your company achieves your vision. What makes your company successful in this future world? How did your organization get to this place? Be flexible and speculative in your answers. Many possibilities could explain this future reality. Consider how far into the future your film projected. Should you extend the time frame because your horizon is too close? If your perception is too vague, should you draw it back to clarify the path? Now focus on the details that defined your success. What technologies, customers and their needs, or competitive realities exist that your company exploited to get ahead?

Action Idea 5.8: Produce your own movie.

What should your organization begin to do differently now to realize the success you saw in the future world cinema? Chart a course with any and all possibilities that could work. What do your organization and its members have to learn now to compete? How does your organization develop or acquire the necessary technologies? Create several versions of a movie that portrays how your organization succeeds. Cut and edit your script to determine which picture gives you the most useful course. Have several "pre-screenings" of your movie. Ask trusted colleagues to review and critique your ideas before broadcasting them to a larger audience.

Action Idea 5.9: Watch the message board.

Imagine your organization is a message board continually blinking with information about opportunities and solutions to problems that people might typically miss. "Watch the message board" means spending time each day consciously focused on any signals or cues and then using your discrimination to determine their meaning. You already have significant experience in message board responsiveness. Consider how you react to your ringing telephone, e-mail, the blinking light on your answering machine, or the beeping sound from your microwave oven. Most people jump to acknowledge these messages, but they turn off their homing device of consciousness to a myriad of other messages blinking, beeping, flashing, and ringing all around them. Use the same receptivity to traditional message indicators when you watch the entire organization as a message board

Action Idea 5.10: Place the Pala bird on your shoulder.

In the Nobel Prize-winning novel Island, Aldous Huxley described Pala, a mythical paradise in which a strange black bird flew about squawking in a high, nasal monotone the phrases, "Attention, Attention" and "Here and now, here and now." Place an imaginary bird on your shoulder to let its call remind you to observe. Focus your attention power. Maintain your awareness on the messages of the present.

Action Idea 5.11: Remember the Challenger.

Warning messages were sent about the faulty seals on the Challenger space shuttle in 1985, but those messages were ignored in favor of other "priorities." Remembering the Challenger may help you pay close attention to your own priorities about the relevance of information.

Action Idea 5.12: Practice perceiving with double vision.

Identify an organization-wide, long-term issue that you believe needs attention. Then specify a detail in your immediate environment that requires concern. Spend 10 minutes each day consciously connecting the big picture issue with the detail. Play with ways to integrate and enfold them into each other. This practice will help you develop the spontaneous ability of the dual-angle-focused Quantum Leader-as-perceiver.

Action Idea 5.13: Practice "up periscope" on a daily basis

Imagine you are in a submarine deeply submerged in potentially dangerous waters. What do you do to determine whether it is safe to surface? One valuable option is to use the periscope on your vessel to get a look at the type and extent of possible challenges. The submarine periscope would allow you maintain some degree of safety and also to see in all directions. In a similar fashion, consider times when you need to "look up," "expand your field of awareness," or rotate your focus of awareness 360 degrees. Each of us has an "internal periscope" that enables us to raise our perspective to observe situations from multiple angles. We do not need to take any action at that point. We only need to observe, consider, and map our environment to ensure we are not missing something important in all areas of our environment. Once we have a better sense of what is going on through an "up periscope" analysis, we can take more conscious and effective action.

7

Go Into the G.A.P.

"We can only achieve quantum steps of improvement if we get the organization looking at the issues in totally new ways."
George Gerhard Schulmeyer, president and CEO of Asel

What enables Quantum Leaders' consciousness to perceive what others don't? What allows Quantum Leaders to process information from a unique perspective? How does their consciousness operate in distinctive ways?

The Quantum Leadership model indicates that leaders move their consciousness into the G.A.P. They interact with the leadership arena and "gain another perspective" of awareness. Going into the G.A.P. means opening awareness to new ways of observing, interpreting, and evaluating information. From the G.A.P., Quantum Leaders break the boundaries of conditioned perception that restrict attention and limit or negatively affect judgment. Operating from the G.A.P. allows Quantum Leaders to get into a state of "not knowing" so they can then adopt an information-receiving attitude of finding out.

Quantum Leaders use expanded levels of consciousness to go into the G.A.P. They step outside an existing paradigm to create an organizational vision and consciously observe the important interactions that make up day-to-day work activities.

Three Approaches Into the G.A.P.

Quantum Leaders go into the G.A.P. from three approaches. They:

1. Seek information from alternate sources.
2. Expand their interpretative range.
3. Increase their response options.

Seek Information From Alternate Sources

J. W Marriott, Jr., visits his hotel chain's kitchens, laundry, and telephone reservation centers to find out what is working and if anything is not up to standard. These are not the typical stomping grounds for CEOs of global corporations. Marriott's behavior illustrates the process of seeking information from alternate sources.

Quantum Leaders go into the G.A.P. by seeking information from new, different, untapped, forgotten, previously overlooked, or typically ignored sources. The process compares to expanding from a 30-channel cable TV to a 500- or 5,000-station offering. Quantum Leaders hook their consciousness into the broadest range of information available to get more and different input from more and different sources. This is a conscious, intentional process. Rather than waiting for apples to fall, Quantum Leaders shake the tree.

Opening up the channels of awareness might seem obvious. Yet many efforts falter because people stop processing or do not fully process the environment's available information-energy. Consider the Iraq war initiated by the Bush administration in 2003. Almost everyone agreed that the U.S. had the military might to easily defeat Saddam Hussein and overthrow his brutal government. However, countless members of the State Department and the Pentagon and numerous experts warned the administration of the dangers the U.S. would face *after* it "won" the war. These obvious and important channels were either discounted or ignored. As of January 2008, almost five years after the invasion, American forces continued to face combat conditions in Iraq. Quantum Leaders do not make such mistakes. They apply the commonsense practice of seeking information from alternate sources which, for others, is not common practice.

Four general mechanics describe how Quantum Leaders go into the G.A.P. and enhance their information seeking:

1. Stop, Look, and Listen.
2. Audit with the five senses.
3. Attend to new channels.
4. Mine the consciousness in others with question power.

Stop, Look, and Listen

Quantum Leaders stop, look, and listen to the information-energy that flows through their organization. They stop their normal routine, look around their operation, and listen to what people are saying. Stop, look, and listen (SLL) turns up information receptivity so people can take in all the signals. Many of the action ideas in previous chapters guide you to stop, look, and listen. For example, fix your sights on nonprescribed areas (Chapter 2). Expand your field into different parts of the organization (Chapter 3). Adopt a daily opportunity - problem search. Conduct an attention analysis. Join "AA" for 15 minutes a week (Chapter 5). Watch the message board (Chapter 6).

Audit With All Five Senses

Quantum Leaders go into the G.A.P. by using their full range of sensory input. They audit all five of their five senses to open their perception to new sources of information. They consider how situations feel, sound, look, smell, and even taste to gain another perspective.

I once asked an R&D scientist in the Procter & Gamble food division how he knew he had a good cookie, cake mix, or other bakery product. He smiled, then stuck his tongue out at me. I was puzzled by the meaning of this gesture, but I figured it meant something. So, I did not respond. His smile turned into a big grin as he said, "I taste it!" He then gave a full belly laugh and said, "How else could I know if it was any good!" He further explained that if his taste test caused him to spit the food out, the lab kept working on the product. If he chewed it but would not swallow, he talked with the rest of the R&D staff about possible improvements. If he took the food home to his wife and kids and they liked it, he might then talk to the marketing group.

A five-sense audit tunes your attention to sensory data that others no longer recognize or discount. I have consulted with many organizations that have work areas so noisy you have to shout at the person next to you to be heard. I wonder whether anyone else's eardrums ring after being in those noisy work areas. I have sat with managers in hundreds of meetings for thousands of hours on extremely uncomfortable chairs. I wonder if anyone else is in touch with how difficult it is to keep the upper part of the anatomy alert while the lower end becomes numb.

We have watched dozens of presenters strain the eyes of their audience. They project slightly out-of-focus images on screens. They use tiny typefaces that no one beyond the second row can read. They keep the lights so bright the projected image is washed out. We wonder what these presenters see when they look out at the audience. We are always amazed when we walk past the seafood department in a grocery store and our noses get filled with the smell of rotten fish. Quantum Leaders do not miss these signals of poor quality. They go into the G.A.P. with heightened sensory alertness. They hear, see,touch, smell, and taste a need or potentiality for action. Consult Field Guide 6 for specific actions on how to use all five senses.

Tune in to New Channels

Quantum Leaders consciously accept information from new or different channels They intentionally expose themselves to alternate data sources. The leader within them makes being open to new information sources a regular practice. For example, part of Japan's rise to economic excellence in the 1980's stemmed from its unflinching willingness to take in data from new channels. This willingness to go into the G.A.P. originated in 1868 when the Emperor Meiji announced the Five Articles Imperial Oath: "Japan will be receptive to knowledge and technology from whatever source it comes. Japan will send students to the United States and Europe, and will invite foreign experts to come to Japan and disseminate their knowledge to the Japanese." This oath, says Chin-Ning Chu in *The Asian Mind Game*, has served as the focus of Japanese economic and political objectives ever since.

The process of attending to new channels is quite simple. Turn your attention power to information sources you normally do not use. Field Guide 6 offers choices on how to do this.

Mine the Consciousness Around You With Question Power

Quantum Leaders do not have to seek information directly. They know that their time and energy limits their ability to use stop, look, and listen, conduct five-sense audits, and tune in to new channels. They also know that, even if they had no limits on their capacity to apply these methods, they could still miss important waves of information. Quantum Leaders rely on others to feed them information that will help them go into the G.A.P.

Quantum Leaders realize that people who are sure they have the answers stop asking questions. They also know that people who stop asking questions rarely venture beyond the prescribed path. Consider the now well-know statement, "It's a slam dunk, Mr. President," by George Tenent, then CIA Director. In 2002, George W. Bush had asked Tenent if he was sure Saddam Hussein had weapons of mass destruction (WMD). Apparently no further questions were asked since the President announced to the world that he had "proof" of WMD. A few more questions might have revealed more information about this "proof" which has never been verified.

A positive example of question power comes from Dr. Joseph Hoeg when he was head of the Range Directorate at the Naval Air Warfare Center in Patuxent River, Maryland. Hoag regularly mined the consciousness of others. The Range Directorate employs over 200 people located in ten offices all over the sprawling naval base. Every Friday, Hoag drove from office to office and visited various work sites. He constantly asked questions to help him tune in to alternate sources of information.

Questions excavate ideas, choices, possibilities, solutions, and alternatives. Questions drive the software of consciousness to combine and integrate information. They also determine what we pay attention to. So good questions lead to more focused attention power. The result in more refined discrimination. They help us discover better answers.. Quantum Leaders do not have all the answers. They can ask questions to uncover possible answers.

Quantum Leaders use questions to focus others' awareness toward uncovering problems and finding potential ways to solve them. Brian Dumaine, writing in *Fortune* magazine, explained how Mike Walsh used question power while he was CEO at Union Pacific. Walsh regularly reached into the ranks and asked anyone he could contact, "If you were CEO of this company, what would you do?" Walsh explained his motivation: "The people inside your company know a lot more than you think they do."

Quantum Leaders use question power to plug into critical information from all sources. They rely on secretaries, customers, suppliers, managers, as well as line and staff employees. Quantum Leaders view every person as a satellite dish that is connected to some meaningful wavelength of information-energy. These people become idea givers who can fuel the Quantum Leader-as-perceiver's awareness.

Walt Disney mastered the use of questions to gather input from others. Whenever a new project, script, or idea was launched, he would display it on a wall-sized whiteboard. He scrawled the question, "How can we improve this?" at the top of the wall as an invitation for everyone's response. People wrote their ideas, suggestions, solutions, and comments all over the wall. Then Disney would review the wall and use the best ideas. He involved the collective consciousness of his entire team to help him get into the G.A.P. and to expand his perceptual capacity.

Any questions can uncover the potentially useful information pulsating within your organization. Eight categories of questions can be used to maximize your ability to go into the G.A.P. The question categories are: understanding, solution, action, meaning, dumb, possibility, alternative, and necessity questions. The acronym U.S.A. M.D. P.A.N. can help you remember all of them.

Ask U - Understanding questions.
Understanding questions direct people to clarify the facts or information needed to comprehend a situation. They focus attention on the details that help make important distinctions. Sample "U" questions are: "What do we need to understand about this situation?" "What don't we know about this situation?" "What facts are we missing or misinterpreting?" "What is the difference or similarity between this and that?"

Ask S - Solution questions.
Solution questions create awareness of specific ways to overcome problems. They funnel creativity and clarity into potentially workable choices. Use S questions to converge thinking on particular choices to chart a course. Examples include: "What choices might solve this problem?" "How can we improve the outcome in this case?" "What direction would help us take advantage of this situation?"

Ask A - Action questions.
Action questions translate thoughts into behavior. They clarify the specific steps needed to carry out solutions. Ask action questions to chart a specific course toward a goal. For example: "What actions do we need to take?" "What specific behaviors do we need to perform?"

Ask M - Meaning questions.
Meaning questions help people consider what is important. The clarify why people should take any action or consider any choices. They get at core values and purposes. Ask meaning questions to clarify intentions and define underlying motivations. For example, "What is important to us?" "Why does this matter to us?" "Why would we want to do this?"

Ask D - Dumb questions.
Dumb questions invoke the wisdom of the old adage, "The only dumb question is the one you don't ask." After asking a variety of U.S.A. and M. questions, you can ask. "Are there are any questions that have not been asked.?" People usually do not ask questions because they are afraid they will look foolish. They think they should perhaps already know the answer. Instead, ask every dumb question you can think of. That means never *not* ask a question. As Aristotle said, "When you ask dumb questions, you get a smart answer."

Ask P - Possibility questions.
Possibility questions stretch thinking beyond existing boundaries. They open up new vistas. They ask people to imagine what might be or what could be. Sample possibility questions are: "If there was a way to do it, what would it be?" "If you could improve this in any way possible, how would you do it?" "What might be a way to solve this problem?" Possibility questions are especially potent when consciousness stalls or will not move further. For example, use a possibility question the next time you hear someone close the doors of perception. Suppose someone says, "It won't work," or "There's no sense in focusing on that." Consider using these responses. "Okay, and if it could work, what would we do?" or "You might be right. And, if there was a useful way to focus on the issue, how would we do it?" In our experience, asking possibility questions has a powerful impact. People who initially shut down their awareness often pause, then immediately restart their thinking. Consciousness moves with possibility questions.

Ask A - Alternative questions.
People usually do not bother thinking of additional answers after they fix on the "right answer." Quantum Leaders search for the second, third, and fourth "correct answer" to break the boundaries that limit awareness. Ask alternatives questions to accomplish such breakthroughs. These questions are especially important because of the classical

physics conditioning that guided most people's schooling. The Newtonian assumption of linear, cause-and-effect reality has led most people to think that problems have one solution. People are programmed to believe that there is one right answer to each question. Indeed, the hundreds of murderous multiple-choice tests we took in school were written to comply with the one-right-answer logic of the classical physics mind-set. Habituated to this approach, we close up our thinking shop (and we feel good about it!) when we get the "right answer." Quantum Leaders shatter such thinking by accepting that other answers could have value. They use what Roger Von Oech, in *A Whack on the Side of the Head*, calls "the second right answer." Ask alternatives questions to accumulate multiple answers. Sample questions include: "What else is a correct answer?" "What are some answers?" (as opposed to "What is the answer?") and "What else would solve the problem?"

Ask N - Necessity questions.
Necessity questions focus on what must be done to carry out possibilities and alternatives. They direct attention to the practical actions needed to make things happen. They balance the divergent, no-holds-barred thinking of possibility and alternatives questions. They provide convergence to guide practical application. Examples include, "What must we do to accomplish this?" "What specifics must we consider?" and "How must we respond to this particular issue now?"

These mechanics do not guarantee finding any particular information. Rather, they are the instruments Quantum Leaders can use to hunt more effectively as they map the territory and chart a course.

Field Guide 6 outlines a process to apply U.S.A. M.D. P.A.N. questions.

Expand Your Interpretative Range

Quantum Leaders gain another perspective when they consciously interpret or evaluate information from a new, different, overlooked, or previously discarded level of awareness. They expand their interpretative range of consciousness to comprehend information from another perspective. This process is structured in the way our mind's work.

The mind has evaluative filters through which information is recognized, accepted, ignored, or rejected. The brain responds to data by comparing new information with an existing, accepted framework of past experience. Humans have a storehouse of impressions or established set of mental models coded into our brains. For example, a production supervisor might evaluate marketing projections for new product orders based on the orders from previous years. Or a strategic planning group might evaluate the impact of new technological trends in its industry by comparing them to established technologies and existing trends.

Most people reject, ignore, perceive as meaningless, fail to consider fully, or even denounce and demonize new information. They do so because they cannot create a reasonable match with new information and their past experiences. They discount new information when it does not fit their mental biases or internal hard-wiring.

For example, the production supervisor might evaluate the new product order projections as "way out of line" because they do not fit the fairly stable number of orders that marketing has taken over the past several years. The supervisor might even question marketing's motives by thinking, "Marketing is probably trying to impress someone upstairs." Similarly, the strategic planning group might evaluate a new technological trend as unimportant for the industry. They might interpret the information as not fitting into the established technology or direction of the existing trend. The strategic planners might even denounce the proposed new trend as "pie in the sky" and something that "will never happen."

Consciousness stalls when information does not fit with an established mental set. People literally do not even consider the information since it is off their existing mental scan. People have little chance to gain another perspective when trapped in the logic of such an evaluative filter.

To illustrate the process of how evaluative filters work, consider Figure 7-1. How would you interpret the three data points that fall outside the more clustered group?

Figure 7 -1. The impact of evaluative filters

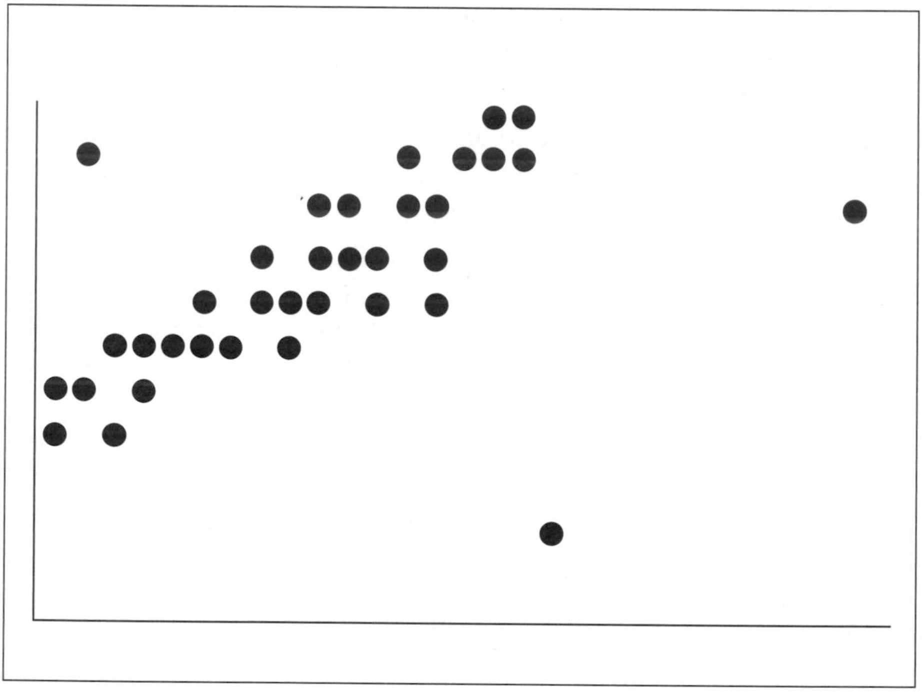

Most people do not consider data outside the boundaries. They translate the three points outside the cluster in Figure 7-1 as outliers. They propose the three points simply represent measurement error or some anomaly in the data. Thus, people say, the three points should be eliminated. They believe the points are unimportant. They do not or cannot attribute any meaning to the points because they do not fit the linear line created by the majority of the data points. However, it might be that these three points are the significant first indicators of a new, larger, more important pattern of the data, as suggested in Figure 7-2.

Figure 7-2. New patterns of information

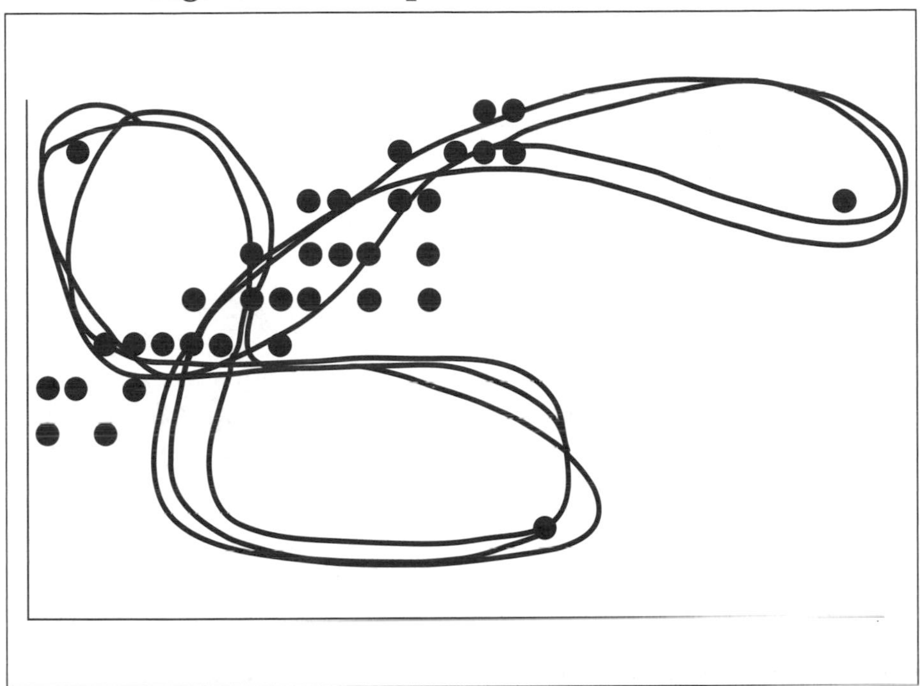

Ignoring information that does not fit an established pattern can spell disaster. In the early 1970s, heads of the American car companies assumed the supply of cheap oil would last for many years. As a result, they discounted the Arab oil cartel as a possible threat to their industry. U.S. auto industry moguls also believed that American car buyers' tastes were standardized and stable. Their judgment suggested no radical changes in cars were needed. They did not believe the innovations available in Japanese autos would dent Detroit's market share. Thirty years later, the U.S. automakers repeated this dysfunctional thinking. They failed to move quickly into hybrid vehicles. Toyota and Honda took the lead to capture much of the initial market in this area.

Quantum Leaders recognize the hazards of restrictive interpretations. Quantum Leaders restructure their interpretative range. They process information from a more expanded level. Restructuring requires the full power of intention directed toward the information evaluation process. It demands the full power of attention focused on the interpretative filters used to accept or reject information. Quantum Leaders consciously focus on establishing a more open and flexible range of interpretation in terms of three factors:

1. Assumptions
2. Beliefs
3. Judgments

Assumptions

Assumptions underlie one way we interpret issues. We make assumptions about whether a particular person can perform a task, and we respond accordingly. We assume a certain group will respond to conflict negatively, and we prepare for a battle. A competitor announces a new product, and we make assumptions about how the product will affect our market share.

Some assumptions are obvious to us. For example, a person might suggest to a friend that they go to a particular restaurant for dinner. When they arrive and notice the restaurant is closed, the person would probably not hesitate to explain that he or she *assumed* the restaurant would be open. In this case, the person clearly recognized that her/his action was based on an assumption, an idea in the mind, as opposed to information from an external source.

Other assumptions are deeply embedded in our awareness. We are oblivious to how they guide our thinking and behavior. For example, we assume that an "enemy" is evil without ever questioning the reasons for that enemy's actions. We assume that certain things are "good" because we were told they were good by our parents, teachers, or institutions.

Quantum Leaders identify and challenge assumptions. They seek to uncover faulty or inappropriate ways of interpreting information. They clarify and identify limiting premises that inhibit them. They define and overcome biases that restrict their judgment. These efforts may not always indicate a clear path to success. And, they can restructure one's awareness and provide the possibility to perceive what others don't. Quantum Leaders, aware that assumptions are a necessary part of thinking, bring these assumptions to the surface to minimize being guided by faulty assumptions.

Field Guide 6 describes actions to clarify assumptions so that you can enhance your range of interpretation.

Beliefs

Beliefs reflect an integrated network of assumptions that guide our interpretation of reality. They provide the ability to succeed, because people with strong beliefs can overcome almost any obstacle. Beliefs also control how we evaluate information. Limiting beliefs virtually imprison our awareness in outdated or useless ways of interpreting information. For example, at one time, no one believed humans could run a sub four-minute mile. Science even "proved" this by analyzing the human muscle structure and the body's wind resistance. Yet one year after Roger Bannister broke the "impossible" barrier, thirty-seven others did it. Within two years, over 300 people had run as fast. Now even high school students crack the four-minute mile every year.

Limiting beliefs become mind-numbing barriers to new frontiers and alternate avenues of interpretation. Reigning scholars of his time scoffed when Copernicus suggested that the sun, not earth, was the center of the solar system. His scientific evidence was dismissed because it ran contrary to the beliefs of the day.

Quantum Leaders embrace the maxim, "What you believe, you achieve." Quantum Leaders go into the G.A.P. to operate from an "all possibilities" belief system. They restructure their awareness and open themselves to believe that solutions and prospects exist. Cynics often mock those who hold "all possibilities" beliefs. Doubters claim they "know better" than those who adopt the mind-set of a "naive enthusiast." John Wooden, winner of eleven NCAA basketball championships in 12 years of coaching at UCLA, offers another belief in his book, *They Call Me Coach*: "It's what you learn after you know it all that counts."

Field Guide 6 describes actions to uncover and expand your beliefs so that you can enhance your range of interpretation.

Judgments

What ideas are you in love with that cloud your mind? Judgments form cognitive filters and biases. Judgments can solidify such that decision making becomes rigid and relies on limited categories. Quantum Leader-as-perceivers go into the G.A.P. to restructure their judgment and open it up to alternative rulings.

Quantum Leaders expand their interpretive range by focusing on learning rather than disagreeing. When they disagree with an idea, they adopt an inquiry approach. For example, they respond, "What else can you tell me about that?" They know that to simply argue for their point of view does not help them understand another's perspective.

Field Guide 6 describes actions to understand your judgments so that you can enhance your range of interpretation.

Increase Your Response Options

Once Quantum Leaders perceive a problem or a possibility, they can chart a course for action. The third way Quantum Leaders go into the G.A.P. is to increase their response options to information. They follow Sun Tzu's advice in The Art of War: "Don't be bound by established procedures."

Quantum Leaders thrive on figuring out how to combine, integrate, and use information in new response modes. Response options naturally increase with more information and a more open interpretative range. Quantum Leaders enhance their potential options by consciously responding with new, untried, or previously abandoned ways to respond.

Quantum Leaders increase their response options when they:

1. Take an experimental approach.
2. Rely on intuition.

Experimentation and intuition may result in success, or they may not. In the quantum reality, no response provides a certain outcome. No guarantees can be made about what will happen. The purpose of experimentation and intuition is to open streams of consciousness that offer new ways to chart a course of action.

Take an Experimental Approach

Quantum Leaders experiment with choices. They are willing to try an approach, knowing that they cannot predict the outcome. They experiment with various possible paths and with new ways to act. They consider multiple scenarios. Quantum Leaders know that the first step toward mediocrity is a culture of conformity. So, they try something new. They experiment with something they believe in. If the action bombs, Quantum Leaders review the experiment to find out what they learned.

In a 1992 *Los Angeles Times* article, Barry Diller, then head of the QVC network, described his experiment to create a winner in the global entertainment and communications business: "Who knows if any of what I'm saying makes sense? That's the most important lesson in this business: That these morning-line prognostications are invariably wrong. Nobody knows what's going to make a good movie. Forget about all the deals and all the theories. All I know from is, this is a good idea, and I'm going to pursue it."

Rely on Intuition

Intuition is often seen as some magical ability possessed by only a few rare individuals. We believe every has intuition. But many people never rely on it. This limits their capacity to increase response options. It keeps people from gaining another perspective.

We define intuition as the quality of thinking that we cannot explain rationally. Logic is the outcome of the learning process, not the process itself. We think logically about a problem only *after* we understand it. George Gilder in *Microcosm*, explains that understanding comes from an "elusive process of pattern matching and association." That is another way to describe what we label as intuition. No reason can describe the flashes of insight and synergistic realizations people sometimes have in response to information.

The quantum power of intuition is also supported by the most widely used psychological assessment instrument on the market known as the Myers-Briggs Type Indicator (MBTI). This scale measures the preference for intuitive thinking. The thirty-year MBTI research data base at Florida State University reveals that less than 30% of the U.S. population demonstrates a preference for intuition when taking in and processing information. Quantum Leaders rise above this limitation. They use their intuition when it signals something. They draw it out when it lies dormant. And, they rely upon its signals to add value to their thinking and action.

These flashes are quantum leaps of awareness that defy classical physics logic. We label them intuitive because no linear logic describes them. Quantum Leaders learn to trust these experiences when responding from the G.A.P.

Lee Iacocca's intuition drove Chrysler back to the convertible car line. Iacocca had a hunch about the marketability of ragtops.. He believed having the top down could bring sales up. However, all American auto manufacturers had eliminated such cars years before. Iacocca decided to test intuition with an experiment. First, he directed the production plant to make him a convertible. The production chief explained that it would take some time to design the convertible, retool the manufacturing line, and build the prototype. In response. Iacocca clarified the meaning of his directive: He wanted the car tomorrow. "Just cut the top off a car and make it look presentable," he ordered.

The next day Iacocca wheeled his makeshift convertible through the streets of Detroit. By the time he got back to the office, the decision was clear to him. Iacocca "just knew" the car would sell based on the positive looks on the faces of those who saw the car. Take a ride on a warm sunny day in almost any big city and you will observe how Iacocca's intuition was right.

Takami Takahashi, founder of Minebea, the world's largest maker of miniature precision ball bearings, used his intuition to guide the development of a new company. Takahashi thought he could apply his manufacturing genius in ball bearings to achieve large-scale manufacturing of DRAM computer chips. Many experts said it could not be done. Takahashi forged ahead anyway. He launched a new firm, NMB Semiconductor. He built a totally automated production facility. By 1988, his company had profitably produced 70 million chips per year. Takahashi's response to his critics, wrote George Gilder in *Microcosm*, is, "Successful people surprise the world by doing things ordinary logical people think are stupid. If I listened to logical people, I would never have succeeded."

Perceiving with intuition means sometimes forgetting what you know and relying on inspiration. Paul MacCready designed the first human-powered aircraft. None of his early efforts worked. All his designs were doomed by "traditional thinking." Then he decided to keep aerodynamic principles in mind but to pretend he had never seen an airplane. His intuitive inspiration came from the way red-tailed hawks fly instead of the way machines fly.

Quantum Leaders use their intuition as a *complementary* power of perception. They know over dependence on logic or hard sensory data can create intellectual indifference and unresponsiveness. On the other hand, excessive use of intuition can lead to idiosyncratic and arbitrary thinking. Taken together, logic and intuition enable the Quantum Leader to command a wider perceptual response range.

Field Guide 6 describes actions to increase your response options with experimentation and intuition.

Pick Your Spots

You don't have to go into the G.A.P. twenty-four hours a day. Nor do you have to ask questions of every person you meet in a nonstop, machine-gun fashion. It is not essential that you continually restructure your interpretative range or ceaselessly try new response options.

Quantum Leaders pick their spots. They go into the G.A.P. for selected periods each day or week. To get started, try just one or two of the action ideas in this chapter's Field Guide. Go into the G.A.P. for just a few minutes each day.

It is uncertain what you will find. No one can say if you will find anything that requires leadership initiative. But if you do not try to perceive anything, you will not find anything. The starting gun for the leadership process will not sound without someone's initiating an interaction with the leadership arena. Organizations could change very quickly if everyone would spend just 15 minutes every day actively going into the G.A.P.

FIELD GUIDE 6

Action Idea 6.1: Take an SLL pause.

Take a break from your busy schedule each day and get out of your office, away from your normal routine. Then go somewhere different in your organization. Visit the loading dock. Stop by the employee cafeteria. Go into the stock room. Talk to someone you usually do not talk to maybe the receptionist or the server in the cafeteria. Pick the brains of a mail clerk. Visit with the company president. Contact your customers directly. Look for information to identify a problem or an opportunity. Listen for a way to resolve the difficulty or exploit the possibility. Take an SLL pause at different times during the day. Vary your SLL routine as you focus on looking and listening in different places.

Action Idea 6.2: Perform "curiosity calisthenics."

Set aside 10 to 15 minutes perhaps once a month for curiosity calisthenics, an inquiring mind. Nose around, snoop, and explore things that are new or not part of your standard routine. Pretend you are in the attic among a bunch of stuff that you might recognize but have not looked at lately. Curiosity calisthenics build up attention power to focus the power of the Quantum Leader within.

Action Idea 6.3: Work the night shift.

Work the night shift (or any other different time slot) to seek insights about activity during different times and to expose yourself to new sources of data.

Action Idea 6.3: Reshuffle your calendar.

Vary your daily routine. Instead of holding the standard 10:00 A.M. meeting every Tuesday, next week schedule the meeting at a different time or in a new place to bring a new perspective to the meeting. Rather than eating lunch every day at noon, go earlier tomorrow and then a little later the next day.

Action Idea 6.4: Conduct a "what's not working" analysis.

A "what's not working" analysis identifies problems before they blow up. It directs you to confront obstacles that stifle effectiveness. Be on the lookout for what's not working by stopping, looking, and listening for problems. Then find ways to resolve any problems you uncover.

Action Idea 6.5: Conduct regular five-sense audits.

Sit in your staff assistant's chair for a while. Look at a computer operator's screen for a few hours. Use a craftsperson's tools for a typical task. Ride in the work vehicles your staff drive. Eat the cafeteria food your company serves. Conduct your regular work activities for a full day in the office space where your employees work. Listen to the noises hammering away in your organization. Use your five senses to experience what is going on in these areas. Your heightened sensory awareness might reveal a challenge, problem, or possibility that requires leader direction.

Action Idea 6.6: Master focused listening.

Listening is one aspect of a five senses audit. We add this action idea because we know it is very important to reinforce the use of effective listening skills. Our experience is that many people believe that to listen means to think about what they are going to say when another person stops talking. Many people simply do not pay full attention to the what others are saying. This approach to listening obviously limits the capacity to understand the other and to perceive possibilities. In contrast, focused listeners tune their full awareness on what others say to fully understand the message. Focused listening is a discipline that requires concentration and repeated practice. To master this action idea, take a listening skills course. Model yourself on others whom you feel are good listeners. Do whatever it takes to open your ears, quiet your mind, and shut your mouth. Listen so that you really hear what others are saying and so that you understand what they mean.

Action Idea 6.7: Read literature outside your field of expertise or interest.

Reading just about any book, periodical, or information from an on-line source that is outside your technical field can expand your capacity to perceive from the G.A.P. For example, *Scientific American* addresses many discoveries that relate to everyday life. *PC World* describes the latest advances about information processing efforts. *O (the Oprah magazine)* offers insights into various issues that impact how people live and work. We read physics books, search on-line sources about brain research, and review a variety of magazines to expand our understanding of leadership, management, and organizational development.

Action Idea 6.8: Watch different news commentary shows.

News shows offer a variety of angles on current information. Most people have their favorite show and ignore the others. Watch a different news show this week to seek an insight or a new perspective on relevant issues.

Action Idea 6.9: Read about important figures in history.

In reading about Lord Louis Mountbatten many years ago, I learned the importance of building relationships as a foundation in manifesting the leadership field. Mountbatten was assigned as the last viceroy of India when Great Britain agreed to give up colonial rule over the country. He had the difficult task of dividing India among the quarrelsome factions of Hindus, Muslims, and Sikhs. The first time Mountbatten met delegates of each group, he was besieged with unrealistic demands about their needs. In response, he skillfully deflected their comments by claiming that he was completely unprepared to talk business until he “made the proper acquaintance” of the people. This relationship-building action helped him win the favor of each group so that he could work with them effectively. Mountbatten’s model is still meaningful today. Reading about historical figures, if you do not already attend to this channel, can suggest useful approaches to recognize and respond to leadership challenges.

Action Idea 6.10: Identify your assumptions.

Spend time thinking about the assumptions you make when you consider any particular information. To uncover hidden assumptions on a particular issue, think about specific, concrete categories. For example, what assumptions have you made about time, money, equipment, other resources, and the people in your organization? What assumptions do you have about what will work, will not work, or cannot work? What do you take for granted as "true?" What do you discard as "meaningless?" Answers to these questions reveal some of your assumptions. Identify them and list them on paper. Then define them in terms of an initial set of assumptions. Plot out assumptions that branch off from the initial set. Be self-referred; recognize that these are assumptions you created. Then from this self-referred place, try the next action idea.

Action Idea 6.11: Clarify the relevance of your assumptions.

Answer these questions for assumptions you discover. "What makes this assumption relevant now?" "What causes me still to consider this a meaningful assumption?" "Why is this assumption no longer valid?" "Do I want to operate with this assumption?" These questions direct your attention to clarify existing assumptions. Refer back to your inner self and ask, "Are these really valid assumptions?" Then take the next action step.

Action Idea 6.12: Generate alternate assumptions.

Generate a list of alternate assumptions for those you identified in Action Idea 6.11. Consider assumptions that are contrary to the ones you created above. Then view the list and ask yourself, "How could the alternate assumptions be true?" "How could both sets of assumptions be valid?" "What new assumptions can be created by combining the assumptions?" Challenge yourself to break through restrictions created by limiting assumptions.

Action Idea 6.13: Enroll in "Toyota Tech"

"Our current success is the best reason to change things," a statement by Iwao Isomura of Toyota, is the motto of "Toyota Tech," the educational division of Toyota Motor Company. Enroll in this school. That is, adopt this way of thinking to direct your consciousness toward the assumption that continuous improvement is essential. Make your course of study a process of on-going innovation. Make a deliberate commitment exploit possibilities that you recognize.

Action Idea 6.14: Distinguish your beliefs from information.

Distinguish beliefs from what is actual information. This avoids being guided by faulty beliefs which are those that are not based on the pulse of the most useful, most relevant information. Identify your general beliefs or those that relate to a particular leadership arena using the same process described in the "Identify your assumptions" action idea. Then identify the most current, relevant information that is based on facts not fancy. Next notice how your beliefs shape your interpretation. Focus on considering how useful, valid, and positive those beliefs are. Using the procedure described in Action Idea 6.12, create a set of new, more effective beliefs. Reshape your beliefs about the updated information you have generated.

Action Idea 6.15: Adopt an "impossible belief" system for a specific time period.

Spend a few minutes every so often suspending a belief about what is "impossible." For example, if you believe doubling your market share is impossible, suspend that notion. Adopt the belief that it could happen. If you believe your agency would never be able to count on Congress to fully fund your needed budget, discard that belief. Adopt the belief that it might happen. Then consider how you would operate from these new beliefs. The idea here is to just give your mind a chance to stretch beyond its current beliefs and give it a chance to go into the G.A.P.

Thinking in the "impossible range" helped Texas Instruments dominate the semiconductor industry over giants such as RCA, Sylvania, GE, Westinghouse, Philco-Ford, and Raytheon. George Gilder wrote in his *Microcosm* that Mark Sheppard, a TI manager, explained, "Those companies all knew things that were impossible. We didn't." A few minutes each day in the "impossible range" reengineers your awareness.

Action Idea 6.16: Look back 100 years.

To open up your belief system, recall that in 1890, there were no space shuttles, no satellite television, no computers, and no frozen meals you could prepare in a microwave oven. In 1890, very few people would have believed those technologies were even possible. What beliefs do you hold today that limit the extent to which you consider possibilities?

Action Idea 6.17: Consider how the past cannot be a meaningful guide for the future.

Almost any busy person in today's changing, complex, competitive environment knows that the past is not a precise predictor of the future. Certainly the past can provide useful insights, but relying on it in a deterministic way is inappropriate. Yet the classical physics belief in a cause-and-effect world still remains deep within our awareness because it offers stability and security. Tinker with this programmed mental model. Spend some time considering how the past cannot be a meaningful guide for the future. Imagine that yesterday, last week, or last year has no impact on the future. What information comes to your awareness to guide you now? Consider ways to incorporate this information into the course of action you chart.

Action Idea 6.18: Do some belief busting.

Belief busting directs you to explore possibilities that normally are unbelievable. Imagine that your organization has no morale problems, or that all work is done exactly on time and exceeds all expectations. If this "impossible" reality were true, what would you do differently to create it?

Action Idea 6.19: Develop 100 possibilities.

Limiting beliefs can be overcome by exploding boundaries. "Develop 100 possibilities" means generating 100 potential ways (that is what it says: "100") you could overcome an obstacle or exploit an opportunity. This action idea works best for those who really want to think big. To hit 100, imagine that you have no restraints. Do not let normal reality loom too large while you are developing your list. After you have your 100, propose ways to turn at least some of these possibilities into realities.

Action Idea 6.20: Challenge your own judgments before you disagree with another

When you and another person disagree, review the reasons you take issue with that person. Consider the assumptions and beliefs behind your judgments. Ask yourself how valid they are in the current situation. Most of your judgments are probably very useful. That is why you have been successful. Continually verify and validate those judgments to be more successful.

Action Idea 6.21: Create a judgment list.

Over the next week, keep a list of all the judgmental statements or comments you make or think. Judgmental thinking may cloak your openness to new, potentially useful information. Consider which of these judgments you might suspend in the future. Establish the intention not to use those judgments for a specific time period.

Action Idea 6.22: Reverse your position.

Suspend your world view when you an someone else have a different perspective. Then take that person's position for awhile. Pay attention to the judgments that caused you to take your initial position. Consider how those judgments might restrict your perceptual alertness. Focus on eliminating a particular judgment for at least a short time frame to help open up your awareness.

Action Idea 6.23: Be your own devil's advocate.

Switch the tables on yourself. Play the devil's advocate with your position. Adopt the opposite of your point of view to gain an alternate perspective. Making this switch avoids overzealous attachment to one judgment. Being your own devil's advocate avoids being limited in your ability to recognize new possibilities or alternate approaches to problems.

Action Idea 6.24: Find 10 reasons why the other person is right.

This action idea redirects your awareness to new reference point of judgment. It compels you to get outside the boundaries of your own thinking.

Action Idea 6.25: Become a new Mr. Wizard every day.

Mr. Wizard was a wily TV scientist who performed incredible science demonstrations. His demonstrations revealed knowledge that previous research had already discovered. Mr. Wizard was teaching us about what was already known rather than taking us into the unknown. However, most viewers were amazed at Mr. Wizard's experiments because they were unaware of the verifiable facts that his experiments revealed. Become a "new" Mr. Wizard by performing "experiments" to find out would happen if you tried something different in which the answer is unknown. Experimenting with a new response, rather than verifying old knowledge, could offer insights that increase your options about what to do and what NOT to do in the future.

Action Idea 6.26: Adopt a learning approach by experimenting.

Every experiment provides data. Adopting a learning approach means making use of those data. Anchor this idea into your awareness Whatever happens, you will gain useful information when you experiment with a response.

Action Idea 6.27: Follow a hunch to test your intuition.

Follow the next hunch you have about how to respond to a particular issue. Hunches, feelings, inklings, and premonitions are intuitive signals. By following a hunch, you can gauge your intuitive skill. We find that the more you use intuition, the better it gets.

Action Idea 6.28: Contact your intuition.

Intuition lies within the deeper layers of consciousness. Contact your intuition by sitting quietly with your eyes closed and letting your awareness simply be. Pay attention to the signals you get from that settled place of awareness; then consider how to respond to a situation. When you open your eyes, reconsider what your quiet consciousness revealed in the light of practical reality.

Action Idea 6.29: Visit your local play ground or toy store

Children may not immediately come to mind as very useful models for the challenges of corporate action or government service. Yet, children are typically unencumbered with the negative baggage that most adults drag around on a daily basis. Tap into your "child within." Visit a play ground or toy store. Consider how the boundless world of child's play could give you an insight from the G.A.P. Use the eyes of child to consider how a kick ball game offers insights into effective team work.

Consider how transformer toys represent a possible model for organizational change. Notice how children become engrossed in repetitive play with the same toys as a way to understand the attraction and possible detriment of routine work for adults.

8

Gain Commitment Through Enlightened Action

"You have to be able, frankly, to sell yourself and the logic of your approach to all those constituencies. You become the human bridge to absolutely everybody."
Mike Walsh, former CEO of Tenneco

Dudley Hanson opened the envelope and noticed the word "rejected" stamped on the cover of his budget proposal. None of the division chiefs and none of his staff colleagues had supported his request. Hanson was chief of the Planning Division of the Army Corps of Engineers in Rock Island, Illinois. The corps was responsible for the navigation facilities of the upper Mississippi River inland waterway system. Significant bulk commodities pass through the system, including agricultural products en route to users in the eastern United States.

In 1986, Hanson had recognized that the system was deteriorating from lack of adequate repair. He believed that, without attention, it might fail to meet increasing carrying-capacity demands. The waterway system compared to a two-lane road in an age of multilane expressways. Hanson perceived what other's don't when Congress passed the Water Resources

Development Act that year. Hanson saw the congressional appropriation as a key opportunity. He decided to request funds for an investigation on how best to make capital improvements to improve the navigational system. He submitted his budget proposal request in 1987 for the fiscal year 1989 budget. The proposal outlined a request to fund a Planning Division study that would investigate future capital improvement projects. Hanson believed that everyone involved would perceive the budget proposal in the same light he did. He assumed the request would be accepted because of the importance of upgrading the facilities.

Hanson tried to sort out what happened after getting the stunning rejection. He had clearly perceived that many factors complicated any proposal regarding waterway improvements in this area of the Mississippi. The area is an environmentally sensitive region. It is recognized by federal law as both a significant national ecosystem and a commercial navigational system. The costs of capital improvements could exceed hundreds of millions of dollars. Moreover, the upper Mississippi is managed by an array of federal, state, and local governmental agencies and advised by a number of pro bono public groups. Any proposal for improvement would have to meet multiple, competing demands from a variety of sources.

But Hanson thought his proposal had taken these complex issues into account. He decided to go into the G.A.P. to analyze his assumptions and beliefs and perhaps understand how others had interpreted the proposal. The analysis suggested several reasons for the rejection.

As chief of planning, Hanson naturally assumed that funding a planning proposal should be the first step. Hanson also assumed that all of the other division chiefs and senior staff in the Rock Island would recognize and support this approach. Hanson found out that the chiefs and the staff held the same beliefs he did. That is, the navigational facilities needed to be upgraded. Yet, they interpreted Hanson's budget request as primarily an attempt to support his own Planning Division.

Hanson knew his intentions were not self-serving. And, he quickly understood why the other division chiefs and senior staff members did not support the budget. From their frames of reference, they believed the allocation would not serve interests they valued.

Hanson also uncovered a lack of support from his staff colleagues. The Rock Island District played an important role in maintaining and upgrading the national assets the waterway system represented. Everyone associated with the operation was vital to it. Yet he realized that his exhortations to his staff to support the budget request communicated a different message. He had tried to influence them by explaining that, without the funds, the Rock Island District would become a "mere operation and maintenance, custodial organization." Hanson now recognized how this message violated their values. The operation and maintenance divisions were very capable and vitally important. Hanson had framed his points in a way that alienated the bureaucratically powerful operation and maintenance personnel.

A few months after the budget rejection, Hanson was still intent on improving the navigation facilities of the upper Mississippi River inland waterway system. He initiated a revised budget for 1990 armed with the increased insights he gained from the analysis of the previous request. The request was approved. By June 1992, studies were underway to ensure the full viability of the navigational systems in the twenty-first century.

Enlightened Action

Dudley Hanson's story shows that it is not enough to map the territory and chart a course to perceive what others don't. Leaders must influence others to follow their course of action (the first natural law of leadership). The Quantum Leadership model indicates that the Quantum Leader - Follower interaction involves performing enlightened action to gain follower commitment (Figure 8-1).

Figure 8-1. The Quantum Leadership model: Gain commitment and perform enlightened action

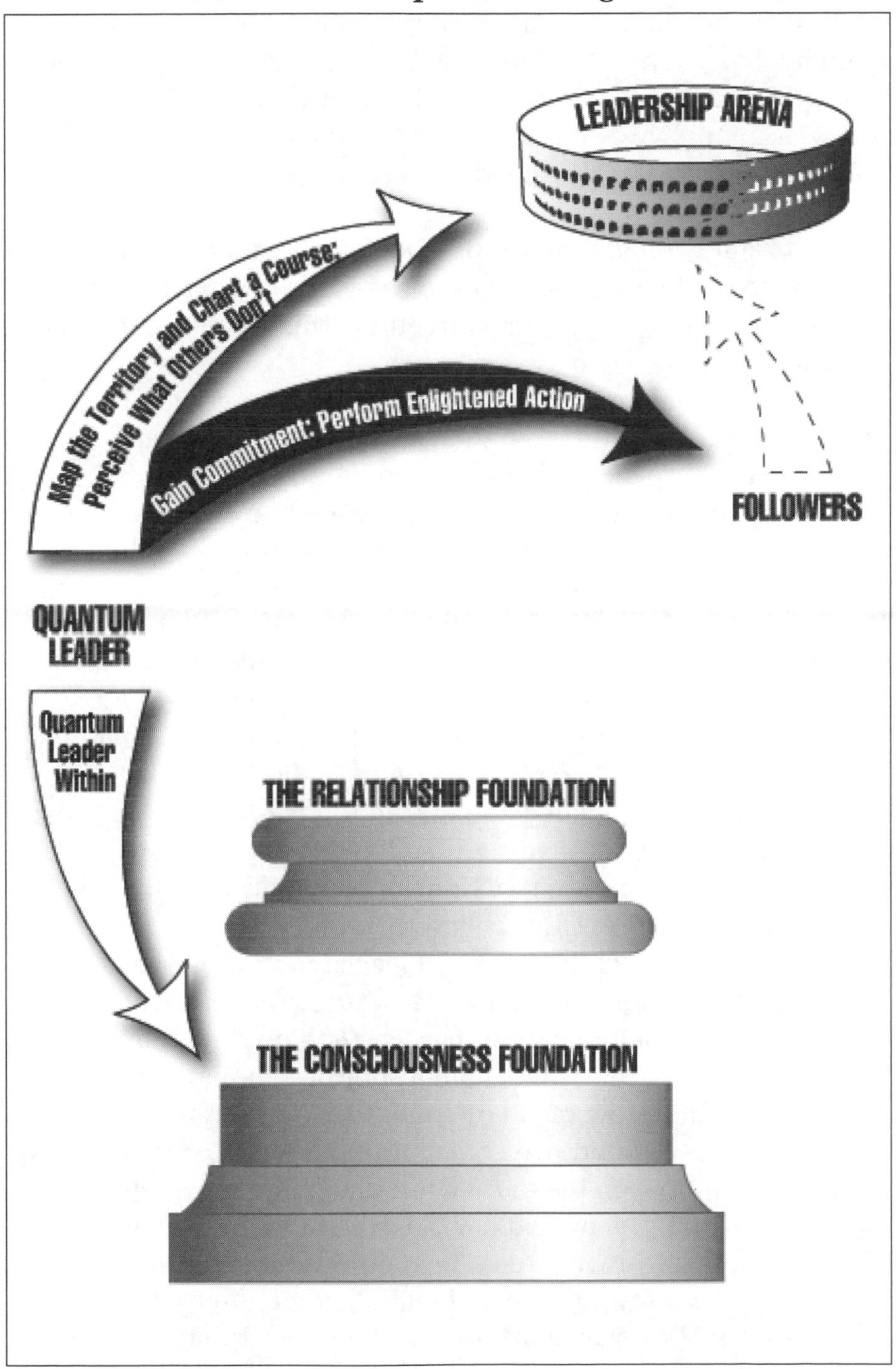

The Light Switch

Performing enlightened action resembles turning on a light in a pitch-black room. Few people will move very quickly, if at all into a dark, unfamiliar room. Yet even a brief flicker of light provides enough awareness to enable them to move ahead. The leadership arena is a risk-filled, uncertain territory. The light of the leader's action minimizes its ambiguity.

Performing enlightened action dispels the darkness of uncertainty. It enables followers to see value and have a clear perspective about the leader's direction. This motivates them to commit.

Quantum Leaders enlighten followers with a variety of actions. Inspirational words, such as Martin Luther King's "I Have a Dream" speech, can inspire commitment. Metaphors can illuminate the followers to accept the leader's direction. Mary Kay Ash, founder of Mary Kay Cosmetics, uses the bumblebee as a metaphor to inspire the women who join her organization that they can realize their full potential. Bumble bees should not be able to fly because their body is too heavy for its wings. However, since the bee does not know this, it flies anyway.

Leading by doing also can motivate followers. During a raging forest fire in Utah in 1978, Martha Hahn of the Bureau of Land Management (BLM) gained committed followers without saying a word. The huge blaze had scorched over 4,000 acres. The BLM needed help from any source. Convicts were brought in and Hahn was given a crew. Her task was to guide these men to contain spot fires which are small blazes that jump over an established fire line. Hahn noticed how the convicts eyed her with suspicion when they first met. She had no time to respond to this signal. They had to contain a spot fire about a mile away.

Hahn and her crew raced by truck to the fire. Hahn quickly gave directions to cut down some burned trees to create a line of demarcation between the burned and the green areas. But the men stood silently, gaping at her. So, Hahn grabbed an axe and started chopping down a tree. The men watched her in amazement for a few minutes. Then they joined in to do the work. After the job was done, one of the men explained to her,

"We aren't used to seeing a girl cut down a tree." Hahn's action inspired the convicts to get to work.

Symbols can also turn on the light to guide followers. Ray Kroc wanted his McDonalds' shift managers to spend more time at the counter interacting with customers. Kroc felt his vision, "Quality, Cleanliness, Service," could not be achieved without face-to-face customer contact. To get his message across, Kroc had the backs of the manager's office chairs sawed off. He felt the managers might not spend so much time in the office if the chairs were uncomfortable. Similarly, a production plant quality team facilitator created a powerful symbol. He used the organization's primary competitor's most successful products to communicate the need for his team to do better. He displayed the competitor's products at the door of the plant so that all could see them. The display served as a symbolic reminder of the quality level the company's products had to achieve to win in the marketplace.

Dudley Hanson's second budget was approved because he took action that enlightened others. His request enlarged his argument for funding to include the full range of responsibilities that the Rock Island District had. He made a case for ongoing attention to upgrading the navigational infrastructure by improvements in operations and maintenance, major rehabilitation and repair, and capital improvements. Hanson gave recognition to all members of the organization and to their professional duty as stewards of a portion of the operation. His arguments appealed to the strong sense of service in the corps. His new approach also recognized and acknowledged their professionalism. He expanded his frame of reference beyond its impact on the Planning Division to eliminate any perception of parochialism. And he established the important role each group had to play in shaping the future of the corps. For these key followers, Hanson's revised approach had new meaning that attracted them to support him.

The Communication of Meaning

Quantum Leaders use words, metaphors, symbols, and action to enlighten followers. These methods, however, only represent the surface level of leader - follower interaction. The real impact of performing enlightened action occurs at the level of meaning.

Enlightened action is the communication of meaning. Figure 8-2 demonstrates the role of meaning in the communication process. Communication involves the Quantum Leader's idea translated into a message. The message reflects how the leader maps the territory and the leader' course of action. It is transmitted by the leader's words, symbols, and behaviors. The follower receives the message and translates it into the follower's idea about the meaning of the leader's direction.

Figure 8-2. The communication of meaning

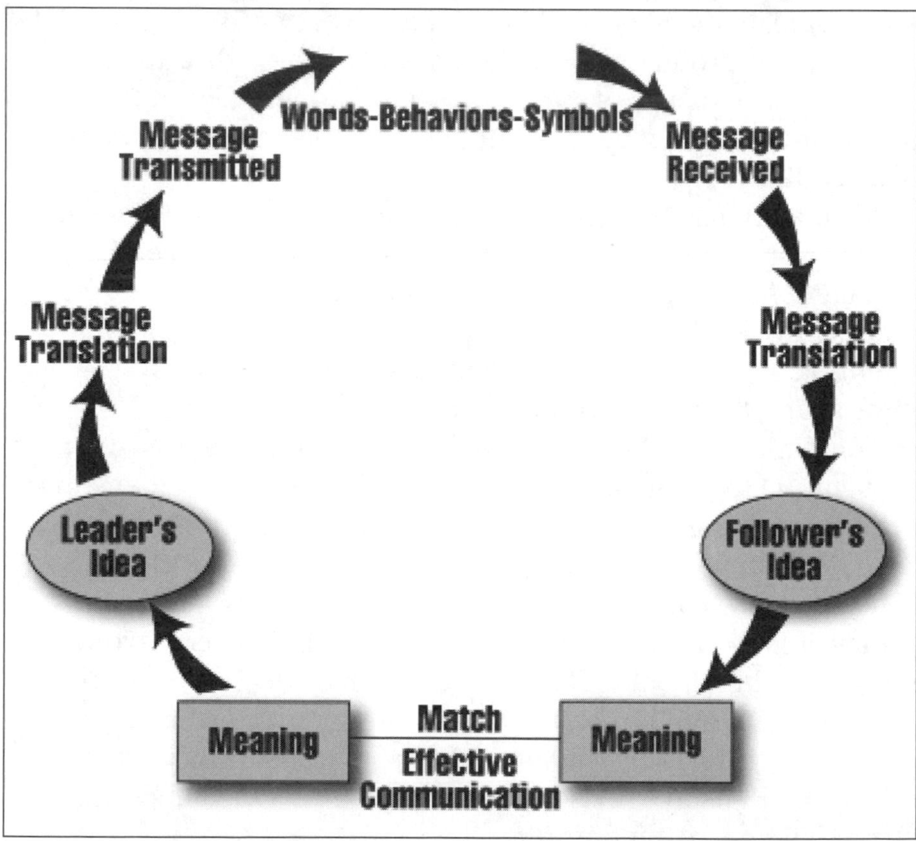

Quantum Leaders gain committed followers when the meaning as interpreted by the follower is the same as the desired meaning underlying the leaders' idea. If people get the wrong meaning, they will not follow. They may even go in the wrong direction. When a young FBI agent was put in charge of the supply department, he decided to cut costs by reducing the size of the borders on the memo paper. He believed that agents could put more information on each memo if the borders were more narrow since that would allow more room to write. FBI Director J. Edgar Hoover received one of the reformatted memo sheets and disliked it. He expressed his reaction in a note on the narrow margin, "Watch the borders," he scrawled. For the next six weeks, FBI agents increased surveillance along the Mexican and Canadian borders.

The FBI memo story illustrates that the substance of communication describes what is actually said or done to transmit the message. Yet, the actual impact of communication occurs in terms of its meaning to the followers. If a message is confusing, the meaning transmitted can negate a leader's impact. Followers interpret meaning from every message they receive. The meaning defines their reaction to the leader.

Consider the reaction created by former Vice President Dan Quayle's infamous rewording of the United Negro College Fund's slogan, "A mind is a terrible thing to waste." Quayle state, "What a waste it is to lose one's mind, or not to have a mind, how true that is."

The Quantum Connection

A connection of meaning occurs with followers when Quantum Leaders perform enlightened action. Meaning is structured in consciousness. It is subjective. It is based in the mind. It is not objective or defined by matter. Each person's unique, self-referral information processing procedure creates meaning for him or her. For example, downsizing efforts that result in an improved balance sheet are interpreted favorably by stock holders. Employees typically interpret downsizing to mean lost jobs and unemployment.

The classical physics paradigm assumes an objective reality. It biases our thinking to believe we can communicate the "facts" and that everyone will accept them as valid. However, leaders gain followers based on the meaning followers assign to facts, not the facts themselves. Quantum Leadership fields do not exist unless the leader's intended meaning resonates with the followers on their level of self-referral consciousness (the ninth natural law of leadership). For example, George Bush's assertions during the 1992 presidential campaign that the United States was not in an economic recession were technically correct. The United States had broken out of the recession months before the November 1992 election based on the traditional economic explanation of number of consecutive quarters of economic growth. Yet, the American people did not accept the objective "correctness" of this information and Bush lost his bid for reelection. In 1994, Bill Clinton made justifiable declarations about having accomplished many of his stated campaign objectives. The budget deficit was down. The crime bill and the North American Free Trade Agreement had been passed. However, many analysts believed that the Republican's ability to gain a majority into both houses of Congress in 1994 was a sign of rampant dissatisfaction with Bill Clinton.

The word communication shares the same root word with community, commune, and commonality. Enlightened action communicates the leader's meaning so that followers understand, accept, and identify with it. The basis of Quantum Leader power, influence beyond authority (the fourth natural law of leadership), lies in a quantum connection. This connection defines the unity created when the follower's consciousness is enlightened by the meaning of the leader's direction.

The quantum connection creates rapport. Rapport means followers perceive the leader to be like them. Rapport generates the sense of trust and comfort followers feel towards the leader. Followers commit when they can "relate to," "identify with," and "have confidence" in the leader. It enables followers to believe the leader's ideas "make sense" to them.

Quantum Leadership explains that the meaning of the message is known in the response the leader gets. Quantum Leaders increase the probability of getting the response of willing followers by communication flexibility. They use a variety of communication channels to transfer meaning. Quantum Leaders also gain commitment as congruent communicators. They speak and behave in ways that mutually reinforce and correspond to the meaning they want to get across. Mixed messages create confused meanings. Communication flexibility and communication congruence transmit the Quantum Leader's message more accurately.

Communication Flexibility and Congruence

Quantum Leaders are flexible communicators. They rely on a variety of communication channels to get the meaning of their message across. Quantum Leaders communicate with congruence. What they say and how they say it transmit a consistent message. Communication research, reported by Albert Mehrabian in *Silent Messages*, shows that only 7 percent of a message's meaning is transmitted by words. Thirty-eight percent of meaning is transmitted by tone of voice. Fifty-five 55 percent is conveyed by nonverbal behavior or body language.

During one of the 1992 presidential debates among George Bush, Bill Clinton, and Ross Perot, analysts counted the number of times each candidate blinked while speaking. The number of blinks is said to reveal the speaker's tension level. Blinking indicates a lack of certainty or conviction about the words being spoken. Each of the candidates' eyes fluttered often when they responded to certain questions. This implied that their statements meant something other than what the candidate's words implied. Quantum Leaders transmit their meaning more effectively when the words, tone, and body language are congruent.

Field Guide 7 provides twenty action ideas to improve both communication flexibility and communication congruence.

Matching Meaning

Enlightened action matches the way followers create meaning. Matching is the Quantum Leader's ultimate power tool to influence others beyond authority. You create shared meaning by meeting your followers at their level of consciousness. Then you can lead them to your own level of consciousness so they will follow your direction.

◆◆◆

FIELD GUIDE 7

Flexibility

Action Idea 7.1: Use symbols to illustrate your direction.

Symbols, such as the competitor's product display placed at the plant door by the quality team facilitator, offer a powerful channel to get across the meaning of your message. Symbols capture the full range of meaning in a kernel of action. Use symbols to capture the meaning of your direction.

Action Idea 7.2: Create a theme event.

Every society has many traditional theme events. The United States celebrates events from President's Day to Thanksgiving. China observes its New Year celebration in February. India honors Mahalakshmi Day. Create a theme event such as an Employee Empowerment Week" or a "Customer Satisfaction Week" to reinforce your leadership direction. Establish a slogan for the event. Create appropriate trappings such as pictures, decorations, music, or food to get the message of the event across to your staff. Make it a memorable event to transmit the meaning of your course of action.

Action Idea 7.3: Collect and use stories or metaphors.

Everyone loves a good story that makes a meaningful point. A well-crafted metaphor can also create an image that depicts the idea behind your leadership direction. A manager we know in a large retail operation loves to tell the story about opening a new store on a Saturday. He recounts how the local banker did not believe the manager really needed fifty specially locked cash bags to store the funds collected over the weekend. The store, the banker said, would never do that much business. She was only willing to give the store manager twenty money pouches. On Monday, the manager arrived at the bank and dumped the twenty full cash bags on the banker's desk. He then piled forty plastic trash bags bulging with even more money. The manager uses the story to illustrate the need to think big.

Action Idea 7.4: Display artifacts into your office.

A personal artifact placed on your desk or office wall can communicate a powerful message. Louis Katopodis, president of Fiesta Mart, the Houston-based grocer, has a baseball bat leaning in the corner of his office. Katopodis believes people need to "step up to the plate" to meet the challenges of the fast moving grocery business."

Action Idea 7.5: Develop a stump speech.

Politicians develop a "stump speech" which is message that they repeat over and over to get across their key ideas as they race along the campaign trail. Your stump speech should contain the two or three core ideas you want to communicate about your leadership direction. Deliver your speech often enough to reinforce its meaning but not so often it becomes boring. The speech will help put your message across effectively. The line between reinforcement and boring is, of course, part of the art that you have to continually address when you implement any of these action ideas. Always consider this action in the larger context of your audience, the situation, and the goal of your communication. Focus on how to use the stump speech effectively by ratcheting up your power of conscious attention and discrimination.

Action Idea 7.6: Write for your readers.

Written communication is an important source of message transfer. Writing for your readers means considering how they will interpret the words you place on the page, not what you think the words mean. Consider how much time the reader has to review your document. Think about whether the writing would be more potent if it were formatted in bullets, or as short paragraphs, or using a table or other graphic. Ask yourself, "When they get this document, how will they make meaning of the direction I am suggesting, based on the words I have written?" A few minutes of reflection will sharpen your written communication.

Congruence

Action Idea 7.7: Listen to a radio talk show.

Radio talk show hosts have mastered the art of communicating meaning through sound. They know how to alter their tone of voice and cadence of speech to reinforce the meaning behind their words. Listen to them speak. Model your own speech on those radio talk show hosts you admire.

Action Idea 7.8: Vary your speech pattern.

Most people can listen much faster than most people talk. Speed up your speech to keep attention. When you want to emphasize a particular point, slow down your speech. Varying your speech pattern keeps followers tuned in to you. It gives you a chance to help your listeners better understand the meaning of your leadership direction.

Action Idea 7.9: Take a presentation skills course within the next three months.

Public speaking is not most people's strong suit. Furthermore, no one can ever be too good at it. You may have to communicate your leadership direction to others in a stand-up presentation. A course on presentation skills can transform your capacity to get across meaning in a congruent and cogent fashion. Local junior colleagues and community colleges regularly offer courses in these areas.

Action Idea 7.10: Join Toastmasters.

Toastmasters is an organization that has mastered the art of developing people's ability to speak in front of groups both large and small. It even provides skills to communicate more effectively one-on-one.

Action Idea 7.11: Move your head and body more when you give a presentation.

Many people present information in a wooden fashion. Think of all the "death by PowerPoint" presentations you have had to sit through in which the speaker drones on and simply reads the words on a slide. Such presenters rarely use any body movements. Avoid this approach. Move your head and body in ways that emphasize your points to increase your communication congruence. For example, nod your head up and down to affirm your point. Raise three fingers when you indicate your have three key ideas to share. Spread your arms wide apart to reinforce that you are making a point that impacts the entire organization.

Action Idea 7.12: Take an acting lesson in the next two months.

Actors know how to speak, behave, and emote in a fashion that convinces us they are the character. An acting lesson will improve your ability to be a more convincing communicator of the meaning of your message.

Action Idea 7.13: Watch one live theater performance this month.

Actors use their full range of voice, body action, and the stage space to get their ideas across. Notice how different actors do this to communicate their character's message. Then model what you see on the stage. Practice, just like an actor rehearses, different methods you observe. When you feel comfortable with the behaviors, try some of them the next time you want to communicate your message.

Action Idea 7.14: Watch a TV comedian perform for 10 minutes with the sound turned off.

Some TV comedians do not say things that are funny, but many of them know how to use their nonverbal behaviors to reinforce their message congruently. Watch them with the sound off to notice how they communicate nonverbally.

Action Idea 7.15: Watch the body language of kids at play.

Children are almost totally uninhibited in their body motion. They jump, shake, wiggle, and contort themselves in concert with how they feel. By watching them play, you might notice a nuance of behavior you could adopt that would be appropriate to communicate more effectively.

Action Idea 7.16: Analyze five TV commercials on video in the next month.

Television commercials are brilliantly crafted morsels of meaning. In 15 seconds, the advertisers can say everything they want you to know to motivate you to purchase the product. Analyze TV commercials on video so you can watch them in fast and slow motion to discern how they get a powerful, congruent message across in a few moments.

Action Idea 7.17: Study five magazine advertisements a week.

Analyze printed advertisements with the same intention as TV ads.

Action Idea 7.18: Consciously relax your facial muscles three times a day.

When your face tightens, your message is much less positive than when your facial muscles are relaxed. Many people do not realize that they walk around with a stone-faced, impassive look on their face, or that their forehead is furrowed, or their mouth pulled down in a frown. By relaxing your facial muscles, you communicate a more positive picture. You also actually use less energy when you smile. Research indicates that it takes a lot of exertion to contort our faces into some of the hard looks we hold. To get additional feedback on your need to take this action, ask trusted co-workers to tell you when they see an pinched or "hard" expression on your face.

Action Idea 7.20: Double your smile rate.

People who consistently smile are often thought to have positive attitudes. Doubling your smile rate communicates greater certainty about your ideas. Smiling can mean greater confidence to followers. A smile draws people to you. A frown or scowl pushes them away.

9

Create Shared Meaning

"If you cry 'Forward,' you must make clear the direction you want to go. Don't you see that if you fail to do that and simply call out the word to a monk and a revolutionary, they will go precisely in the opposite directions."
Anton Chekhov, Russian playwright

We attended a meeting with a group of eight managers, who were essentially peers, while consulting with a large manufacturing company. The company had gone through an extensive downsizing. Joel, one of the group's managers, had been charged to develop a new approach to restructure work processes. Joel presented his plan to the group. A brief question-and-answer period ensued. It was decided that the managers would discuss the plan with their staffs and then reconvene the next day for further discussion. The meeting was then adjourned. I noticed that one manager, Liz, very obviously favored Joel's plan while another, Robert, was clearly against it. I asked each in private to explain their positions.

Liz thought that Joel's plan was "the right thing for employees whose morale was most important now." She believed that, "Joel's point of view minimized the trauma of what was a tough situation." In contrast, Robert believed that the plan was "a bad approach at this time because it hurt the organization's chances to improve efficiency." Robert said, "Joel's frame of reference is too narrow given the radical changes that had occurred." I probed for deeper insights about both their comments. Liz and Robert referred to the same facts and statistics Joel presented to support their completely different interpretations. This difference arose because Liz and Robert processed Joel's information differently.

Values and Frames: Sources of Meaning

Every person processes information within their own consciousness. Quantum Leaders cannot directly control a follower's information processing methods. That means leaders cannot dictate the meaning a follower attributes to a message. However, Quantum Leaders *can* consciously match the way a follower processes information to influence the meaning that the follower interprets.

Followers create meaning in terms of their values and through the frame of reference they use. Values serve as a filter people use to assign meaning about what is good or bad, right or wrong. Frames of reference act as windows through which the meaning of information is filtered. Frames are like lenses that bring the meaning of information into focus.

Joel influenced Liz to follow because his presentation matched her values and frame. Joel failed to gain Robert's commitment because his presentation did not match Robert in these two critical areas.

Quantum Leaders create shared meaning by performing action that matches the follower's values. They can also reframe their initiatives to match or create a frame that a follower can identify with as useful. Meaning gets translated more effectively when the leader creates a better match of values and frame of reference. Followers will more likely support the leader when the match of meaning is more complete.

Quantum Leaders meet followers at their level of consciousness and then lead followers to the leader's level. The mechanics of performing enlightened action involve Quantum Leaders' tuning their attention to understand how others create meaning and then adapting to match the follower's process. At times, the leader only has to find the critical 1 percent match to achieve a 100 percent endorsement for a specific direction. Matching values and reframing are the Quantum Leader's power tools to forge that connection and thereby create shared meaning.

Matching Values

The Values Filter

Values define what people believe is important. Values indicate what people regard as good or bad, worthy or unworthy, right or wrong. Liz valued employee morale. Robert valued organizational efficiency.

Values lie in the deep fabric of consciousness. They form an executive level of judgment. People process information through their core values. Those critical values affect the creation of meaning. Values guide behavior. People use values as touchstones to measure if they are on or off course. Values serve as a filter through which we translate information and evaluate its content. People doubt those who do not support their values. We are suspicious of those with different values.

Followers identify with the Quantum Leader's message when it is personally significant to them and it taps into their core values. When President Kennedy visited Berlin in 1963, he astutely matched the values of the democratic population held hostage within the divided city of the communist-controlled portion of Germany. His words had meaning at a deep level with the West German people:

> There are many people in the world who really don't understand, or say they don't, what is the great issue between the free world and the Communist world. Let them come to Berlin. There are some who say that

> Communism is the wave of the future. Let them come to Berlin. . . . And there are even a few who say that it is true that Communism is an evil system, but it permits us to make economic progress, "Lass sie nach Berlin kommen." Let them come to Berlin. Freedom has many difficulties and democracy is not perfect, but we have never had to put a wall up to keep our people in to prevent them from leaving us.

The crowd went wild. They shouted and cheered their enthusiastic acceptance of Kennedy. His refrain, "Let them come to Berlin," resonated with their core values.

Resonating With Follower Values

Quantum Leaders identify follower values and then reinforce those values with their message. When Jim Renier became vice chairman of Honeywell in 1985, he encountered a company with falling productivity and low morale. He identified the values employees felt were most important: truth, trust, and respect. He also noticed that they were absent from the workplace. Indeed, he perceived that his organization suffered from a malady that had spread across the United States. People felt an increasing narcissism. Everyone cared only for themselves at times at the expense of others. So Renier promoted the theme, "Respect for People" to indicate his disdain for the "paddle-your-own-canoe" values dominating the workplace. Honeywell employees identified with this message. As a result, they supported Renier's direction based on a report by Noel Tichy and Mary Anne Devanna in *The Transformational Leader*.

Successful political candidates match voters' values. They personify the public's concerns and passions. Bill Clinton's 1992 campaign theme focused on the domestic economy. His message matched a core value for voters. In 1940, Winston Churchill gained the prime minister post by tapping into the value held by the British people that they could win the war against Hitler.

Rudy Giuliani has emerged as a highly respected public figure since 9/11 in large part because he communicated important values in the days and weeks after the attacks. However, I was in

New York in August of 2001 three weeks before the World Trade Center attacks. The newspapers were filled with negative stories about the Mayor. Yet, during the 9/11 crisis, Giuliani masterfully communicated messages that clarified core values to the people of New York. He create a connection of meaning that caused the public to both admire him and move away from disapproval of him to willingly support of his direction in the days after 9/11. Giuliani continually reasserted those values in the 2008 Presidential campaign. He was well aware that the 9/11-Giuliani connection reinforced key core values of many Americans.

Identify Values

Quantum Leaders clarify their own values. They can more efficiently create shared meaning with followers when they have a clearly defined set of their own values. Quantum Leaders then realize which values they share with others. They use that shared reality to draw followers to them. Aware of their own values, Quantum Leaders can recognize when they have minor value clashes or more serious values conflicts with others. Recall the seventh natural law of leadership: Not everyone will follow. When you cannot match another person's values, that may be a signal to move on and try to attract other followers.

Quantum Leaders identify follower values in various ways. They listen carefully for "values messages" which are statements that reflect deeply held beliefs. For example, "I love all the different things I do in my job," reflects the value of job variety. "I want to finish this project and show it to my boss," reveals the values of achievement and a desire to be recognized. "I will take the extra time to do it right," suggests values such as a willingness to work hard and to serve the customer. Quantum Leaders also observe others to identify core values. A picture of one's family on the wall or desk, an artifact such as a tennis ball, or copy of a current business or management book could all suggest values such as concern for family, the importance of fitness, or life-long learning. Quantum Leaders seek clues to reveal fundamental values. They discuss which values are the most important to others. They help people understand, clarify, and prioritize their values.

Field Guide 8 provides six action ideas to apply these suggestions and identify values.

Match Values to Create Shared Meaning

Quantum Leaders match follower values when they communicate their course of action. One of the senior partners in a medium-size law firm wanted to expand the business. That required hiring more lawyers with different specialties. Some of the lawyers resisted this idea because it went contrary to two core values. The attorneys perceived growth in the number of personnel as a threat to their autonomy. They worried that a larger organization would be more rigid and structured. Thus, increased staff was contrary to the core values of autonomy and flexibility. The senior partner met with the resistant attorneys. He listened to their concerns. He then worked with them to map the territory. This analysis revealed that a few more attorneys would actually allow for greater autonomy and job flexibility. New staff would be primarily new law school graduates. They would be assigned much of the more routine work that the more seasoned attorneys found less enjoyable but were forced to do because of staff limits. The senior partner further explained that more attorneys would allow the firm to broaden its base of operations into different areas of legal counsel. This would allow for an expanded client base. The attorneys would have more options about the types of legal issues they would address. The senior partner ultimately gained the willing support of all the attorneys. He demonstrated how his direction would actually support their core values.

Field Guide 8 provides four action ideas to apply these suggestions and match values.

Reframing

Leon Moore exudes energy and enthusiasm. In May 1991, I asked Moore, then regional commissioner for the Internal Revenue Service's Central Region, how he felt the IRS was doing.

"Well," he replied, "we need a $7 billion capital investment for our modernization efforts!" His comment startled me, not only because of what he said but also by the way he said it. Moore seemed almost upbeat. Intrigued, I asked him to explain. Moore replied that when consumers have problems with their bank, they can telephone the institution and almost immediately get a response regarding the cause of the problem. But when taxpayers have problems with their returns, they cannot get such a speedy reply. "We haven't had the computer hardware and software in place to help explain the situation to the taxpayer. Now we know what we need. It will cost us $7 billion to become fully computerized." This did not sound like a very good situation to me, so I said nothing. Then Moore completely changed my perspective. He smiled broadly and said, "What an exciting time to work for the IRS!"

Frames and Reframes

Leon Moore illustrated how Quantum Leaders create shared meaning by reframing. They create an attractive and positive perspective by putting information into a different context.

Our "mental frame" defines the perspective through which we perceive the world. The frame clarifies the picture like a lens that brings an image into focus. We process information and create meaning based on the frame we use.

Leon Moore painted a picture of the IRS situation as an exciting and challenging period of change. He focused on the IRS's expansion of capacity and ability to serve the public. He could have lamented the problems associated with the use of unsophisticated technology. Instead, he chose a frame that highlighted the positive aspects of the IRS transformation. Moore's action with me was not an isolated incident. In speaking with those who work for him, I discovered that Leon Moore lives the image he presented to me. He consistently views the IRS as an exciting, challenging place to work.

Reframing relabels and redefines events. It enables people to think about things differently, to see another point of view, and to take different factors into consideration. Meaning changes when the frame changes. Consider how almost every investor got on the dot.com bandwagon during the late 1990's. One business person exclaimed to me, "Everyone should invest in tech stocks. There is no end in sight to how much money people will make!" That frame totally changed when the dot.com boom went bust. Quantum Leaders create shared meaning by reframing events so that followers connect with the leader's direction. They reframe to help followers understanding the utility of their direction. Their reframe helps followers recognize the attractiveness of their course of action.

Quantum Leaders know there are multiple ways to perceive any experience or situation. They select a frame that is valid and useful to them and to their followers. Katherine Graham, publisher of the *Washington Post*, clarified the subjective reality of a mental frame. She noted that "a mistake is simply another way of doing things."

It is easier to perform action that enlightens others when people initially share a similar frame of reference with the leader. In such cases, the leader only has to reinforce the existing, similar frame to establish shared meaning. For example, we have met several other managers at the IRS who share Leon Moore's enthusiasm regarding the organization's status. They do not perceive his comment as a reframe. Instead, they heartily agree that it is an exciting time to work for the IRS.

Quantum Leaders reframe situations when they need to change the focus of attention. Reframing creates shared meaning for those whose prevailing view limits their willingness to follow. Reframing elicits a positive response that unites the leader and follower.

On April 4, 1968, African-Americans smoldered with justifiable anger about Martin Luther King Jr.'s murder. Fear of a violent backlash spread across the country because a white man had gunned King down. Bobby Kennedy, on the campaign trail for the presidency, was scheduled to speak in a predominantly African-American neighborhood in Indianapolis. He was the first to bring the news of King's assassinations to this crowd. Kennedy effectively reframed the tragedy to soothe those deeply hurt supporters of the inspirational King. His powerful reframe calmed the crowd:

> For those of you who are Black and are tempted to be filled with hatred and distrust at the injustice of such an act, against all white people, I can only say that I feel in my own heart the same kind of feeling. I had a member of my family killed, but he was killed by a white man. But we have to make an effort in the United States, we have to make an effort to understand, to go beyond these rather difficult times.

Effective reframes result in comments from followers such as, "Well, when you look at it that way, I do agree" or "Yes, from that perspective, I do feel okay about taking this course of action." Reframing requires stepping out of trained patterns of perception to change the meaning of events.

Perceptual processes can become trapped in routinized models or maps. This limits our capacity to perceive information. Quantum Leaders direct their consciousness to break through their bounded cognitive patterns when they map the territory and chart a course to perceive what others don't and by going into the G.A.P.

Quantum Leaders then perform enlightened action by reframing situations so that others also discard limiting models and accept the leader's direction. Quantum Leaders reframe to redraw the follower's mental maps.

Understand the Follower's Existing Frame

Reframing begins by identifying the follower's existing frame. Quantum Leaders seek to understand the context or backdrop that establishes the follower's existing perspective. They ask a series of probing questions to understand what the person's comments actually mean.

For example, Jose, a supervisor in a service company, recently told me that Bobbie, a new manager, "doesn't support our real mission." I asked Jose, "What do you mean, 'doesn't support?'" He responded, "Bobbie is more interested in costs than customers." I sought further understanding of the frame by asking, "What do you mean she is 'more interested in costs than customers?'" Jose clarified his frame. He told me, "Bobbie has held dozens of meetings with the finance people, but she hasn't visited our location once. She only focuses on cutting costs and doesn't care about customer service." For Jose, the meaning of Bobbie's behavior was a lack of customer focus. Understanding Jose's context was the initial step in being able to reframe.

Reframe to Create a New Level of Meaning

Quantum Leaders arm themselves with the knowledge of a person's existing frame to determine the degree of shared meaning. When the overlap is insufficient to attract followers, Quantum Leaders reframe the situation to change the meaning. They use several methods to do this. They clarify how a negative can be a positive. They restate problems as opportunities. They change the backdrop or context of a situation. They reinterpret a situation from a more useful perspective.

Thomas Edison reframed a tragedy that had struck his brand-new, state-of-the-art factory. A fire had burned it to the ground. Worse, Edison had no fire insurance since he had been convinced the building was fireproof. When someone commented to him that the destruction of the plant was a terrible occurrence, Edison shook his head and replied, "No, we just burned down a lot of bad ideas." Edison provided two other very powerful examples of reframing. He was asked how he was able to persist during his 10,000 failures at inventing the light bulb. Edison replied that he never failed once during the process. He actually found 10,000 ways that did not work. Edison also once said, "I'm not discouraged, because every wrong attempt discarded is another step forward."

Stonewall Jackson reframed his troops' retreat during a vicious enemy attack. He said, "We're not retreating, we're advancing in a different direction." As it turned out, this was not an idle change of meaning. Jackson's strategy was to string his attackers out in line as they chased the "retreating" Union troops. Then Jackson turned his troops around and assaulted the flank of the thinly dispersed enemy lines. Jackson's reframe was necessary to inspire his troops to stay with him during the supposed retreat.

Almost any experience can be useful and worthy of support in the proper context. I consulted with a medium-size automobile parts manufacturer. A group of plant employees complained that a new employee was continuously on sick leave. This person continued to receive a salary and accrue other benefits because of the organization's liberal policy in this area. The team had to work very hard to meet its quotas. It was disgruntled about what they perceived as an inequity. I discussed the situation with their group supervisor. We came up with a reframe that she agreed to try. After allowing the group to air their feelings about the issue, the supervisor explained that the company had a good health care program. She clarified that if any of them got sick, their family would be provided for until they get better. She explained that many companies do not have the substantial health care program their organization provided. She expressed they were fortunate because the company would take care of its employees, even new ones. The reframe caused a few heads to nod in agreement as she spoke. Then one of the longest tenured workers said, "1 guess you're right. At least we know the company cares." The reframe worked in this situation.

Managers at 3M used reframing to encourage salespeople to emphasize how their products help customers make it through a recession. Robert Hershock, a group vice-president, told Fortune magazine writer John Huey how he reframes an economic slowdown. Hershock explains that a slack off in sales allows salespeople "a real opportunity to go in and talk about the labor and cost saving aspects of our products."

Reframing also creates meaning that enables, empowers, and excites people to join with the leader and move forward together. An R&D lab's quality team leader used reframing to motivate the group to follow her lead. At one point, the group became disgruntled because they had to rework a quality proposal to include new guidelines. This would take many hours of extra work. The team captain agreed that the unexpected rework would take extra time. She agreed that the new guidelines might not add anything of real value to the existing proposal. She then reframed the situation by saying, "I also believe that with the additional effort, we can refine what we already have done to make it even better." One of the group members then spoke up: “I agree. There are some changes I would like to make to what we have, in spite of these new demands.” That comment brought a strong enough wave of agreement from the rest of the group to align them behind the team captain.

Recall the story about Jose, the service company supervisor. He felt that Bobbie, the new manager, did not “support the company mission.” We reframed the situation with positive results. Jose’s current frame was based on Bobbie’s cost-cutting focus. Also, she had not held any meetings with the customer service group. I suggested that perhaps Bobbie’s cost-reduction efforts would ultimately serve customers. It might allow the company to reduce prices or uncover operational inefficiencies that ultimately damaged customer relations. This reframe worked for Jose. He asked Bobbie to meet with the customer service group and explain the cost-cutting measures. Bobbie responded positively. She gave a presentation to the group in which she emphasized that customer service was a high priority. The reframe had an important secondary impact because it gave Jose a sense of empowerment that he could create change. Jose felt empowerment was an important core value. Reframing has an even more powerful effect when it reinforces one of the follower’s values.

Reframing Drill

Reframing is a skill that can be honed with practice. Here are some sample situations you can use to practice. Write out your reframe to each situation. Then compare your reframes with those listed below.

Imagine you, or those you want to lead, face the following situations. Further assume that people interpret the situations as a problem. Reframe in a way you believe others would be inspired to follow you:

1. Your department must trim 20 percent of its workforce.
2. Your boss wants your department to stop working on a project that the employees really enjoy.

3. Your organization has flattened its hierarchy so that twice as many people now report to you.

Here are possible reframes:

1. Your department must trim 20 percent of its workforce means.
   - The cutbacks give you a chance to cross-train people which could enrich their jobs and increase work satisfaction
   - The rightsizing will get rid of some of the dead weight in your department.
   - The smaller workforce gives people a chance for more responsibility and therefore greater visibility. This could improve chances for future raises and promotions.
   - The reduction in force enables the group to rethink the way it works and develop more efficient work procedures.
   - Those who are not let go are the most valuable members of the group.

2. Your boss wants your department to stop working on a project that the employees really enjoy:
   - The department can seek out other projects that are even more enjoyable.
   - The boss is finally paying close attention to you and your work, which gives you a chance to shine.
   - By your giving up this project, the boss might be willing to negotiate with you on other matters that you care more about.

3. Your organization has flattened its hierarchy, and twice as many people now report to you:
   - The increased staff size gives you more influence within the organization.
   - The flatter organization eliminates the mis-communication from the senior ranks.
   - You can now get approval for advanced computer technology to create more efficient means for fast

communication with more people. The new technology will also be an aid to other aspects of your job.

Manipulation or Motivation: Humpty-Dumpty Talk

I once overheard someone giving advice about how to manipulate others. The person said, "Sincerity is the secret. You say whatever you have to so that you prove you are sincere."

Reframing can be used to manipulate information in the worst sense, or frame, of the word manipulation. Some people reframe information to gain followers when they do not have the followers' best interests at heart. I call this Humpty-Dumpty talk, based on Humpty-Dumpty's comment, "When I use a word, it means what I choose it to mean, nothing more, nothing less." I do not consider manipulation to be the positive intent of an enlightened Quantum Leader.

Humpty-Dumpty talk is the spin control politicians use. A joke about Washington politicos is that a political rival is slick when the rival can fool the public more successfully than the opponent can. Spin control in the culture of Washington, D.C. helps people merely look and sound good in the image they project rather than demonstrate that they are successful. In business, Humpty-Dumpty talk avoids substance in favor of form or to mask what is going on.

One of the explanations suggested as contributing to General Motors's decline from a premier auto manufacturer to a struggling dinosaur during the 1970's was the use of slick accounting procedures. According to Maryann Keller in *Rude Awakening*, GM executives toiled endlessly to present their numbers in the most favorable light. Those who got ahead in the organization were not creating value. Rather, they had the greatest talent for sprucing up their balance sheets to simply look good.

Humpty-Dumpty talk creates blame rather than present a frame that solves a problem. Humpty-Dumpty talk occurs when advertisers spew hype to hawk a product rather than clarify valid benefits. Ads that tout, "new and improved," "100 percent natural," and "low in sodium, fat, and cholesterol," often simply hype their product news for marketing purposes rather than signal substantive changes.

Quantum Leaders recognize the potential misuse of reframing. They know that they control their intentions. They know they can choose to manipulate, misguide, mask, or otherwise mislead. Or they can reframe to create shared meaning that adds real value to followers. Quantum Leaders do not abuse the process with Humpty-Dumpty talk. Field Guide 8 provides six specific action ideas to apply the concept of reframing.

When Reframing Does Not Work

Reframes might not work for three reasons. First, a reframe may fail when it suggests a meaning too far afield from the follower's existing frame. For example, almost any reframe will fail to convince a strong pro-choice person that abortion is murder. Similarly, no frame will influence a strong right-to-life proponent that terminating a pregnancy is a woman's right.

Reframes may also fail if they lack elegance. Reframes fail if they do not offer a compelling new meaning for the situation. A manager in a computer company recognized the firm's low sales revenues and backlog of work. He bungled an attempt to influence his boss when he reframed the need for more staff by saying, "We would be helping the local economy by hiring more people."

The third reason that reframing may not have impact stems from a lack of trust. When we hear a person say, "I don't care how it sounds, I don't believe that guy," we know the reframe may be elegant, but the person will not follow because of a lack of trust. *Strained relationships result in rejected reframes.* Without some degree of trust and common ground, possible followers mock the reframe because they perceive it as a manipulative ploy or insincere attempt to change the followers' minds about an issue. In this situation, no leadership occurs. The quality of leader-follower relationships is an important foundation of Quantum Leadership, and it has a direct impact on reframing.

"Wet-Finger-in-the-Air" Leadership

Matching followers' values and frames of reference does not mean leaders simply guide the followers where the followers already want to go. Quantum Leaders do not practice "wet-finger-in-the-air" leadership: holding a finger in the air to test the direction of the wind and then pointing in that direction. Quantum Leadership transcends simply telling people what they want to hear.

Quantum Leaders perform enlightened action while engaging the full power of the Quantum Leader within. Their intention is to make a difference, not to assume the posture of the sycophant. Quantum Leaders focus attention on ways to overcome difficulties and exploit opportunities that realize meaningful results, not merely to pander for followers. Quantum Leaders use expanded judgment to create choices, select options, and take initiatives designed to inspire, motivate, and produce beneficial outcomes rather than to simply gain popular support.

◆◆◆

FIELD GUIDE 8

Action Idea 8.1: Clarify your core values.

Spend time determining your core values. Define those values that are ends in themselves. Probe what matters to you by asking, "What parameters do I use to guide my decisions, my thinking, and my approach to life? What is most important to me?" List these values on paper. Then clarify the more primary values behind those on your list by considering, "What does this value provide me?" For example, you might value professional respect, because it provides you with a sense of self-confidence, which you desire as an end in itself. Self-confidence would represent a core value.

After you develop an initial list of values, self-refer. That is, turn within your consciousness to the source of your intention, and prioritize your values. Which values are most essential to you? And are these the values that you really want to guide you? By consciously self-referring to your values, your capacity to make meaningful judgements is more able to choose the values you want. Revise and refine your most essential core values to select a set of your highest-priority values. Review this refined list on a regular basis, perhaps once a month, to reinforce it and/or update it with further clarification.

Action Idea 8.2: Hold values clarification sessions.

Set aside time to discuss values with others. Ask "meaning questions" from the USA MD PAN technique described in Chapter 7. That means, ask people to explain what is important to them at work. Discuss which values they rely on to interpret events. Propose a list of values for discussion (e.g., teamwork, expertise, concern for others, honesty, participation) to find out which values they find most compelling. A group of people may have a variety of different values. By clarifying their values, you gain the possibility of finding ways to match those that are important to each person. Furthermore, the values clarification session gives you a chance to define your core values to others. This helps set the tone to guide the discussion toward primary values. That is, when you apply Action Idea 8.1 you will have determined your own primary values (those that are ends in themselves). You can communicate those values to others as part of the process of discussing their key values.

Action Idea 8.3: Listen for the values messages.

Values are subtle. They can be difficult to uncover. You must consciously listen for them. The statement, "I don't care how long it takes, I just want to get it done," suggests the speaker values good follow-through or results. The statement, "I hope the layoffs are over because I can't go through much more of this," suggests the speaker values stability. "What are the numbers? What's the bottom line here?" suggest a person who values precision, accuracy, and accountability. "We need to pull together" suggests the speaker values teamwork and cooperation. Clarify the accuracy of your perception when you think you have identified the values behind the words. State the values. For example, after someone says, "I don't care how long it takes, I just want to get it done," restate the core value. Say, "It is obvious that follow-through is very important to you." The person's response will verify if you have accurately discerned the value message.

Action Idea 8.4: Probe to clarify deeper values.

Clarify values by probing the deeper meaning behind each one. Consider a person who says she values money. You can probe this value by asking, "What is important to you about money?" Suppose the person responds, "The ability to take care of my needs." A further probe might be, "What's important about taking care of your needs?" The person might respond, "A sense of security," which could be the deeper, more primary value. Probing digs into deeper layers to help fully clarify core values.

Action Idea 8.5: Prioritize values through pairing.

All values do not hold equal weight. Achievement might be of paramount importance at work. Love and respect might be more important at home. Understand followers' values by asking them to prioritize values in pairs. For example, ask followers, "In this situation, which is more important to you: being respected or having a challenge?" Making such distinctions helps you identify the highest-priority values.

Action Idea 8.6: Identify the behavior-value connection.

Once you have identified a person's important values, explore the behaviors he or she believes reflect those values. Define the behavior-value connection to help reveal the difference between values and behaviors. Values are invisible filters. Behaviors are observable. Identify the behavior-value connection by asking a person to define the specific behaviors that demonstrate a specific value. For example, assume being respected is one of a person's most core, fundamental values. Suppose the person indicates being respected means asking people for their opinion. You now have a clear way to match that core value. Ask for the person's opinion. Solicit the person's input. Thank the person for providing ideas.

Action Idea 8.7: Translate your direction to match follower values.

Translate your course of action into a message that reinforces values. For example, if people value expertise, communicate your direction by demonstrating your expertise: "I know this direction will payoff because. . . [demonstrate your expertise]." You could also communicate your direction to reinforce how it affects their expertise: "We will learn more about. . . if we do. .."

Action Idea 8.8: Communicate values with congruence.

Practice aligning what you say and how you say it to be congruent with the values you are trying to match. For example, use a sincere tone and expression to communicate more honesty. Make eye contact and get out from behind your desk to communicate more openness. Your desk implies a barrier between you and others. Speak with enthusiasm about a challenging situation to communicate a "can do" spirit. These action ideas sound like common sense. But, congruent communication takes practice. Refer to the action ideas in Chapter 8's Field Guide regarding congruent communication to improve your skills in this area.

Action Idea 8.9: Perform action that demonstrates followers' behavior-value connection.

Specific behaviors are indicators of values. Create shared meaning by behaving in ways that followers have identified as linked to core values. For example, consider a group that values openness which they explain means being able to spend face time with managers. Assume they have described two specific behaviors that directly demonstrate this value: 1. The manager's door is typically open; 2. Employees can pop in for an unscheduled meeting. Do these two things to demonstrate the behavior-value connection.

Action Idea 8.10: Say it again Sam.

"Everyone wants to do a good job. Everyone wants to make a contribution." Ron Ovitz was a manager at Public Service Organization of Oklahoma, a utility company in Tulsa. He made this statement dozens of times during a six-month consulting project I conducted with his company. The statement expressed one of his core values. He repeated it often to create shared meaning with the group he wanted to influence. He knew they valued quality work and being a part of something. Ovitz's example reveals how to create shared meaning by frequent repetition of key values. Repeat your message to transmit core values. Let people know you really believe in specific values by reminding them again and again of the value's importance.

Action Idea 8.11: Clarify the existing frame

Ask potential followers to explain the context or backdrop for their interpretations of events. Funnel your questions to get at deeper layers of meaning. Keep asking the question, "What does that mean?" until you discover the specific events, behaviors, and circumstances that create the current frame.

Action Idea 8.12: Reframe one negative situation each day.

Reframe a negative situation into a positive one each day. The ability to reframe a negative as a positive is critical today because of the dominance of negative news. Watch any television news show or read the front page of any paper, and you will recognize how we are bombarded with negative images. Reframe one negative situation each day to practice creating a more useful perspective.

Action Idea 8.13: Clarify the usefulness of existing frames.

Effective reframes often begin by clarifying the usefulness of the follower's existing frame. For example, consider a person who states, "The company's empowerment effort has demoralized me, it has taken away the authority I worked so hard to gain over the years." An effective reframe might begin, "Yes, your situation has changed dramatically, and it is going to require a readjustment." This statement provides a match of meaning between you and the other person. You can then reframe by expanding the context of the existing frame so that the other person gains a new, more useful meaning. You could say, "You were able to make it in the old system that had so many rigid boundaries. I'm sure you will be successful in the new structure because it has fewer restrictions. In fact, you could have more influence because everyone has lost formal authority in the restructuring, but you have such good relationships with people, they will probably listen to you."

Action Idea 8.14: Affirm the negative framers.

Some people tend to frame almost everything in a negative context. "Life's a pain and then you die" or "Sometimes you get the elevator, but mostly you get the shaft" are among their favorite mottos. It is difficult to respond to negative framers, but there are ways. One is to affirm the negative frame. For example, when someone complains about the difficulty of a situation, affirm the frame by saying, "Yes, it's tough, isn't it?" or "You're right; it won't be easy." The phrasing of these reframes draws the negative reframer to you because, in effect, you are matching this person's frame. This builds rapport because it creates the sense that you and the other person are alike. With this foundation, you then might be able to suggest a reframe that is more useful and positive.

Action Idea 8.15: Reframe parts of the situation.

Effective reframing sometimes requires breaking up big problems into manageable pieces. Consider what has happened to many organizations today: a drastically cut workforce, a radically restructured hierarchy, a revamped authority system, and rightsizing, reengineering, and restructuring can be viewed as profanities by those who fear even more change in the workplace. Trying to reframe the meaning of all of these situations would overwhelm even the most hearty. Instead, cut the problem into small pieces, and reframe only a part of it. Refocus attention on a small area of the work redesign. Redirect people to consider one element of the new structure. A series of small reframes can build into a major transformation of meaning.

Action Idea 8.16: Reframe to bring out the sweet truth.

The "sweet truth" is the meaning of an event others can easily accept. Very few people accept information that puts them in a bad light. The sweet truth points out the best side of a situation. Years ago, a shoe salesperson gave me a simple example to illustrate the power of the sweet truth. A good shoe salesperson, I was told, always tells a customer who has two different-sized feet that one foot is smaller than the other rather than that one foot is bigger. Few people want to hear they have big feet, but anyone can accept that they have a smaller foot.

Action Idea 8.17: Reframe with congruence.

Reframes have to be communicated in a congruent manner. The words, tone, and nonverbal behaviors used to communicate the reframed message have to complement each other. Using a sarcastic or uninspired tone when saying, “This is really an opportunity,” will not garner much followership. Giving a disapproving or condescending glance when saying, “I’m sure you’re going to find this beneficial,” sends a mixed message that limits the potential for shared meaning. Leon Moore’s reframe about how excited he was to work for the IRS was totally congruent. He was standing straight, smiling broadly, his eyes bright with enthusiasm, and his tone upbeat.

10

Influence Strategies

"If we want to be heard we must speak in a language the listener can understand and on a level at which the listener is capable of operating."
M. Scott Peck, author of The Road Less Traveled

Have you ever tried to convince someone to do something but just could not get through? You thought your direction was in line with the person's values. You provided a useful and attractive frame of reference. Yet, the person still resisted your direction. Quantum Leaders recognize the need to match values and reframe to create shared meaning. They also understand and rely on more subtle strategies to perform enlightened action and attract followers. These persuasion strategies are designed to match the way followers actually structure information in their consciousness. They involve a deeper level of meaning creation.

Internal Information Processing Codes: Private Mental Languages

People use specific internal codes or modalities to portray experiences in their minds. For example, some people portray experiences visually. Such individuals actually see pictures in their mind. Others make sense of information auditorily. They literally represent information by sound. Still others process information kinesthetically or based on actions and feelings. They create meaning in terms of a physical experience.

Internal information processing codes are the subtlest level at which people assign meaning to their experience. Unlike values and frames of reference, internal information processing codes are the fundamental routines that define how people take in, sort, store, access, and configure "raw data." These internal codes are similar to codes used by Western Union operators to make sense of the telegraph line beeps. They also resemble the source codes of a computer program.

Internal information processing codes form a person's private mental language. For example, individuals who rely on visual signals and are detail-oriented have to *see* every fact, figure, and bit of information available. They do not *notice* or know how to recognize generalities very well.

Quantum Leader influence involves speaking the follower's private mental language. People learn their internal language, just as they learn English, Spanish, or Chinese. Quantum Leaders can learn these internal codes because only a finite number exist. Quantum Leaders can then speak the follower's private mental language to create shared meaning that attracts committed followers.

Four key internal codes form the foundation of the private mental languages people use to create meaning:

1. Visual - Auditory - Kinesthetic (action-feeling) code
2. Detail - Generality code
3. Approach - Avoidance code
4. Similarity - Difference code

Understand the Visual - Auditory - Kinesthetic (Action-Feeling) Code

The visual - auditory - kinesthetic (VAK) code reveals that some people create meaning as pictures. Others rely on sound work. Still others use feelings or actions. It is important to know that everyone uses a combination of VAK. No one code is more effective than another. Visual, auditory, and kinesthetic are simply different ways to structure information. However, many people rely more heavily on one of the three.

Visual people want to "see" what you mean. They "get a good picture." They "show" you things to make them "perfectly clear." Things "look good" or "look bad" to them. Ideas may "appear insightful," or information may be "hazy" or "foggy."

Auditory people like to "tell." They want you to "listen." They "hear" you when things "sound good." They "purr like a kitten" and "ring a bell." They do *not* "tune in" when you "sound" bad or "blabber."

Kinesthetic (action-feeling) people want to "get moving," "take a step," and "hang in there." They recognize how times are "tough," action is "rough" or "hard to handle." They "get close," "catch on," and "walk hand in hand" when they follow. They "slip away" or do not want the "hassle" when they choose not to follow.

Quantum Leaders recognize visuals by attending to words and phrases and observing physical actions. They pay attention to typical phrases, such as "a dim view," "the naked eye," "plainly see," and "the image." They look for a person's degree of eye contact. Visual people usually look you directly in they eye. They stare or look closely at things to understand them. It is common for a visual person to peek into your office, look over your shoulder, or request to see documents or other materials.

Quantum Leaders tune in to auditory types when they hear typical comments such as "hold your tongue," "listen up," "give me an earful," and "explain it word for word." Auditory people often turn their ear toward a speaker. They may even cup their ear while listening intently. They do not need to make eye contact when talking to someone. In fact, those who are dominantly auditory may even close their eyes while listening. This heightens their hearing ability. An auditory person likes to converse by telephone and will have long conversations.

Some IBM executives might have responded better to CEO Lou Gerstner had they understood that he probably has a strong preference for the auditory mode. According to a story in Paul Carroll's *Big Blues: The Unmaking of IBM*, Gerstner forbade executives from using overhead slides. He insisted that if somebody had something to say, he or she should just "say it."

Quantum Leaders catch on to kinesthetic people by typical comments such as "touch base," "point out," "turn things around," "get my mind around it," "control it," and "all washed up." Kinesthetic types like to make physical contact. They willingly shake hands. They touch an arm or shoulder. They pick up objects and feel their texture. They rub their hands together without the need to warm them. They often stretch in meetings, run their hands along a table, or tap on objects.

Field Guide 9 provides five action ideas to help you understand the VAK code.

Understand the Detail - Generality Code

This internal code reveals that some people create meaning in the form of details, while others favor a general overview to interpret information. Detail people make presentations using specific facts and figures. They read everything and examine the fine print. For them, every bit of information is important. Detail people review information again and again so that they do not miss any point of information.

In contrast, a generality person's briefing emphasizes only "the highlights." They make a few short statements about "the key points" which they feel tell the entire story. They need only an overview of the main points to understand information. Generality types first review the summary graphs and charts when they pick up a book or a report. They feel that a quick, cursory inspection of a situation gives them the whole story.

Consider a human resource manager in a large corporation who wants to review a new training program. A manager who prefers details will attend the entire program, read every word in the participant manual, and make notes about multiple details. A generality manager will slip into the back of the room and observe for 10 to 15 minutes. The manager will flip through the participant manual and note the overview and summary pages. The manager will explain, "That's all the time I need to know if the program is worthwhile for us."

Although people do use both elements of this code, most tend to be more comfortable with one or the other. They make meaning using their dominant mode. Quantum Leaders recognize this code by noticing how much information people request and by observing how people respond to the information they are given. Field Guide 9 provides three action ideas to understand the detail - generality mode.

Understand the Approach/Avoidance Code

The approach/avoidance code is concerned with whether people experience (approach) or do not want to experience (avoidance) something. This internal meaning creation code stems from the desire for comfort and the dislike of pain.

People who represent information in the approach mode "move toward" something in order to realize more pleasure and to minimize pain. The statement, "I really want to get home early tonight," indicates the approach person moving forward towards something he or she thinks will be positive. People who represent information in the avoidance mode structure information by "moving away" so they experience less pain and more pleasure. An avoidance person might say, "I hope I don't get home late tonight." The avoidance person perceives some discomfort getting home late and wants to avoid that. Both approach and avoidance people aim for the same thing. They want more comfort and less discomfort. Their internal code structures a different reality and reaction to their experience.

Everyone uses a combination of approach and avoidance. Most people consistently favor one or the other. A vice president of human resources recently said to me, "I believe the new employee assistance program will help our people feel better about the company." This suggests an approach interpretation. Another vice president in the same company remarked that the employee assistance program, "Should limit the potential for employees to make claims that the company is unfair." This comment suggests an avoidance interpretation. The first vice president wanted a new human resources management software package to help analyze data more easily. The second wanted the same package for the opposite reason. She hoped it would help minimize errors that might create problems with employee records. The approach vice president attended association meetings as a way to network and build credibility within the industry. The avoidance vice president attended the same meetings because she did not want her boss to think she was not a committed career person.

Avoidance can be beneficial despite its seemingly adverse response posture. People who move away from a lit match do not get burned. Thus, an avoidance person can be very useful when considering ways to minimize losses or to limit problems. Quantum Leaders notice the approach/avoidance code when they carefully attend to people's language, logic, and explanations for behavior.

Field Guide 9 offers three actions to understand the approach - avoidance code.

Understand the Similarity - Difference Code

This code involves meaning creation in terms of similarities and differences. Similarity people make comments such as, "This is just like the last one," or "We did this yesterday." They process information in terms of perceived commonalities. Difference people say, "It's completely different from what we did before," or, "I've never done anything like this." Their private mental language forms meanings based on perceived contrasts.

The similarity - difference code has two subcodes. Some interpret exceptions to a similarity. For example, such a person comments, "They are all the same size, except this one, which is a little larger." The second subcode means people interpret exceptions to a difference. Such a person might comment, "Every one of these is a different size, except these two, which are the same." People can switch around among the variations of this code depending on the situation, but most favor one of the four.

Quantum Leaders notice the similarity - difference code and its two subcodes when people describe how they compare things and how they make distinctions about events.

Field Guide 9 offers two actions to understand the similarity - difference code.

Speak the Follower's Private Mental Language

Quantum Leaders gain entry into the follower's private mental language when they recognize and understand the preferred codes being used. Quantum Leader's have influence when they speak the follower's language. They match the follower's internal codes to create shared meaning.

Matching another person's private mental language is like speaking his or her native tongue. We easily understand that people who are raised to speak Spanish think and speak in Spanish. People brought up in Germany think and speak in German. People raised in China represent their world in Chinese. We quickly realize how hard it is to communicate with people who speak a language that we do not know. However, if, for example, we speak Spanish, we can easily communicate shared meaning when Spanish is the native tongue. The subtle, internal codes that make up our private mental language also have to be matched to create the powerful quantum influence connection of shared meaning.

Jay Stark Thompson is CEO of Life Technologies, a supplier of tools to life sciences researchers. He understands the need to match the private mental language of others. According to *Fortune* magazine writer Faye Rice, Thompson states, "I've learned that just because you think it, write it, or say it doesn't mean employees hear it or believe it." Thompson explains that a graphic picture or image may be required. He recognizes that a behavioral portrait might be needed to get across the meaning of an idea. Thompson also understands that internal codes must be matched individually. That is, he discounts general exhortations such as, "achieve better quality." Thompson favors talking directly to shop workers to hammer home the importance of sending precisely correct amounts of chemicals in every vial leaving the factory.

Matching internal codes requires a high level of attention power from the Quantum Leader within. Quantum Leaders pay attention to the signals that indicate each of the codes. Then they use their judgment to recognize subtle private mental language differences. They discern when people switch modes, such as an auditory person who suddenly wants a picture to be *shown* a direction. Quantum Leaders are intent on matching the follower's private mental language and they take initiative to do so.

Match the VAK Pattern

Quantum Leaders match the follower's VAK code. They show the visual people, tell the auditory types, and make contact with the kinesthetic people.

Match the Approach - Avoidance Code

Quantum Leaders match approach people by explaining what they will gain by following. To match avoidance people, ensure them they will not have to experience specific outcomes if they follow.

Match the Similarity - Difference Code

Quantum Leaders match similarity people by emphasizing how something resembles something else. They match similarity-with-exception people by asserting the larger degree of similarity and by agreeing to the portion that is different. Matching difference people requires some finesse. For example, assume you try to influence a coworker to help you with a report. The person's response is, "I don't want to do that. It's too different from what I am working on." To match the person might involve saying, "You're right it is different." That could be interpreted as confirmation of their desire not to work with you and limit your capacity to influence the person. However, by definition, difference people will respond by disagreeing. That means the response to, "You're right it is different," might be, "Well, it's not that different." The person's automatic difference response now indicates they are more willing to be influenced.

Match the Detail - Generality Code

Quantum Leaders match detail people with mounds of data, facts, and statistics. Leaders match generality people with overviews, summaries, and bottom-line statements. An easy metaphor to remember here is: "Detail people recognize all the trees. Generality people perceive a forest."

The Quantum Reality of Matching Internal Codes

Internal codes represent broad categories that people use to create meaning. The way any particular follower makes meaning of any single bit of information cannot be absolutely determined. Uncertainty and probabilities govern this subtle layer of life.

Human information processing has great flexibility. Human consciousness can take a quantum leap and change from one code to another. A generality person might suddenly say, "I need more information. Let's get into some of the specific numbers," after you have prepared only a short general overview of financial data. An auditory person might blurt out, "Is that all you can show me? I need to see this more clearly," after you told the person everything you thought she/he needed to hear.

To speak the follower's private mental language requires experimentation. Quantum Leaders accept the risk associated with trying to influence others (the sixth natural law of leadership). They thrive on the challenge because of their intention to lead. They keep their attention sharply focused to recognize a change in the use of any code. They expand their judgment by preparing more response choices.

To reach all the VAK modes, Quantum Leaders may develop a well-articulated speech, prepare several eye-catching graphs, and bring materials that followers can leaf through or hold. They prepare to communicate their direction with both an executive summary and many pages of charts and graphs.

Quantum Leaders can explain how their direction will create possibilities and assure how following will minimize problems. They create comparisons and they are ready to acknowledge and accept the existence of differences. The better the match is, the greater is the possibility that their action will create shared meaning and enlighten others to support their leader initiative.

Quantum Leaders change the follower's consciousness with their influence initiatives, their methods to create shared meaning, and their techniques to perform enlightened action. These tools connect leaders to followers at the follower's level and then guide the follower to the leader's level of consciousness. Despite the best efforts, it is not always possible to change follower consciousness. The seventh natural law of leadership states that not everyone will follow. When people are locked into a particular state of awareness, it may be very difficult and extremely time-consuming to gain their commitment.

Quantum Leaders also know that they can increase the probability of influencing people to follow by cultivating relationships that create a sense of common ground, trust, and credibility. By developing the relationship foundation, Quantum Leaders strengthen the impact of performing enlightened action.

FIELD GUIDE 9

Actions to Understand Each Mode

Action Idea 9.1: Pay attention to VAK words and phrases.

Watch for *visual* words and phrases such as see, look, watch, eyeful, clearly, from my point of view, image, hindsight, focused, catch a glimpse, or make a scene. Listen attentively for *auditory* words and phrases such as soft, idle talk, to tell the truth, hear, amplify, tune in/out, be all ears, rings a bell, or manner of speaking. Tap into *kinesthetic* words and phrases such as make contact, get a hold of, catch on, turn around, concrete, smooth out, come to grips with, control yourself, firm foundation, get the drift, keep your shirt on, pull some strings, or too much of a hassle. The simple act of your close attention will reveal a person's dominant mode. Attention prepares you to respond using the person's private mental language to influence him or her.

Action Idea 9.2: Pay attention to greetings and goodbyes.

Greetings and goodbyes offer fertile ground for understanding VAK codes. Visual types look at you and might remark, "Nice to see you," or "You're looking great." They maintain eye contact when they leave and could comment, "I'll see you again." Auditory types greet you with words such as, "I'm glad to speak to you," or "It's great to talk to you again." They say goodbye with phases such as, "It was great to hear from you" and "I'll call you soon." Kinesthetic (action-feeling) types often greet others by shaking their hands or touching their arms. Kinesthetic types comment that, "It feels so good to be connected." When they depart, they might say, "Keep in touch," as they shake your hand again or make some other physical contact.

Action Idea 9.3: Watch the eyes.

Richard Bandler and John Grinder pioneered neurolinguistic programming (NLP), the science of internal information processing codes. They explain in their book, *Frogs into Princes*, that people's eyes move in different directions based on the element of VAK they use. People look up when they see information in their minds. People look to their right or left, level with their ears, or down and to their left when they subliminally hear information. People look down and to their lower right when they are accessing information kinesthetically. Spend some time observing people's eye movements to determine their preference for VAK.

Action Idea 9.4: Ask questions to validate VAK

Assume you do not get a clear sense of a person's code based on observation, greetings and goodbyes, or eye movements. You can use questions to further explore a person's dominant preference. For example, ask, "What is your experience regarding. . . ?" The question is code neutral since the word "experience" can apply to V, A, or K. The response to the question usually reveals how the person processes information.

Consider a manager's response to the question, "What is your experience regarding the recent downsizing?" Her comment, "Things look pretty grim now. You can see on people's faces that they have a dim view of what happened." This manager is clearly a visual type.

Action Idea 9.5: Pay attention to the VAK sequence.

Everyone uses all three elements of this code. They typically have a preferred sequence or syntax of VAK. Some may hear, see, and then feel. Others might feel, hear, then see. Pay attention to the VAK syntax to expand your capacity to understand and match people's private mental language.

To illustrate, consider this statement: "Look, I don't see how this will happen. It's really frustrating to me. I feel my hands are tied. What can you tell me?" Reread the sentence and notice the sequence of the statements. Visual words appear first. Then kinesthetic phrases pop up. Lastly, you hear auditory comments. The particular sequence of such a statement is VKA.

Action Idea 9.6: Pay attention to the form of requests.

Detail people make requests such as, "Do you have any more information?" "How much exactly did it cost?" or "Can you give me some background?" Generality requests include, "What is the bottom line?" "Do you have a summary chart?" or "What is the one most important thing I should know."

Action Idea 9.7: Notice how people handle written material.

Detail people carefully review almost all of the written material they are given. They take lots of notes. A document returned from a detail person will be well handled. It will have many folded pages, lots of dog-eared corners, and generally be worn-looking. Generality people read the summary or table of contents. They might underline just one or two items. A document read by a generality person will remain in pristine shape. It will have few creases, almost no marks, and only a few pages handled.

Action Idea 9.8: Ask questions to reveal detail vs. general response.

Ask, "What do you need to know about this issue?" and "What information can I give you about this project?" The detail person will reply, "I'll have to go over all the numbers and get some background reports." The generality person will retort, "I need to see the total cost," or "It will be obvious after I review your summary."

Action Idea 9.9: Pay attention to approach - avoidance language.

Focus on language that indicates moving toward something or phrases that suggest an attempt to gain something. They indicate an approach person. Use the same attention power to identify avoidance people's statements. Notice when someone describes what they do not want to happen or do not want to lose.

Action Idea 9.10: Ask questions to determine approach - avoid.

Ask questions such as, "What do you want from your job?" or "What do you want from the organization?" Approach people will explain to you what they want. Those who avoid will describe what they do not want.

Action Idea 9.11: Notice situational approach - avoidance.

Some people may be approach oriented in some situations and avoidance oriented in others. A tax lawyer I know uses avoidance when it comes to dealing with the IRS. She wants to stay away from the possibility of an audit. Yet she slips into the approach mode when she considers entertainment. She seeks out the thrill of rock-climbing and hang-gliding for excitement.

Action Idea 9.12: Pay attention to similarity - difference comments.

Listen for statements such as, "It's all the same," or "It's all different." Attend to comments that reveal exceptions such as, "These are all the ____ (the same or different) except this one."

Action Idea 9.13: Ask questions to determine similarity - difference.

Ask, "How do these [objects/events/people] compare?" or "What is the relationship between these [objects/events/people]?" The answers offer insight into which code people favor.

Actions to Speak the Follower's Private Mental Language

Action Idea 9.14: Make pictures for the visual person.

Use visual language with words such as see, look, and glimpse to create mental pictures that match visual people. Show them pictures, graphs, or charts. Draw sketches for them when you explain your points. Create visual presentations using video or computer imagery. Match the visual person by using colors and bright light. Let the visual person see what you are doing or writing. Make eye contact. Use facial expressions to support your ideas. Adjust your eyebrows in concert with your ideas. And smile. Visual people see the smile, and you probably look better to them that way.

Action Idea 9.15: Make it sound good for the auditory person.

Match auditory people with language that rings a bell for them. Use words such as tell, hear, and listen to create a resounding sense of shared meaning. Adjust your tone to emphasize key words. Speak clearly. Modify your rate of speech to theirs. Repeat words and phrases that reinforce what you want. Restate the words auditory types say to reinforce that you have heard them.

Action Idea 9.16: Get in touch with the kinesthetic person.

Allow the kinesthetic people to hold on to a document or other object that is relevant to your point. Shake hands firmly with them when appropriate. Use kinesthetic phrases such as grab on, smooth sailing, and solid ground to match meaning. Emphasize feelings with statements such as, "I get the feeling. . ." and "This is going to be tough, but we can get through it."

Action Idea 9.17: Match the VAK syntax.

Match the person's VAK syntax by adopting his or her sequence of VAK elements. If the person "tells you how they feel" (A-K syntax) respond by "saying how you feel." If the person "sees that it rings a chord," (V-A syntax) match them by "showing them you are listening."

Action Idea 9.18: Point out how "moving toward" benefits those who approach.

Match approach people with statements such as, "You're really going to gain if you do . . . ," or "You will benefit in this way if you go in this direction," or "By taking this path, you will receive this positive result."

Action Idea 9.19: Clarify how no harm will come to those who prefer to avoid.

Match avoidance people with comments such as, "You can avert that danger by doing. . . ," or "It will be worse unless you do . . . ," or, "When you take this path, you won't have to deal with..."

Action Idea 9.20: Point out similarities.

Say, "This is just like what we did last week," or, "Notice that the changes are almost identical to what happened last week and we made it through that," or "Everything here compares very well with the other program."

Action Idea 9.21: Clarify similarities with exceptions.

Say, "You can see that every one of these requests is almost identical, and this unique one won't be hard to deal with," or, "I know this part is somewhat unique. The rest of this is all the same."

Action Idea 9.22: Allow similarity people to build on your lead.

Similarity people usually reinforce your lead because they will try to find something they can recognize and accept. Match the similarity mode by asking, "What more would you do to get us moving in this direction?" or "How can we make this initiative more effective?" A similarity person will often respond, "I recognize a way to do it."

Action Idea 9.23: Ask for differences.

Ask difference people, "What's different about this?" or, "Does this appear unlike what we have done before?" Difference people will chime in with the many contrasts they notice. Simply asking for difference reinforces their interpretation. This creates rapport because you demonstrate that you understand their private mental language.

Action Idea 9.24: Appreciate the difference person.

Difference people find it hard to get along with others because they disagree so often. By focusing on discrepancies, difference people distance themselves from others. One way to create shared meaning with them is to thank them for their contributions and to acknowledge the validity of their insights. Appreciating difference people because of their uniqueness can bond them to you.

Action Idea 9.25: Acknowledge the difference and ask for support.

When difference people counter your lead, openly acknowledge it: "Yes, that is a difference." Be silent for a few moments. Then ask for their support. The purpose here is twofold. First, difference people may reverse themselves by saying, "Well, it might not be that different," and then support your lead. This sounds somewhat unrealistic, but I have experienced it. It can work. Second, by agreeing with difference people, you join them at their level of meaning. That connection may establish enough overlap of meaning to influence them to follow.

Action Idea 9.26: Rely on matching other internal codes when matching differences gets tough.

The tricky nature of matching difference people could be circumvented by taking an alternate approach. For example, focus on their VAK code or their detail - generality code. You might create shared meaning at this level such that the difference matcher finds a way to get your message.

Action Idea 9.27: Rely on others to help you match detail and generality people.

It can be easy to match detail people if you are one yourself. You can easily talk generality people's language if you are also a big-picture person. Matching your opposite can be difficult. One way is to rely on others to help you. For example, imagine you have to give a report to a detail person. Suppose you can think of only two main points which you know will frustrate a detail driven audience to ask you all kinds of questions. Avert this difficulty Find a detail person whom you trust. Ask that person for help in developing an itemized package of information. Similarly, find a general person to help you if you are a more dominantly detail person.

11

Leader-Quality Relationships

"No matter how busy you are, you must take time to make the other person feel important."
Mary Kay Ash, founder of Mary Kay Cosmetics

Quantum Leaders do not attract followers in a vacuum. Leaders and followers typically have a relationship history outside the events that bond them together in a Quantum Leadership field. They interact when they work together. People socialize together during and after office hours. Good relationships create meaningful bonds. Awkward, uncomfortable, and negative interactions, in contrast, distance people. Association can breed respect, or it can create contempt.

The Quantum Leadership model shows that the quality of interpersonal relationships forms the foundation of the Quantum Leader-follower interaction (Figure 11-1). This relationship establishes a platform that will either support or fail to support the leader's initiatives. Quantum Leaders realize that people are more likely to respond to their call for support when people hold the leader in high regard and are already on their leader's side.

Garry Nelson, now an executive coach, spent over twenty-five years as a senior human resource specialist in several large financial institutions and insurance companies. He made developing positive relationships with others a number one priority. Nelson explained, "If I can't connect with the people I'm working with and let them know we're in this together, they're not going to listen to what I have to say. I'll have little influence if I don't establish positive interactions with people."

Nelson's insight may sound like simple common sense. But as Will Rogers once said, "Common sense ain't so common." Many people, even highly skilled individuals, can forget or overlook the primary importance of relationship building. For example, Jimmy Carter failed to create important alliances with power brokers within the DC beltway when he assumed the presidency in 1976. Carter relied heavily on his "Georgia Mafia," a limited field of relationships with home state cronies. He never established the necessary bonds with the players of national politics in Washington. President Carter was dedicated to his office. He had a highly regarded intellect. Yet, his inability to effectively connect with the crony-oriented beltway limited his sphere of presidential leadership.

The capacity to influence others beyond the dictates of formal authority rests heavily on the quality of relationship. Many leader initiatives fail when this fundamental reality is violated. A 1983 study in *Psychology Today* by Morgan McCall and Michael Lombardo, from the Center of Creative Leadership identified ten factors that caused high-potential executives to derail their career success. The top four reasons were: 1) insensitivity to others; 2) an abrasive, intimidating, bullying style; 3) cold, aloof, arrogant behavior; and, 4) betrayal of trust. Think of your own experience. How do you react to a call for support from a person you do trust? What response do you typically give to someone's initiative when you have a negative impression of the person?

Figure 11-1. The Quantum Leadership model: The relationship foundation.

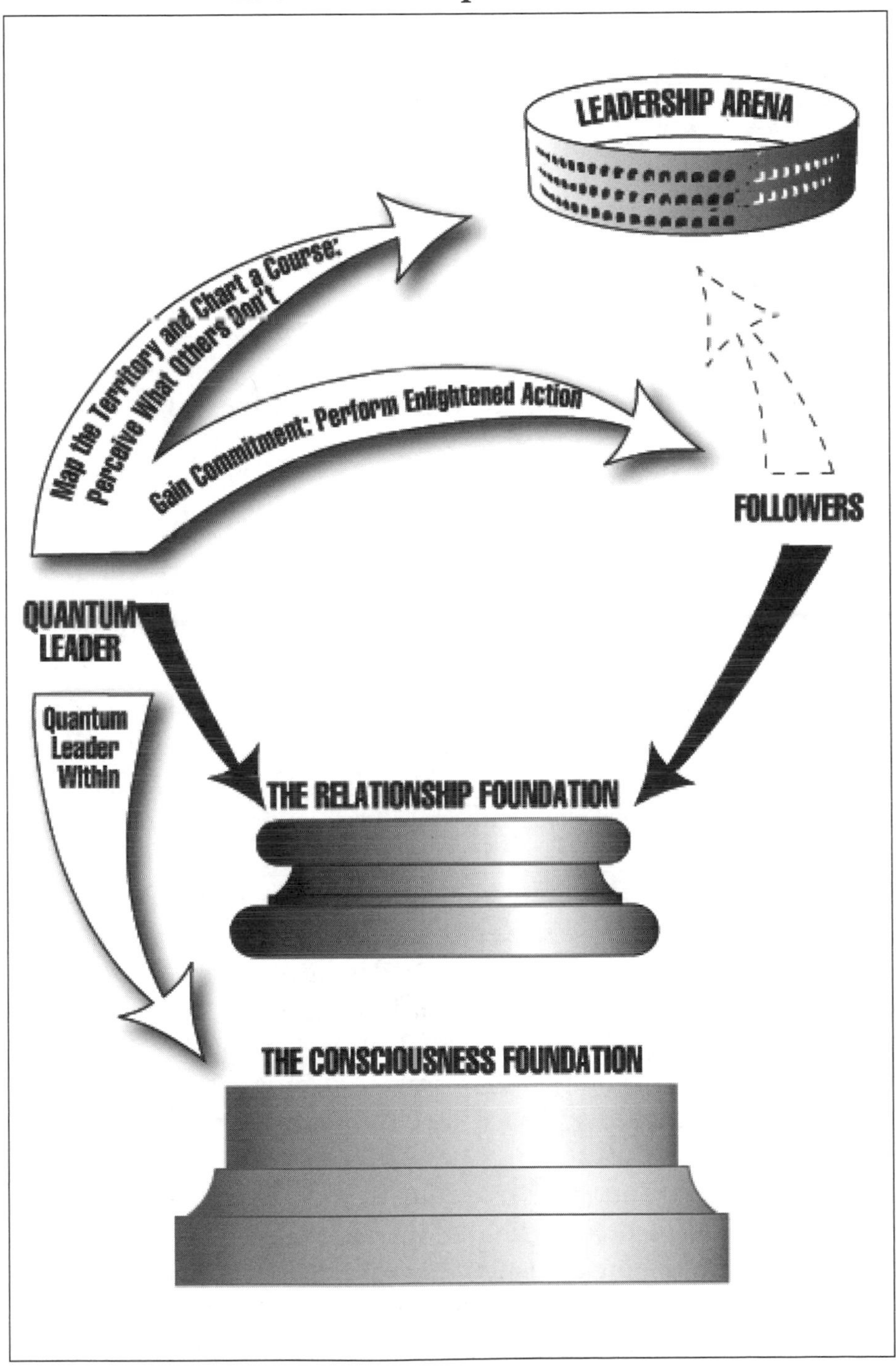

Quantum Leaders know that good relationships do not simply happen. Quantum Leaders must cultivate leader-quality relationships. Such interactions increase the probability of gaining followers.

Four areas are particularly important to achieve this end:

1. Establish a common ground.
2. Provide valued resources.
3. Develop trust.
4. Build credibility.

Establish a Common Ground

Lou Hughes, the president of General Motors Europe, learned German to communicate with local hourly workers. He immersed himself in the language for six months. He required colleagues to use it in meetings with him. Hughes became so competent that he used German even in conversation with English-speaking Germans.

At the Minnesota headquarters of Toro, the lawnmower and snow blower company, CEO Kendrick Melrose tries to eat lunch at least once a month with employees. He puts in occasional sessions on the assembly line and answers customer service telephones.

Every quarter F. H. Behrendt, CEO of Exabyte, the computer tape-drive producer, meets for two and a half hours with all employees for questions and answers. He introduces new employees, shows slides of them, and says something personal and interesting about each. Hughes, Melrose, and Behrendt all demonstrate ways to cultivate a common ground.

Leaders and followers share important common ground when they stand together on a platform of shared experience and understanding. Common ground transforms individual separateness into a holistic field of interaction. With a common ground, individual consciousness becomes unified, collective consciousness. This transforms a relationship in ways that are similar to what happens when disparate energy waves join to form a new, coherent wave. Common ground connects the Quantum Leader with other people's subjective views of reality so that the leader can look through their eyes and listen with their ears.

Retired army general Norman Schwarzkopf admits that he is an impatient man. Yet, he understood the need to establish a common ground with the Saudi royal family during the Persian Gulf crisis. Schwarzkopf spent endless hours philosophizing with the family members because that was their way of making decisions.

A common ground creates a meeting of the minds and a joining of the hearts. When people are like each other, they usually like each other. A common ground develops when people share the same background, compatible interests, or similar goals. Even a common geography can create an immediate common ground. Peter Hart, a public-opinion researcher, discussed in *Rolling Stone*, reasons to explain why John Kerry lost the 2004 presidential election. Hart suggested, "Kerry always thought it was about IQ. But it was about 'I like.' He never connected."

During the introductions to my seminars and speaking engagements, I often mention that I have lived in Santa Barbara, New York, Boston, Chapel Hill, Vero Beach and in the mid-western states of Ohio, Indiana, Illinois, Oklahoma, and Iowa. During breaks, many people say: "You know, I lived in Iowa too," or "Where did you live in Indiana? I grew up there," or "My son goes to school in Chapel Hill. I really like it there." Furthermore, because I travel a good deal, I can usually create a common bond by referring to places where people grew up that I have visited. During a program I conducted in Denver, a manager explained that he was raised in Oregon near the Columbia River gorge. Two weeks earlier, I had conducted a retreat in that area for a senior management group. When I described my experience of the majestic countryside, the manager and I made an immediate connection.

Develop Common Ground

Three key steps enable Quantum Leaders to develop common ground with others:

1. Make the B.I.G. Connection
2. Identify the shared aspect of your experience.
3. Accept people as they are.

The B.I.G. Connection

The B.I.G. connection stands for: background, interests, and goals. Quantum Leaders know everyone has some aspect of their B.I.G. experience that is meaningful to others. Quantum Leaders operate with the conscious intent to find out about other's B.I.G. to develop comfortable relationships with them. Common ground helps us feel comfortable with others. This is essential to good relationships. Quantum Leaders know they have to break down the "strangeness barrier" that can interfere with how they interact with others. Think of your own experience. A degree of tentativeness always accompanies initial meetings unless a person is highly skilled and totally comfortable building rapport with others. As we get to know others, and find we share common aspects of our B.I.G., we start to feel more comfortable with them. We are then more at ease with the other person. We feel glad to be with another person. People rarely follow a person if they feel uncomfortable or "strange" around that person. Quantum Leaders listen to and learn about other's background, interests, and goals. They ask questions and observe people's work space to find some common ground in terms of B.I.G. They then identify the links they have with others in terms of B.I.G. to solidify the base of commonality they share.

Identify the Shared Aspect of Your Experience

Armed with the knowledge of another's background, interests, and goals, Quantum Leaders seek to identify the shared aspect of experience that creates the common ground. In some cases, this is easy. When I meet someone who enjoys traveling, likes baseball, or studies physics as a hobby, we immediately share an interest. In other cases, finding the shared aspect of experience requires some digging.

Fred, a manager in a large chemical plant, plays tennis almost every day. Tennis is such a part of his life that he translates his work experiences into a tennis game. Interactions with others are "matches" in which he "serves" ideas and then "returns" information to them. Fred subscribes to several tennis magazines, and his office is littered with tennis paraphernalia. "Getting the ball over the net" consumes Fred's life. In contrast, I have whacked a ball over a net only a few times in my life. I do not really count my experience as playing tennis. That means I cannot effectively create a common ground around tennis with a buff like Fred. I like sports, but for Fred, tennis is sports. So that did not draw us together. However, I am interested in coaching as a tool for managers to develop job-related skills. One day I asked Fred to explain how he improved his tennis game. He told me about taking tennis lessons. He described the teaching videos he watched. I related what he told me to coaching people at work. He became enthusiastic about my ideas. I saw a way to link with him in terms of tennis. We identified a shared aspect of our common experience. That had an immediate positive impact on our interactions. Quantum Leaders purposefully point out shared experience to create that positive relationship.

Quantum Leaders tell people directly what they have in common. This may sound too elementary even to mention. Yet, I have known people who do not clarify common interests because they think it is not important. For six months, I consulted with a production vice president and his six-person quality team. Two of the team members were attending night school to get advanced degrees. The vice president had attended the same program at the same school several years earlier. He never mentioned this commonality despite the many discussions the entire team had about the program. I discussed the issue with the vice president. He explained to me, "Well, that isn't relevant to producing results in our quality effort." One reason I was brought in to consult with this group was that the relationships with the vice president and his group were strained.

You may not find an initial overlap with some people. When this happens, you have to dig deeper for ways to establish common ground. Fred's interest in developing his tennis game overlapped with my interest in coaching. At times, establishing the overlap may be less direct. I worked with a man from a large wholesale food distributor. He was marketing vice president of fat and oil food products. He had graduated from college with a chemistry degree. Before he joined the wholesale food company, he had worked for a chemical plant that produced food products. I had done work with a chemical plant that produced polypropylene, the plastic-based material used in food-related substances. I talked about my experience at the plastics plant operation. We found the production processes used in both plants had some similarities. This overlap area helped us establish an initial common point of relationship. Quantum Leaders seek related information from people to find overlap areas of experience. They offer information that appears to be connected as a means to introduce a common ground.

Accept People as They Are

It is easy to identify with and accept someone who is already like us. We bond easily with people in the fertile soil of common ground we already occupy. The process becomes tougher with those who differ from us on important issues.

Quantum Leaders work to accept people as they are. They transcend the boundaries that separate them to operate from a more unified sense of their relationship with others. They recognize the quantum field reality. At some deep level of life, we are not separate from anything we experience. Quantum Leaders consciously self-refer. They look within their consciousness and recognize that pure consciousness, our deepest sense of "I" dissolves any self versus other distinctions. From this state, Quantum Leaders can accept others with honor and respect, not judgment.

The quantum paradigm reveals that reality is subjective, based in consciousness. Differences are frames of reference. Quantum Leaders reframe their experience with others when necessary. They honor different interests, backgrounds, or points of view as simply another frame of reality. They may not agree with another's frame. Yet, they accept it as a frame that works for another person based on that person's level of consciousness. The act of acceptance forges the possibility for a common ground because it demonstrates an openness to the person.

It's Not My Style

Some people type themselves as introverts and lament that their style limits their capacity to find and share interests. Introverts can feel less comfortable with relationship building. Their preferences do not immediately guide them to share information about themselves or seek information about others. More extroverted people usually find it easier to get to know others. Yet introverts can improve their skills in this area.

For those who feel, "It's not my style," create a structure for your common ground-building activities. Make specific appointments, attend scheduled activities, and set agendas for yourself to cultivate a common ground. Relationship building typically does not happen by itself for those who prefer to be introverts, but a structure can help the process. Field Guide 10 provides action ideas to build a common ground. These actions are particularly effective for those whose style does not lend itself to spontaneous common ground building activity.

Provide Valued Resources

Quantum Leaders provide others with valued resources to cultivate leader-quality relationships. The operative word is "valued." The value of any resource is defined by the person who receives the resource. Quantum Leaders provide people with resources they want, not what the leader wants. Quantum Leaders also know that resources are more valuable when people cannot easily get them from other sources. Quantum Leaders gain distinction by providing scarce resources.

Identify Valued Resources

Quantum Leaders consciously pursue, ask about, listen for, and observe what matters to others. This may sound elementary, but it is not an elementary reality.

In a June 1991 article in *Fortune*, Faye Rice cited a 1990 poll conducted by the management consulting company Towers Perrin. The poll revealed that fewer than half of the employees surveyed believed their management was aware of the problems they faced. Rice also reported that the Hay Group, another consulting organization, found that of more than 1 million employees from 2,000 organizations, only 34 percent said that their company listened to them well.

Define the Resources You Control and Those You Do Not

No one controls the full range of resources people want from work. The increasing press for "lean and mean" companies has almost eliminated the promise of lifetime employment. Salary increases and promotions, which were never given nonchalantly, are even more competitive.

Quantum Leaders take a proactive approach by defining the resources they can and cannot control. They point out resources they can and cannot provide. Quantum Leader then explain to employees the boundaries of their authority. They describe the limits to their flexibility regarding resource acquisition and distribution.

Provide the Resources That You Do Control

If you control the "hard" resources such as pay, promotion, working conditions, equipment, and vacation time, provide them when people deserve them. However, control over these resources is always limited by forces beyond most people's control.

Our experience with organizations reveals that people have a higher degree of control over soft resources. Most people do have the ability to appreciate and recognize others without limits. They can provide access to information, challenging work opportunities, and involvement in decision making with a fair degree of flexibility. And, these resources are often highly valued. In their 1982 study, *In Search of Excellence*, Peters and Waterman found that excellent companies pay attention to appreciating, involving, and showing concern for their employees.

In our consulting work, employees regularly tell us that they believe their managers do not give them enough voice in what goes on in the company. They tell us they are "sure" their managers withhold information from them. Quantum Leaders recognize the importance of soft resources such as involvement and concern. Quantum Leaders also recognize that they usually have greater control over such resources. Three soft resources seem especially important today: appreciation, visibility, and professional opportunity. Quantum Leaders have significant latitude to provide these resources and they do.

Appreciation

Perhaps the most valued resource you can provide to others is to make them feel valued by appreciating them. People move in the direction where they are appreciated. Appreciation transforms interpersonal relationships, because when people appreciate us, they tune into our particular awareness frequency, defined as MMFG-AM (Make Me Feel Good About Myself). Everyone wants to feel good about themselves. Appreciation helps people possess that feeling. Quantum Leaders tune into each person's specific wavelength of MMFG-AM.

Appreciation and the desire to experience MMFG-AM are imprinted in each of us during childhood. Think about how adults behave around small babies and little toddlers. Adults make funny faces and gurgle sounds to get a baby's attention. They coo soft words and wave or wiggle their hands at babies to create a playful interaction. They smile and speak in a friendly and supportive manner to little children. Babies and toddlers are showered with positive stimuli from all the people around them. If a baby or toddler cries or appears uncomfortable, a gaggle of helpful adults gather to offer suggestions and counsel on how to soothe the baby. When a baby is hungry, or has a wet diaper, or is hurt, most people, even complete strangers, move quickly to remedy the situation and to help the baby feel better. These experiences create a significant impression in the baby's consciousness. The continuous stream of messages from the environment says to the baby: "You matter to us," "We care about your welfare," and "We want to make you feel good."

Yet, as we grow older, our favored-person status begins to fade. People stop taking notice of us. We can be tired, fearful, or hurt, and few people take time to even recognize our discomfort, much less do something to make us feel better. Yet the memory of MMFG-AM remains within our awareness. An instant connection occurs when we meet someone who helps us feel good. The appreciation regenerates that sense of unconditional self-worth we experienced as infants.

Visibility and Professional Opportunity

Two other valued resources Quantum Leaders can fairly easily provide to cultivate leader-quality relationships are visibility and professional opportunity. These resources reinforce each other. Visibility meets our need to be noticed and to feel important. It helps us be a part of what is going on. Professional opportunity offers us access to arenas for achievement where we can demonstrate our skills and experience. It allows us the chance to grow and develop.

Field Guide 10 provides a set of actions to provide others with valued resources.

Develop Trust

Trust binds people together in leader-quality relationships. Trust has impact on all aspects of relationships. Common ground requires a solid confidence that the person is trustworthy. Common ground crumbles when suspicion infects a relationship. The impact of valued resources depends on the beliefs people have about your intentions. Efforts to appreciate others or to provide them with other important resources lose their impact when people suspect your motives. People will hide their interests and will not reveal the resources they value to a person they do not trust.

Trust is a quantum phenomenon. It unites people in a seamless field of interdependence. Distrust drives people apart. It reinforces the classical physics sense of separateness. People do not give unqualified trust to someone who is not and cannot be a part of them. Rather, people operate with wariness, destructive competitiveness, and even harsh aggressiveness. Individuals trust those who are like them. People do not trust those who are dissimilar to them.

Quantum Leaders know that trust begets trust. When they trust people, Quantum Leaders encourage people's involvement. They show confidence in others. That galvanizes others to show more initiative and greater allegiance to the leader. People respond with more openness. Positive results occur. People feel a sense of pride. The Quantum Leader's trust is confirmed. In contrast, when someone distrusts another, he or she tends to overly control and doubt the person. The person responds with apathy, resentment, and hesitancy. Efforts falter, and the person neglects work and operates with secrecy. Distrust is confirmed.

Jack Stack, CEO of Springfield Remanufacturing Corporation (SRC) in Springfield, Missouri, turned SRC around from a losing venture in 1983 to a debt-free, $77 million-a-year company by 1992. One key to his success was to establish a climate of trust. At SRC, all employees, even line workers, are trained to understand company financial statements. They learn about the company's income statements, balance sheets, cash flow statements, and so forth. They help develop standard accounting costs and compute variances for their own work. They calculate and interpret financial indicators and financial ratios. And, they are taught to understand how the company's stock is evaluated and how their work affects stock values. Stack's openness demonstrates his trust in others. That translated into bottom-line results.

Trust building begins within the Quantum Leader's intention to be trustworthy and to trust others. Field Guide 10 provides a set of actions to build trust.

Build Credibility

Credibility represents the unified point value of leader-quality relationships. Like DNA, credibility contains the entire coding structure of a relationship. Common ground, valued resources, and trust converge into the focal point of leader-quality relationships known as credibility.

When a person is credible, others believe in that person. They perceive the person as dependable, reliable, and worthy of support.

Invisible Points

Credibility can be viewed as invisible points that people ascribe to a leader. The more points or credits a leader has, the greater is the leader's credibility. Everything a leader does affects the point total. People give points when common ground gets established, valued resources are provided, and trust is demonstrated. They give points to the leader who matches values and effectively reframes events. Credibility builds when leaders speak in the codes of the follower's private mental language. Leaders enhance their credibility rating when they map the territory and chart a course that meets the follower's needs. People take points away when the leader fails to do these things.

With enough credits or points, the possibilities to gain and maintain the confidence of others increases. A very high degree of credibility provides the leader with tremendous influence. Consider the frightening reality that Jim Jones's credibility was so high at the time of the Guyana tragedy in 1976 that he could convince 900 men and women to kill their children and then commit mass suicide. When credibility is destroyed, little can be done to maintain support. Despite the landslide presidential victories of Lyndon Johnson in 1964, Richard Nixon in 1972, and George Bush in 1988, each of their political careers ended soon afterward. They lost too many credits to get reelected. In contrast, leaders with enough points can maintain support even after they lose significant credibility. Remember that Ronald Reagan's response to the Iran-contra affair in 1986 was, "1 don't remember." Reagan then admitted he lied about Iran contra. His credits declined because of these actions, but he had so much credibility that voters accepted his memory lapse and lack of truthfulness. Bill Clinton also lied to the American people. He was impeached but did not have to resign. Most people still wanted him to be in office. He had such a high credibility rating that he did not have to quit the presidency.

Quantum Leaders know that credits are governed by the follower's subjective consciousness. What might be credible to one person may not signify credibility to another. Additionally, potential followers require varying degrees of credits before they accept the leader as credible. Some people demand a large number of credits. Others require only a few. Until a person passes the necessary credit threshold, that person does not have the necessary credibility to gain willing followers.

Frank, a manager in a wholesale and retail products company, gained credibility very quickly with the company president. Frank had highly effective customer service skills. This capacity meant a lot to the president. It took him much longer to establish the necessary credits with the vice president of operations. Frank finally passed the critical threshold with the operations vice president when he started coming to work early, staying late, and taking on extra projects. These were actions the operations vice president's perceived as key credibility indicators.

Credits can amass slowly over time. They can also be lost in a moment. Gary Hart's 1988 bid for the Democratic presidential nomination seemed almost certain. He had a positive political record. He made a successful showing in the early days of the race. He seemed to have a lock on the nomination. But Hart's credibility was stripped almost overnight because of a personal indiscretion. Similarly, Howard Dean was far ahead of the pack during the 2004 Democratic primary season. However, he lost the Iowa primary. Then he gave a screeching speech with a contorted look on his face that was played over and over on news stations. Dean's presidential aspirations faded instantly.

Quantum Leaders intentionally seek ways to build their credibility. Field Guide 10 provides action ideas to build credibility.

Leader-Quality Relationships in Perspective

Relationship building can be compared to sex. Almost everyone believes they understand the importance of sex. Almost everyone thinks it involves "natural ability." And, perhaps most telling, almost everyone blames the "other" when the experience is not satisfying.

Quantum Leaders know that they hold the responsibility to build leader-quality relationships. That is, they have the "ability to respond" in effective ways. No person can ever cultivate the requisite quality of relationship needed to win over all people. The seventh natural law of leadership explains that not everyone will follow your lead. Quantum Leaders keep their relationship-building activity in perspective. They focus on critical relationships first.

Quantum Leader also know the field of relationships cannot be controlled in a dictatorial fashion. They nurture relationships as a gardener cares for a garden. They plant seeds, tend them as they grow, and accept when some do not sprout.

FIELD GUIDE 10

Action Idea 10.1: Conduct a "Stranger Audit"

This technique helps you assess the quality of relationship you have with important others. It helps you analyze how comfortable you are with others. To say this another way, the audit enables you to assess how much "strangeness" exists between you and key others. To conduct a Stranger Audit, create a grid similar to Figure 11-2.

	1	2	3	4	5	6	7	8	9	10

Figure 11.2 - Stranger Audit

Fill in the first column of the grid with the names of key people you need on your side to accomplish your leadership initiatives. Then rate each person on your list in terms of how comfortable you feel around him or her. Use the scale along the grid's top. Let "1" equal very uncomfortable and "10" equal very comfortable. Our experience is that the extent to which you feel comfortable around others is a fair indication of how comfortable they feel around you.

Make your rankings using what I call the "gut check" technique. What is your gut reaction response to the question: "How comfortable do I feel about this person?" After completing your rankings, think about those people whom you rank below a 5. These are the "strangers" you need to work with to build a common ground. Conduct Stranger Audits regularly.

Action Idea 10.2: Learn one fact about someone each day.

Discover new information about people. Find out about their work background, educational history, professional likes and dislikes. Explore their career interests and aspirations. Ask about their non-job-related hobbies, preferences regarding food, cars, or vacations. Inquire about their future hopes and expectations. People often take it for granted that they "know all about" another person. In reality people usually know very little about another person's background, interests, and goals. Daily fact finding breaks through the boundary of limited knowledge.

Action Idea 10.3: Observe artifacts.

The artifacts in a person's office often provide powerful clues to their interests. Alex Stolley, while CEO of Northlich Stolley, a Cincinnati-based advertising agency, had pictures of airplanes on the wall and a small model airplane on his desk. These artifacts were not accidental. Stolley was an avid aviator who piloted his own plane on weekends. A question about artifacts offers an effective way to connect with someone. Alex Stolley loved to talk about flying.

Action Idea 10.4: Allow small steps.

Accept that some people will disclose information to you in small steps. Let them work at their pace until they feel safe enough to reveal more.

Action Idea 10.5: Respect the boundaries of personal disclosure.

People usually have boundaries surrounding their willingness to make personal disclosures. Some people feel uncomfortable talking about their private lives or view such information as inappropriate workplace conversation. Some people might not be too open about revealing information about professional hopes, aspirations, and interests because of a concern about how their motivations might be interpreted.

Respect the preference for confidentiality. The president of a privately owned company we know does not like to talk about himself or his professional experiences; however, he does have a passionate interest in his company and its activities. We connect by talking about our mutual interest in developing his organization's competitive excellence.

Action Idea 10.6: Disclose important facts about yourself.

Self-disclosure begets self-disclosure. Disclose important facts about yourself to your staff on a regular basis. Your openness can set the stage for others to reciprocate.

Action Idea 10.7: Take a ride in a pickup.

When Floyd Hoelting was director of residence life at Illinois State University (he is now director of housing at the University of Texas at Austin), he would frequently take people for rides in his '52 Chevy pickup. This was one way he established common ground with others. Floyd adores his dented old pickup. It rides like a bucking bronco, but it is perfect for getting around on Floyd's ranch. Emblazoned on the pickup doors in big red letters is "Floyd Hoelting, Professional Auctioneer," an avocation that he loves to demonstrate! When you go for a ride in his pickup, you enter Floyd's world. He allows you to become one with him while jostling down the road in that pickup,

Floyd spontaneously tells stories about himself, his family, and his dreams; his interest in horses and cattle; his love for the outdoors; and his belief that people need to share a sense of community. Floyd's openness naturally warms others to talk about themselves. A ride in Floyd's pickup is a perfect place for him to build relationships with others. What is the comparable pickup truck in your life? Where can you take people to let them know about you and what you value, thus setting a stage for them to talk about themselves? Find that place, activity, or vehicle, and invite people to join you there.

Action Idea 10.8: Practice nonjudgmental acceptance with one person each day.

Resolve to listen carefully and accept whatever you are told without judgement. Naturally, you want to pick your spots carefully with this choice. Try this action idea in a nonbusiness-related context first. This eliminates the chance that the action might compromise you in a bottom-line situation.

Action Idea 10.9: Dance at the other person's rhythm.

It is hard to establish a common ground when people are consumed with protecting their own point of view. People cannot or will not seek to unite points of view if they must always defend their position to the exclusion of others. Quantum Leaders maintain their beliefs and preferences. They also seek ways to get into step with another person, much like two dancers seeking a common rhythm. Practice letting go of your point of view as a means to get in touch with the other person's perspective. You do not have to abandon your own ideas. Just suspend them long enough to let the other person's ideas in and to help the person recognize that you understand and recognize their perspective.

Action Idea 10.10: Double your face-to-face contact rate.

That means get out and talk to people more frequently. Set aside time every week to talk with each person in your area. Create a one-month action plan for face-to-face contact, and stick to it. People communicate so much more of themselves in person. You can understand and appreciate others more fully when you are in their presence.

Action Idea 10.11: Create an interaction space near your office.

An interaction space is a place where people can congregate comfortably for a few minutes during the day. Creating such a place near your office draws people to you. This makes it easier for you to break out of an introversion tendency. The interaction space also saves time. You do not have to go traveling down the hall or to another floor to visit others. One manager placed a popcorn machine in a small area outside his office. He popped corn twice a day, creating that distinctive and delicious smell that attracted others to the area.

Action Idea 10.12: Take the ocean liner approach.

For introverts, building a common ground can take a long time. Give yourself the necessary time. Reframe the process as an extended journey across the Atlantic, sailing on a majestic ocean liner. Realize that you have the entire journey to develop a common ground with certain people. View each day as another step in the process. You can create a link during a lunch break or while strolling through the workplace.

Action Idea 10.13: Conduct a valued resources needs analysis.

Conduct a meeting where you ask people, "What resources do you value?" Give them a list of possible resources (e.g., wages, appreciation, promotion, being kept informed, job security, working conditions, understanding about personal problems) as a starting point. Ask people to add resources to the list if necessary. Then ask people to rank the items from most to least important. There is no magic to this process. It is a nuts-and-bolts question-and-answer session. We recommend revisiting this analysis at least twice a year or after any significant event that affects the organization (e.g., a shift in competitive focus, organizational restructuring, a change of management).

Action Idea 10.14: Focus on acquiring and providing the valued resources you do control.

This is overtly obvious. Just do it.

Action Idea 10.15: Explain the system.

Explain to people, to the best of your ability, how your organizational resource allocation system works. Explain the processes used to mete out wages, determine working conditions, and provide promotions. Describe how softer resources, such as information, access, and recognition get distributed within your organization's . This discussion requires complete candor. Tell people what you know. Clarify what you do not know about your organization's systems. Continuously seek ways to improve your knowledge about such systems. This will help you provide important and up-to-date information more effectively.

Action Idea 10.16: Tune In to MMFG-AM.

Spend 10 minute a day focusing on ways to appreciate people. Praise some aspect of their work you find admirable. Recognize a contribution at a meeting. Tell people you are glad to be working with them when the circumstance warrants.

Action Idea 10.17: Thank people.

Give a sincere thank you when people do even the slightest thing for you. This sounds simple, right? Consider how many times you actually hear someone say thank you like they mean it.

Action Idea 10.18: Create an "applause newsletter."

An applause newsletter recounts people's work contributions. It can include accomplishments that are both major (an increase in customer service efficiency for the entire organization) and more everyday (resolution of a very specific quality issue). Write the first five issues of the newsletter yourself to get it started. Such documents typically become highly valued by others. Once this happens, seek out those who might be interested in writing subsequent issues. This will expand the power of appreciation giving throughout your work group.

Action Idea 10.19: Hold success celebrations.

Formally celebrate the successes of your people on a regular basis. In 2006, the Department of Transportation Volpe Center published a "points of pride" brochure. The document acknowledged the key contributions of people within the organization. In a 1992 *Fortune* magazine report, it was reported how, every Saturday, top executives at Wal-Mart got together to review the week's activities. Then Chief Operating Officer Don Soderquist read the honor roll of stores that showed the greatest improvement over the corresponding week a year before.

Action Idea 10.20: Create a "company hero" program.

Designate an informal reward, "The Company Hero," to be given when someone goes above and beyond the call of duty in even a modest way. Create a certificate to symbolize the award. Present it with the proper ceremony of gratitude.

Action Idea 10.21: Send "I heard something good about you" notes.

When you hear of someone's accomplishments from others, send the person an "I Heard Something Good About You" note. Write 10 notes each month to test how much impact this appreciate action has. Write more if people respond with enthusiasm.

Action Idea 10.22: Help a "10-yarder" across the goal line.

A "10-yarder" is someone who is close to succeeding on an important task. He or she will succeed eventually, but your help can provide a boost. A manager from a large company knew that a staff assistant in his division wanted a transfer to a position that had more challenge and responsibility. She would have gotten the new assignment eventually. The manager placed a telephone call to support the assistant's application. His action sped up the process to have the position offered to this assistant. The manager's effort pushed her request along to expedite the process and helped her "score" this valued resource. This small but meaningful effort by the manager created a sense of very positive regard within the assistant towards the manager.

Action Idea 10.23: Send people with their report.

Sending people with their report provides an avenue for both visibility and professional opportunity. Consider what typically happens when a person pours tremendous amounts of time and energy to develop a truly excellent report. If the information gets presented by someone else, the presenter receives an intense wave of appreciation for the effort. The report preparer gets only a secondhand accounting of the positive reaction. Sending people with their report makes them visible to get the firsthand approval response to the report. It provides a platform for them to demonstrate their professional expertise. However, this action idea will not work for someone who does not like to speak in front of a group. Also, in some situations it is not possible or appropriate to use this action idea. As is the case with all the Action Ideas in this book, use this choice when you think it will make a positive difference.

Action Idea 10.24: Include people at a meeting.

Allow people to attend a meeting with you that they would like to attend but normally do not. Access to the meeting provides an opportunity to be visible. It might also create a platform for the person to demonstrate a unique element of expertise or offer a meaningful contribution to the meeting's agenda.

Action Idea 10.25: Tell the truth.

This one sounds like a no-brainer, but the most important ingredient in building trust is telling the truth. Trust and truth telling go hand in hand. Telling the truth is also easier. It is easy to remember the truth. It may take some thought to remember a lie. Most people will usually get caught when they lie. I believe this happens because most people are not very good actors. They give themselves away when they lie. Do not equivocate. Tell the truth.

Action Idea 10.26: Make and follow through on 10 commitments.

Make 10 observable promises and keep them. People learn not to trust those who do not do what they say they will do.

Action Idea 10.27: Trust others first.

A red flag goes up when you ask people to trust you as a condition for your trusting them. Offer your trust first, as a way to gain the trust of others.

Action Idea 10.28: Extend your trust of others.

If you already display trust, extend that display with greater trust. Increase the latitude you provide to people. Trusting others more makes you more trustworthy in their eyes.

Action Idea 10.29: Protect core interests.

Protect what matters most to people. We trust those who look out for our core interests.

Action Idea 10.30: Eliminate secret meetings.

Secret meetings send a message that you do not trust people. Abolish them.

**Several of the following action ideas are based on ideas in Managing Transitions, by William Bridges.*

Action Idea 10.31: Use your three I's.

Your three I's are involve, inform, and include. Involvement in decision making gives people a sense of ownership. Involve people in discussions about important issues. Information is power. Inform people of what is going on. Inclusion creates a sense of belonging. Include people in decision making. Your three I's show people you trust them with power.

Action Idea 10.32: Get your "but" out of your conversation.

When we use but in our conversations, we negate what was just said. For example, consider these statements: "You did a good job, but I have some suggestions." "I enjoyed this time together, but I have a meeting to go to now." The word "but" negates the previous part of each statement. That sends a mixed message. Such messages limit trust. Take the word but out of your language as much as possible. Replace it with "and." For example, "You did a good job, and I have some suggestions." "I enjoyed this time together, and I have a meeting to go to now." The word "and" changes the meaning. It sends a congruent message.

Action Idea 10.33: Give trust building time.

Trust building takes time. People are cautious as a form of self-protection. People do not give up self-protection easily. Give your trust building efforts time to germinate. With consistent application of the action ideas suggested in this chapter, trust will pervade your relationships.

Action Idea 10.34: Find out what people perceive as credible.

Ask people what they feel indicates credibility. Have them define the specific behaviors that demonstrate credibility.

Action Idea 10.35: Demonstrate your credibility.

After you find out the credibility markers others use, demonstrate your capacity in relation to these markers. For example, if people in your organization tell you that work-related expertise demonstrates credibility, develop your expertise. Then actively seek ways to display it. If credibility means helping others, do so. This action idea does not mean being underhanded or manipulative. Quantum Leaders always refer back to their intention when implementing an action such as this. They use this action idea with the sincere intention of cultivating leader-quality relationships that benefit others. We have total control over our intention at all times.

Action Idea 10.36: Admit mistakes.

Integrity increases credibility. The rash of cover-ups, fraud, and underhanded dealings in government and industry has jaded many people. Cynicism runs rampant today. In a poll reported on June 8, 1985, in the New York Times, only 32 percent of the public indicated they believe most corporate executives are honest. Fifty-five percent said they think executives are dishonest. This survey was done before the massive nationwide savings and loan crisis victimized over 350 institutions and produced 331 convictions of "respectable bankers." Think of the Enron and World Com scandals as more recent indicators of the low credibility of some corporate chieftains. Admit mistakes to distinguish yourself from the unsavory lot who try to conceal their mistakes.

12

Quantum Leaders vs. Classical Managers

"The leader leads, and the boss drives."
Theodore Roosevelt

What are the differences between a leader and a manager? This question plagues countless people we meet.

Managers want to be leaders. They are unclear about what that means. Training directors want to develop leaders within their organization. They cannot clearly define what has to be done to develop the skills or behaviors that identify leaders. And personnel directors want to recruit leaders for their organizations. They have no framework by which to measure potential leaders.

Quantum Leadership explicitly reveals that a manager is not necessarily a leader. The common research approach of discussing "leadership" findings based on an analysis of managers is inappropriate. The media also misdirect us when they label as "leaders" those who hold the title of manager, a position in government, or head of a club, company, or country.

The Fundamental Distinctions

The natural laws of leadership and the Quantum Leadership paradigm provide a clear distinction between leaders and managers: Leaders are better understood as a quantum phenomenon. Managers are well described through the classical physics lens. Quantum Leaders differ from classical managers in five ways:

Classical Managers	Quantum Leaders
1. Have subordinates	**1. Attract willing followers**
2. Use influence based on formal authority	**2. Develop influence beyond authority**
3. Operate within prescribed pathways	**3. Operate outside prescribed pathways**
4. Are given a position	**4. Take initiative to lead**
5. Rely on tradition and procedure	**5. Rely on consciousness**

Subordinates vs. Followers

The first natural law of leadership provides the fundamental distinction between managers and leaders. Managers have subordinates. Managers and subordinates are defined as separate entities by the permanent lines of authority described in an organizational chart. Quantum Leaders attract willing followers. They create a field of interaction, a relationship *(the second natural law).* The manager and subordinate roles exist as a continuous reality defined by position. Specific people who occupy those roles may change, but the roles are an ongoing reality of the organization. Quantum Leadership is discontinuous (*the third natural law*). The leadership field of interaction manifests whenever a leader attracts followers.

Formal Authority vs. Influence Beyond Authority

Managers rely on influence based on formal authority. They use deterministic, predictable rules, regulations, policies, and procedures as the basis of their power. They apply the classical physics concepts of force and pressure to control people's behavior. The manager operates from a "superior" position. The manager is "the boss." Bosses are separate from subordinates. They can command their employees to comply with the authority they are given by the organization.

Influence in the Quantum Leadership field stems from the interaction between leader and follower *(the fourth natural law of leadership)*. Quantum Leaders bond and unite with followers as allies. That unity generates the power of leadership. Quantum Leaders start where the followers are and connect with them. Quantum Leader then direct followers along a specific path.

An organizational chart spells out the prescribed lines of formal authority between managers and subordinates. The chart defines the deterministic reporting relationships. With a classical physics mind-set, people rely on the chart to answer the question, "Where do I fit in?"

The field of Quantum Leadership interaction is better described as a web of relationships. It exists as an intricate network of connections. The central node of the web represents the Quantum Leader in any given leadership event. Threads that bond the Quantum Leader to the followers spread out in an array of linkages. Some of these threads more directly connect leaders and followers while others are more indirect. (Figure 12-1).

Figure 12.1
Classical-manager vs. Quantum-Leader authority.

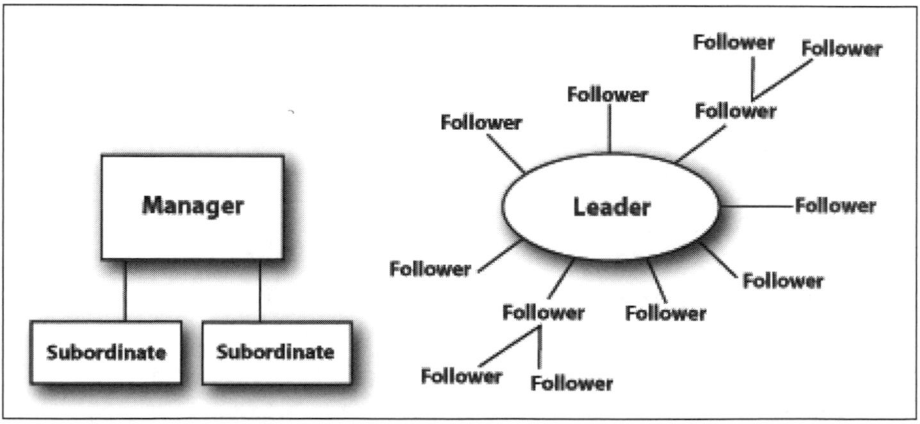

Prescribed Pathways vs. Doing More Than Is Prescribed

Classical managers implement prescribed rules, regulations, policies, and procedures. They see that orders are carried out. They control people and systems to ensure assigned duties are completed. Management theory focuses on orderliness, structure, and stability. Application of this approach defines a good manager.

Established procedures do not apply in the arena where Quantum Leaders operate *(the fifth natural law of leadership)*. Quantum Leaders do more than is prescribed. They operate in the uncertain leadership arena that exists outside the boundaries of organization rules and regulations. Quantum Leadership clarifies the need for awareness of uncertainty.

Both managers and leaders do the right things. They both do things right. Managers deserve credit when they effectively complete established missions along defined pathways. Quantum Leaders deserve recognition because they emerge when the existing pathway fails to provide direction. Leaders operate in the uncertain, probabilistic, changing realm where organizational policies do not apply and people do not know what to do *(the sixth natural law of leadership)*. Managers receive organizational recognition when they get people to do what they are supposed to do. Quantum Leaders gain credibility by guiding followers to take unique action that overcomes nonprescribed problems and exploits opportunities.

Given a Role vs. Taking Initiative

Managers are given a role and asked to fulfill the requirements defined by its prescribed authority, responsibility, and accountability. Subordinates are obligated to comply with the manager's demands. Quantum Leaders take the risk of initiative to resolve uncertainty *(the sixth natural law of leadership)*. They do not always get the commitment they seek from others *(the seventh natural law of leadership)*.

Tradition and Procedure vs. Consciousness

Classical managers rely on tradition and procedure to get things done. They go by the book to determine direction. They demand compliance from others. Quantum Leadership is based on consciousness which is the capacity to process information. They use their consciousness to map the territory and chart a course. They create a connection of consciousness to gain committed followers. The Quantum Leadership field exists as a shared wave of information-energy *(the eighth and ninth natural laws of leadership)*.

Two in One: The Manager as Quantum Leader

Leaders are not better than managers. A surge of manager bashing has denigrated the managerial role as a second-class occupation. This approach reveals flawed thinking about the differences between managers and leaders. We need both effective managers and Quantum Leaders to steer people and organizations forward.

Anyone selected or promoted to a managerial position deserves credit for being recognized as qualified to fulfill the managerial requirement. Managers *also* deserve encouragement to carry out the difficult duties associated with meeting prescribed deadlines. They should be commended for motivating others to complete assigned duties and ensuring that results meet defined goals. In today's challenging times, managers face even greater demands than in the past.

The most productive managers are those who also take the lead to resolve the uncertainty inherent in the leadership arena. Such managers merit even greater recognition. People typically expect managers to function as leaders. People usually look to the person in charge for direction within the confines of prescribed rules. People also typically turn to their boss first when unpredictability and uncertainty emerge. This reality provides an advantage for managers who seek to lead. They will be called upon first to chart a course through uncertainty.

Quantum Leadership is not a better role than management, just as quantum physics is not better or more real than classical physics. Both are valid in their respective domains. The laws of nature that govern quantum physics and Quantum Leadership differ from those that regulate classical physics and management. When you require someone to do something because of prescribed rules, you contend with classical physics. You experience the quantum reality of leadership when you want to move your consciousness and the consciousness of others to take initiative in the leadership arena,

Some people have bifocal consciousness. This is the capacity to process information as a classical physics manager and as a Quantum Leader. Such individuals hold others accountable and enforce their compliance to fulfill the managerial requirement. They are also willing to take the risks associated with venturing beyond the boundaries of established procedures and gaining willing followers.

David Bell, director of the Management Services Division within the Department of Agriculture, models such behavior. When he took over the director's position, he held an off-site workshop for branch chiefs. The group generated ideas about how the division could be more productive and could respond to change and uncertainty. Under Bell's guidance, the group made several important decisions about how to realign the organization for the future. The branch chiefs were enthusiastic about their new ability to participate. They eagerly followed Bell's lead.

Yet Bell also put on his managerial hat when one of his staff members failed to follow through on several directives regarding implementation of the off-site meeting's initiatives. No amount of leader influence had any impact. Bell resorted to his managerial authority. He defined the staff member's responsibility and accountability for results. Bell confided that in some respects it was more difficult functioning as a manager. He found leading the branch chiefs stimulating. In contrast, using managerial force to overcome the staff member's resistance was gut wrenching and draining.

Not all managers operate with sharply honed bifocal consciousness. Many rely almost completely on the brute force power of their managerial position. "Kick butt and take names" is a phrase we still hear throughout the ranks of managers in business and government. This testosterone enriched approach is even glorified in a 2007 book by Donald Trump. We understand the appeal of the tough-guy managerial posture. We do not feel it is the most effective way to begin managing others. Neither is it the most productive way to consistently guide staff.

For example, take Jerry, a manager of a chemical plant. Jerry works from 6:00 A.M. to 7:00 P.M. five days a week. He frequently comes to the plant on his days off "just to see how things are going." Jerry's dedication and willingness to work hard is admirable. Yet, he also has a tendency to over control his staff. Jerry relies on the phrase "Because I told you to," when directing others. He regularly reminds people, "It's my responsibility to make sure you do it right." This really means to do it his way or else.

Jerry ensures that required tasks get done. When situations are "in order," the unit runs smoothly. Jerry "expedites" when obstacles arise and people and processes get stuck in unforeseen ruts. This happens often because of unexpected change and uncertainty. Then Jerry works harder and pushes people even more. He gets results, but he exhausts himself through reliance on force. He also wears others down through constant pressure. He operates within a limited mindset that does not take advantage of all the laws of nature that govern human interaction.

Quantum Leader Effectiveness

All managers and all leaders want to be effective. Managerial effectiveness can be determined by how well the manager carries out prescribed rules, regulations, policies, and procedures. Effective managers meet established requirements, gain compliance from others, and achieve stated objectives.

Effective Quantum Leadership cannot be measured in this way. Its arena transcends these standards. Quantum Leadership occurs in arenas of uncertainty. It requires gaining subjective commitment of followers. It does not mean enforcing the objective manager-subordinate line of authority. Thus, "effective" leadership is subjective. It depends on the viewpoint of the observer. When people evaluate leaders, they act like residents of Missouri which is known as the "show me" state. Leaders and their methods are assessed differently by different people based on what the leader demonstrates and represents to the followers. As a way to understand leadership effectiveness, consider the categories "the good, the bad, or the ugly."

Good Leaders

Think of someone you have willingly followed who helped you to achieve a goal. That person represents a good leader to you. Americans who supported George H.W. Bush in Operation Desert Storm believed the war just. They were glad the Iraqi forces were defeated. For them, Bush was a good leader in this situation for those followers. Those who willingly supported Jack Welch at GE during the massive employment cuts and organizational restructuring and who believed these changes benefitted the company considered Welch a good leader. A "good" leader is someone you follow who helps you to achieve a goal you feel is important to you.

Bad Leaders

Have you ever followed someone and the result was failure. That is, you did not accomplish what you had hoped? For you, that person is a bad leader. You followed, but the leader did not take you where you wanted to go.

In the late 1980s, James Robinson III, CEO at American Express, projected a bold vision for the company: to transform it into a global financial empire. Robinson had the support of many, but according to *Business Week*, Robinson's vision failed. In 1993, he was ousted by the company's board of directors.

Bad leaders are also defined as those who take followers in the direction the leader initially charted; however, when the followers get there, they realize it is not the place they want to be. Consider George H.W. Bush again. The majority of Americans supported him in 1988 on a presidential platform that essentially argued America needed to stay the course. Voters agreed with Bush that no major domestic crises faced America. Bush focused his efforts on international affairs. By 1992, staying the course appeared to be a mistake. Americans felt their president needed to focus attention on domestic issues. In 1992, Bush was seen as a "bad" leader. He had led his followers in the direction they initially supported, but they did not want to be where he had taken them. Consider the "other" Bush, George W., whose approval rating rocketed to 90% after 9/11. By March 2008, his approval rating was 19% which was the lowest rating of any U.S. President in history.

Ugly Leaders

To understand the ugly leader, think of someone you would not follow, but whom others do follow. For example, few Americans would say they were willing followers of Adolph Hitler. For Americans, Hitler was an ugly leader. However, Hitler did possess a huge numbers of followers. What is ugly to one person can be good to another.

Ineffective Leaders

Leadership effectiveness is subjective. It reflects a quantum phenomenon. Leaders can be good, bad, or ugly depending on how people look at them. The continual quest to define effective leaders explores barren territory until we accept the quantum reality of leadership.

It might simply be that the term *ineffective leader* is a misnomer. Perhaps we need to define leadership ineffectiveness as a failed attempt to gain followers. Ineffective leadership could also be defined as a situation in which no leader emerges and a leadership vacuum exists. That is, when people hope, expect, and need direction but they get nothing, problems remain or opportunities pass. No one takes the risk of initiative to lead. No one has a chance to follow. The group or organization falters in its need to address challenges.

Are You a Quantum Leader or a Classical Physics Manager?

To answer this question, consider why people do what you ask. Is their behavior performed as compliance with your formal authority? Are you directing them to carry out the prescribed path of their job and to fulfill the organization's established strategy, goals, and plans? If you answer yes to these questions, then you are a manager. Good! We need effective managers who get others to do what they are supposed to do and who fulfill their organization's stated mission.

Now also consider: Are people willingly following your direction? Is your influence based on commitment to you, the person, regardless of your position? Are you directing others to go beyond the boundaries, to join you in the risk of taking advantage of an unknown opportunity or of finding a way to overcome an obstacle? If you answer yes to these questions, you are in the Quantum Leadership arena.

13

Develop the Quantum Leader Within

"Before we start talking, let's decide what we are talking about."
Socrates

Can leaders be developed? Or are some people "natural-born" leaders? Quantum Leaders can be developed through the expansion and development of consciousness.

Quantum Leadership Development as Consciousness Expansion

Quantum Leadership development involves expanding consciousness in terms of the "three C's:" *chemistry*, *character*, and *culture*.

Chemistry refers to our neurophysiological processes. Chemistry sets the *capacity to be conscious*. To use a computer metaphor, our mind-body chemistry, its neural and structural faculties, represents the human hardware of consciousness. Quantum Leadership development requires that we restructure the human hardware. Consciousness expansion begins by upgrading the human bio-computer.

Character refers to our information-processing methods. Character defines *the ability to apply consciousness*. The mind-set we use to perceive represents the human software of consciousness. Quantum Leadership development requires new or reprogrammed versions of our quantum sense. We need to enhance our capacity to perceive what others don't. We must refine our ability to go into the G.A.P. We need to transcend the conditioned response of knee-jerk thinking. Developing character enhances our skill at performing enlightened action to create shared meaning.

Culture affects the flow and display of group consciousness. Organizational culture reflects the collective mind-set and organizationally structured methods of interaction. Group norms and organizational systems represent the network of consciousness. Quantum Leadership development requires alterations in organizational systems so that both leaders and followers are rewarded as co-creators of leadership power.

This threefold approach of developing chemistry, character, and culture, or hardware, software, and network, offers a solid foundation to develop Quantum Leadership.

Upgrade the Human Hardware

The brain and nervous system make up the human hardware. They represent the circuitry of consciousness. We function with an active, focused awareness when our mind-body operates properly. We feel stable and relaxed even when engaged in activity. Consciousness cannot flow effectively when the human hardware breaks down. We experience the breakdown as feeling dull, fatigued, and inflexible. Our capacity to pay attention is restricted. Judgment becomes cloudy. Initiative wanes. Performance suffers. We react by trying harder. This often exacerbates the problem. We strain a fragmented system.

The impact of a stable circuitry and an effectively functioning biochemistry on consciousness is typically unnoticed until the system breaks down. Burnout is usually viewed as a psychological malady. Yet the lack of energy, motivation, and concentration symptomatic of burnout is associated with dramatic changes in blood pressure and other biochemical changes.

Quantum Leadership development begins with a comprehensive fitness program. This improves the circuitry and biochemistry that form the capacity to be conscious. Today fitness programs are recognized as important to performance. Yet to expand consciousness, a workout program needs to go beyond simply toning up or slimming down. Continual maintenance and improvement of the human bio-computer circuitry are needed through a mind-body fitness program.

An integrated program of diet, exercise, and behavior management can upgrade the human hardware. Whatever methods one uses must suit the needs, interests, and desires of the practitioner. Quantum Leaders find a routine that works for them where they are. They upgrade the human hardware by improving some very fundamental habits for eating, exercise, rest, and life-style. I suggest going into the G.A.P. to explore the utility of any mind-body program that has been shown to develop consciousness.

Field Guide 11 provides a set of action ideas to enhance the chemistry of consciousness through a mind-body fitness regimen.

Reprogram the Human Software

Our mind-set establishes the perceptual framework through which we receive, interpret, and respond to information. The approach we take to Quantum Leadership is structured within our personal paradigm. We map the territory and chart a course based on our mental set. The way we go into the G.A.P. and perceive what others don't reflect our quality of thinking. The flexibility to reframe and match the follower's internal information processing codes refer back to how we make sense of our world. Many of the action ideas in Field Guides 4, 5 and 6 specifically focus on ways to reprogram the software of consciousness. Review those action ideas as part of your program for consciousness expansion.

Restructure the Group Consciousness Network

Individual leadership development is reinforced when leaders are developed throughout an organization. The network of group consciousness, an organization's culture, provides a platform to enhance leadership. It can also create constraints on leadership.

Quantum Leaders can shape organizational change but must also reflect collective consciousness. The leader cannot be too far ahead of the pack, or few followers will have any idea where the leader is. To develop Quantum Leaders means to create an organizational culture that develops consciousness in everyone. Several steps can be taken to restructure the group consciousness network. Because of their scope, these steps will have to be taken by those at the top of the organization or those who can gain followers from senior levels.

Field Guide 11 offers action ideas to restructure the group consciousness network.

Initiate a Quantum Leader Consciousness Development Plan

When Do You Begin? Now!

While playing for the New York Mets, Tom Seaver once asked Yogi Berra, "Hey, Yogi, what time is it?" Berra responded, "You mean now?" Quantum Leadership development begins now. And it begins again the next time you realize it is now. The process never ends.

Quantum Leaders establish a continuous consciousness improvement plan. Ray Kroc, founder of MacDonald's said, "When you're green you're growing. When you're ripe, you rot." Quantum Leaders stay green. They initiate a lifelong learning plan and then stick to it with regular and dedicated practice. Do not ride the waves of change; make the waves.

How Do You Begin? A Workout Plan

Establish a workout plan to develop your Quantum Leadership capacity. Define your goals. What aspect of Quantum Leadership do you want to master? Improved neurophysiological functioning? The ability to go effortlessly into the G.A.P.? The capacity to recognize and match the internal codes of private mental language? Write your goals on paper in clear, specific, measurable language.

Use the "perfect practice makes perfect" approach. The widespread belief that "practice makes perfect" is incorrect. Some people have years of practice doing things wrong! To use the "perfect practice makes perfect" approach means to apply a skill based on the well-designed mechanics behind it. Quantum Leadership development requires practice with guidance. In whatever way you choose to improve yourself, continually refer back to the mechanics that describe the process. Effective Quantum Leadership practice requires artful implementation based on an application of the mechanics that guide that art.

Quantum Leaders are not stymied by the blocks of the past. Think back to an action plan for any task that you did not follow through to completion. Identify the causes for your lack of completion. Then set up the conditions to break through these causes. For example, perhaps you did not follow through because you did not allow adequate time. Get past this block by scheduling time on your calendar for your Quantum Leadership consciousness development workout.

Any process of meaningful change can create a sense of awkwardness. It can be difficult to alter your diet or life-style regime or implement a new set of behaviors. When people do something that is new or unfamiliar, they can become frustrated by the intense effort and lack of comfort they feel. The awkwardness created by personal change efforts can throw people off course. Anticipate this awkwardness. Prepare yourself so that you are ready to overcome it. Reframe the experience before it happens. Acknowledge that everyone feels this way sometimes. Feel good about the fact that you recognize the awkwardness for what it is: a part of the developmental process.

Set your own standards to measure progress instead of external standards established by others. To keep on track, compare your progress only with yourself. It might take a peer only a few weeks to master reframing. Your progress might be slower. You could become discouraged if you use this peer as your standard. Remember the subjective nature of quantum life. Develop an inner standard to determine your progress. Compare where you are to where you were, not to someone else.

Include variety in your workout. Practice applying your skills in different situations with different people. Being able to focus your attention into the G.A.P. on the shop floor does not necessarily translate into doing so in a meeting with senior management or critical customers.

Create a support system. It is much easier to meditate or get to the gym every day if you have other people to do it with you. It will be easier to stay on your Quantum Leadership consciousness development workout if you involve others. Ask people to join your effort. A support system has the added bonus of developing the leadership capacity of others within your organization.

Accept that you will make mistakes. Use your mistakes as learning opportunities. Mistakes do not become problems unless you refuse to accept them for what they are: learning events. An old adage is that success comes from good work, good work is the result of experience, and experience is often the result of doing poor work. By definition, the leadership arena involves risk and uncertainty. You will not always do the "right thing" in terms of getting the outcome you expected or hoped to get. Use your mistakes to redirect your thinking and action so that you continually do better.

Find out from friends the methods that they use to enhance their mind-body fitness. Review the appropriate literature. Look for references to consciousness, mind-body medicine, or executive health in books, magazines, and on-line sources. Ask your doctor for suggestions. Review all the alternatives to find something that appeals to you. Then start it right away.

Avoid the "no pain-no gain" approach to exercise. "No pain-no gain" assumes that you have to push yourself to your limit and then let the system recover. Recent mind-body fitness innovations suggest this approach may be antithetical to overall biochemical adaptability and stability. Dr. John Douillard recommends a more enlightened approach to exercise in his book *Body, Mind and Sport*. He suggests that exercise should rejuvenate mind-body effectiveness, not reduce its energy. He clarifies that a workout should remove stress, not create it. Mind-body fitness should improve mind-body coordination, not break it down.

Learn a meditation technique. Voluminous scientific research supports the beneficial impact of meditation. Some form of meditation is essential to your mind-body fitness program. Research on the Transcendental Meditation (TM) technique shows it has a positive impact on neurophysiological functioning. TM improves cardiovascular efficiency. Those who practice TM report feeling more energetic, alert, and able to focus sharply while maintaining broad comprehension (essential for going into the G.A.P.). TM is easy to learn and very simple to practice.

Quantum Leaders work to change the systems within their organization to support mind-body fitness efforts. They also work on reforming their organizational culture to eliminate barriers that restrict leadership initiatives.

Set up in-house programs that provide mind-body fitness knowledge and techniques. Corporate wellness programs or companies that provide stress management training are a step in this direction.

Reward both leaders and followers. Reinforce individuals who take the risk of initiative, perceive from the G.A.P., and develop influence beyond authority. Recognize and reward followers as vital contributors to the Quantum Leadership field. Such efforts change the organizational culture from one that rewards only managerial activity to one that rewards leadership action.

Redirect the "boo rulers." Those who process information as negative doubters, destructive critics, and hopeless cynics restrict the flow of collective consciousness. Quantum Leaders challenge and question. They do not limit information flow with incessant booing. Redirect the information processing assassins who negate Quantum Leadership practices. Confront phrases such as, "We've done okay without it," "I do this now anyway," and "It's a gimmick, a fad, a trick." Institutionalize behaviors that are proactive, positive, and progressive. Change the organization's reward system so that "boo rulers" are not positively reinforced.

Create a discussion around restrictive culture roots. Organizations with destructive information processing cultures can be recognized by various roots. Consider organizations that have the following ways of doing things as part of "they way it is around here." They have a tendency to let information sort itself out rather than sorting it out themselves. They wait until pressures from any source define what to do rather than proactively deciding what to do. They rely on outside experts and wait to be told rather than referring to their individual instincts and being proactive. They lack of cooperation and trust. They fail to reward innovation and do not support new ideas. If these culture roots exist, consciously label them as outdated. Identify behaviors that reinforce the negative roots. Change those behaviors with skill training and facilitation.

The Invisible University

Albert Einstein said, "Wisdom is not the product of schooling but of the life-long attempt to acquire it." Any arena can be a learning event to develop Quantum Leader consciousness if you enroll in what Ron Gross calls the Invisible University. In his book *Peak Learning*, Gross clarifies that everyday life experiences represent a world of invisible classrooms and instructors. Students in the Invisible University can learn from any source, at any time, in any place. The motto of this all-inclusive institution is, "Bloom where you are planted." To take an Invisible University class means you define your leadership learning goal, select the teachers and classroom where you want to learn, and set out to master the lesson.

For example, you might study the art of advertising to expand your consciousness about performing enlightened action. Skillful advertisers know how to persuade people to purchase products. Learn from them to enhance your capacity to influence others beyond authority. You do not have to enroll in a marketing class at your local college or university, although that is one option. Rather, you can create an Invisible University study program in your office or living room. Analyze on-line advertisements and the ads in magazines. Videotape television ads and analyze how the director gets the meaning of the message across. Ask others to give you their impressions of specific ads to understand how ads affect people differently. The point of the Invisible University is to make every day a learning day. The idea here is to create as many learning events as you want without the constraints of formal, institutional boundaries.

Match your learning experiences to your information processing styles. If you are a visual person, you may gain insights by watching films that illustrate different elements of leadership practice. If you are an auditory type, cassette programs can be an important learning source. Producers of audiocassette programs have created tapes that fit the modern life-style. Because the average car ride is 20 minutes, most cassettes are packaged with complete 20-minute segments on each side. You can take an Invisible University course as part of your daily commuting activities.

Kinesthetic types learn best by feeling and action. Use an outdoor challenge experience such as a ropes course or Outward Bound to learn through this mode. For those who learn best by reading, the bookstore and library become an Invisible University feeding ground of food for thought. What books are worth reading, and which one should you read first? One way to decide is to select any book that has a title you find appealing. Skim its Table of Contents. Flip through the pages. Read a few passages. If you read something that you believe is important and you do not absolutely own that knowledge in theory or in practice, read that book. Study it. Do not get a second book until you master the content of the first.

The Hope for the Future

Can we develop the type of people needed to lead organizations to greater prosperity, to lead others to greater happiness and fulfillment, and to lead themselves with more inner contentment?

The development of consciousness holds the key to foster more and better leadership. The difference between human DNA and chimpanzee DNA is said to be only 2 percent. A small percentage of development in consciousness can yield quantum leaps forward in the quality of leadership power in organizations.

You have the capacity to create that leap. You can contact and develop the leader within you. Your consciousness is the source of Quantum Leader power in your organization. This power does not rely on any charter, vision statement, or constitution. This power is not a position someone holds. You have complete access to your consciousness. Goethe said, "Whatever you can do or dream, you can become it." You are the Quantum Leader. You own your consciousness. That makes you a custodian of leadership power. If you do not take the lead, who will?

Each of us has a choice. We can take the lead, even though we may not always gain followers and we may not achieve our goals. Or, we can languish in the background, unwilling to step forward and map the territory, hesitant to chart a course. Goethe also said, "Unless one is committed, there is hesitancy."

The Japanese believe that samurai warriors are as solid as the earth and as fluid as the water. The fully awakened leader within operates like a samurai. Quantum Leaders have a solid intention to lead. They focus their full attention on mapping the territory and charting a course that they believe will resolve problems and exploit opportunities. Quantum Leaders also have the fluid adaptability of water. They meet the followers at the followers' level of consciousness. They use their refined judgment to try out alternate interpretations and to experiment with various routes.

Perfection is a moving target. A Quantum Leader's initiative is adaptable and generative because consciousness is always moving. Quantum Leader take initiative with a full understanding of the natural law of successful action:

**If you do not get the results you want
with one course of action,
try something different.**

14

Evolutionary Leadership: Lessons Learned

"All creatures evolve over time."
Charles Darwin

"Growth is worth any price, even a little temporary discomfort."
Robert R. Carkhuff

Since the original publication of the first edition of "The 9 Natural Laws of Leadership" in 1995, we have learned many additional ways to understand leading and enhance leadership. This chapter describes a variety of our most significant "lessons learned." These lessons illustrate the evolutionary nature of leadership development: real and lasting success comes only with an on-going commitment to continuous improvement over a long period of time. No one is too good at the leadership game. Few people achieve mastery without substantial perseverance and dedication to improve.

Our insights come from over three decades' worth of training, coaching, and developmental interventions that involved over 30,000+ individuals who have attended our leadership programs and seminars. These programs ranged from one day to two weeks in length. Our participants included those who had managerial positions and those who did not. Some were at the beginning of their careers while others were seasoned veterans with many years experience.

The types of issues our participants presented required that we continuously adapt the Nine Natural Laws and Quantum Leadership Model to various organizational settings. These included public sector and private sector, large and small, new and well established organizations. We also had the benefit of getting direct feedback from our participants and their organizations. We conducted six month follow-up evaluations from those who completed of our leadership programs.

We describe these lessons learned as additional tools you can use to enhance your own understanding, application, and positive results in using the leadership laws and Quantum Leadership model.

Lesson One: Focus on Facts not Fads

Since the publication of the first edition of "The 9 Natural Laws of Leadership" in 1995, hundreds of books, models, and frameworks have been published on the subject of "leadership". Most are still written on the premise that you must be a supervisor or manager in an organization to be a leader. Many are extensions or modifications of previously developed models or approaches that were originally created during the past 40 years. These books do offer some useful ideas that could be of practical use.

Yet, many are anecdotal or "too cute" for their own good. They often use attention grabbing titles that include references to cheese, elephants, eagles, fish, penguins, cows, mice, and icebergs. However, many of these works are simply fads and not based on facts. While the metaphors can be powerful teaching tools, to be useful in the real world, they must be based on viable models or frameworks. Once the make-up and rouge has been removed, many of these books and models do not apply to the complex world of today's organizations or are insufficient to address the vexing challenges leaders face. We know this based on the frustrating comments we would hear from our training and consulting clients. They took a course about cheese or eagles and the concepts sounded useful, but in the "real world" the ideas had limited application.

We based the natural laws and quantum model on many of the classic and most widely used leadership models and frameworks developed over the past 40 years. These include: The Managerial Grid, The Leadership Grid, Situational Leadership I, Situational Leadership II, The Supervisors Window, Social Styles, The DiSC Personal Profile System, and Theory X-Theory Y. Each of these models and frameworks offer useful aspects of the "science" of leadership.

We also provided what we call the "art" of leadership by suggesting multiple choices to implement the laws and model (the science). This balance allowed our participants to forge a strong bond between knowledge and experience. It enhanced the full leadership polarity.

The lesson we learned is simple: *avoid the fads and look for the facts*. Avoid being swept up in catchy metaphors and simplistic approaches. Continue your growth as an effective leader by using three simple guidelines before you invest in another book, training course, or consulting expert.

1. Does the knowledge framework being presented have a firm foundation in verifiable information - what are the facts (the science) to back up the concepts?
2. What is the process to apply the knowledge being presented - are the application suggestions adaptable (the artfulness) to your situation?
3. Do the concepts, principles, or models allow for and make it clear that continuous improvement is part of the process and essential for success?

Lesson Two: Continuously Expand Self-Awareness

In all of our work, we make a strong case for leadership law 8: Consciousness creates leadership, and leadership law 9: Leadership is a self-referral process. We know these laws are abstract, so we include awareness building modules in our programs. This allows us to operationalize laws 8 and 9 into understandable and practical information. We assess personality, temperament, behavioral preferences, values, ethics, personal beliefs, physical wellness and emotional intelligence.

These instruments help people know themselves better so they can be more conscious of how to lead, gain followers, and succeed. The instruments also help people recognize how to enhance their leadership skill by knowing how they and others perceive and respond to leadership challenges based on each person's self-referral identity.

Lesson Two is absolutely essential today. Over 70% of today's organizational members have a limited accurate awareness of how their personal preferences impact the people around them. This has shown to be true for managers at all levels and for non-managers regardless of educational level or years on the job. More importantly, a lack of such awareness can have serious negative effects during leadership moments. We have come to understand this as the "B. L.M.!" reality.

B.L.M. stands for Be Like Me. We know that most people want to work with others who are similar physically, intellectually, emotionally and substantively. This is understandable based on the importance of one element of rapport: that having things in common with others makes it easier to relate to them.

"B.L.M." becomes problematic, we think it is in some ways like a disease, when people cannot "get out of our own skin" and see the world through someone else's eyes. In such cases, B.L.M. transforms into a chronically debilitating reality. B.L.M. transcends the usual differences identified in traditional diversity training such as gender, age, race, culture, creed, ethnicity and size. B.L.M. includes differences in personality, behavior, habits, personal beliefs, values, etc.

To apply Lesson Two: Continuously Expand Self-Awareness, we provide participants with several powerful instruments that we have found over time are valid, reliable, generalizable and practical tools for self-understanding. We suggest you consider using these instruments to help you. Always utilize a qualified person to administer, score, and help you interpret your results.

The Myers-Briggs Type Indicator is perhaps the most widely

used personal awareness instrument organizations rely upon today. It helps participants understand their individual personality and temperament preferences.

The FIRO-B Instrument is the second most widely used instrument found in organizations today. This instrument helps individuals gain insight into their behavioral preferences. It addresses the areas of the need for Inclusion, need for Control, and need for Openness.

The DiSC Personal Profile assesses behavioral preferences in the areas of Dominance, Inspiration, Steadiness, and Compliance.

The Ethical Type Indicator analyzes how we make our decisions. It provides insight into our moral frameworks.

The Bar-On EQI is the most validated instrument that examines our level of emotional intelligence and development.

The Leadership Skills 360 Survey is based on the book, *The 108 Skills of Natural Born Leaders*. This multi-rater 360 degree survey gives valuable insight into your individual development level in nine leadership skills areas which reflect *The 9 Natural Laws of Leadership*.

We use these instruments as well as simulations, activities, video clips and one-on-one feedback/coaching in 20 different leadership programs to help participants expand consciousness and gain greater self-awareness.

Lesson Three: Focus on the Whole to Achieve the Goal - The "P.I.E.S. Model"

Charles Darwin's observations of the natural world led him to the conclusion that those who adapt best to the environment around them SURVIVE and THRIVE! We have found this "Survival of the Fittest" law to be true in the organizational world as well. Those individuals who have become whole and balanced people in their daily lives, greatly improve their opportunities of survival as leaders and first followers in their organizations and communities.

Our career-long observations and experience have shown us that human development occurs throughout our lives in four distinct dimensions. Those dimensions are the: Physical,

Intellectual, Emotional, and Substantive. Lesson Three guides us to make sure we address each area to realize benefit.

We honed this insight by recognizing the impact of each dimension on individuals who attempt to take leadership initiatives and gain willing followers. (See ffigure 14.1.)

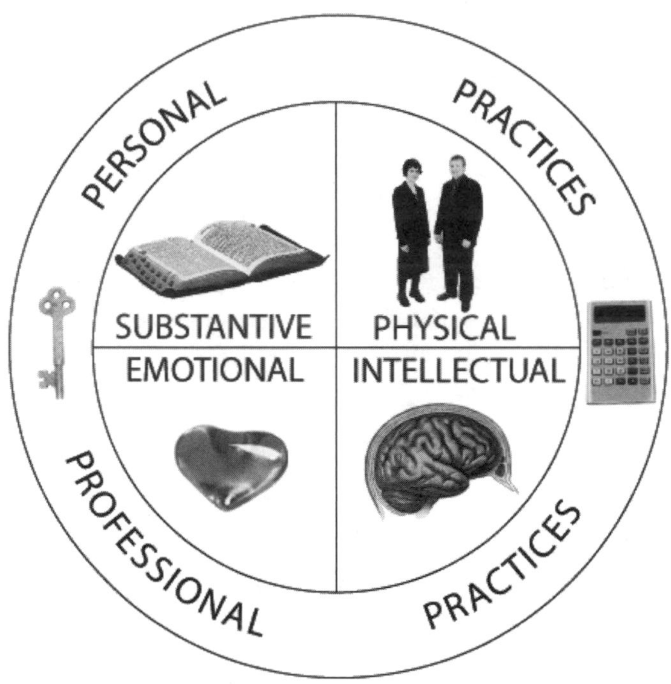

Figure 14.1
PIES Developmental Model

"The Physical Dimension"

The physical dimension of life and leadership could be called the lost dimension. Even though it is the foundation of the other three dimensions, the physical dimension is often overlooked or ignored as a primary element in the leadership equation of success.

Simply stated, it takes more energy to lead then it does to maintain the status quo or to do nothing. We often ask participants in our training programs if they have ever been part of a team responsible for starting or creating something brand new or for fixing/correcting a major problem area in their organizations. Many hands go up in an affirmative response to these inquiries. We then ask these individuals to explain how much physical energy it took to begin and complete a "fix it" or "start-up" that involved several weeks or months of effort. Over 95% of the responses indicate the physical demand was enormous. This indicates the critical importance of this dimension to overall leadership effectiveness.

The Physical Dimension also includes how we handle stress, recover from sickness, and maintain reserves of energy when concentrating during intense problem solving. The physical dimension crosses over into our personal lives in many ways. We can only have the necessary energy to sustain ourselves if we fuel our body with nutritious food and adequate exercise on a daily basis. We are only able to make it through hectic workdays and still have reserves for our families, friends, communities, and personal interests during the evenings and on weekends or vacations if we feel fit. The balance of our physical dimension throughout our lifetime also determines the level of activity that we can take into our next career called retirement.

Consider the quality and capacity of your Physical Dimension of Leadership. Take a lesson from the suggestions we make in our one and two week leadership training seminars. Assess you diet and how it makes you feel. Review your rest and activity cycle to determine how it impacts your energy level. Analyze the extent to which you engage in at least moderate physical activity (e.g., brisk walking and stretching on a daily basis). Also, ask yourself, "Would you willingly follow someone who did not possess the physical energy necessary to sustain leadership initiatives?" Then consider how well you radiate an enthusiastic physical appearance and quality of action.

"The Intellectual Dimension"

The Intellectual Dimension of Life and Leadership includes not only your intelligence or IQ level but also how "hungry" and agile you are as a continuous learner. We believe Quantum Leaders are curious about life, growth, and personal development. They welcome new ideas and information into their intellectual matrix. They explore a variety of on-line sources, journals, magazines, and books. They belong to various professional organizations. Attendance in training programs is frequent. Quantum Leaders develop their intellectual capacities.

Enhance your Intellectual Dimension by utilizing a technique we implement in our training sessions: *Read to Lead*. Review sections of this book on a regular basis to help you recall concepts and ideas that slipped by. Reconsider some of the action ideas and try those you overlooked or did not even try. Consider reading *The 108 Skills of Natural Born Leaders*, Published by AMACOM in 2001. This text builds on the foundations of *The 9 Natural Laws of Leadership* and takes the core elements of Quantum Leadership to new levels. It offers over 1000 action ideas for leaders at all levels of today's organizations. The book answers an age-old question: Are there individuals who are natural born leaders? Get a copy of *The Leadership Event: The Moments of True Leadership that Transform Organizations*, published by the Leadership Group Press, 2004 (now it its second revised edition published in 2007). This book presents a comprehensive model to assist leaders in gaining followers in critical circumstances. The book explains how to create leadership events, reinforce leadership events, and block negative leadership events. It offers 90 action steps, and a Leadership Development Plan Template. If your goal is to understand the inner mechanisms of true leadership, this book will help you. *Leadership for Smart People: The Five Truths*, published by the Leadership Press, 2007 is the first in a new series of practical guides for leadership success. This book will clear the air for all to hear that Smart People Lead…Dummies Don't"! The book describes the "truths," the realities which never change, regarding how and why people are leaders.

"The Emotional Dimension"

This dimension addresses how we behave and interact with others. Author and psychologist Daniel Goleman popularized the term "Emotional Intelligence" in his 1995 book that brought this dimension to the forefront of individual achievement in life and for leadership. Research over the past 25 years has shown that EQ is as equally important as IQ in living a successful life. We focus on the emotional dimension when we ask our clients questions such as, Do you have the empathetic awareness to see the world through another person's eyes? Do you know, understand, and appreciate yourself? Do you know, understand, and appreciate others?

How would you answer these questions? And, would you willingly follow someone who did not know, understand, respect, or appreciate you as the unique individual that you are?

"The Substantive Dimension"

Core beliefs, values, ethics, and morals make up the Substantive Dimension of Life and Leadership. This dimension reflects what we stand for as a person. Many call this the "role model" dimension. It represents our personal credibility to the world. It explains who we trust in our relationships and why. Consider your own substantive dimension. Would others describe you as honest and a person of integrity? Do you "walk your talk" especially when times are tough? Is there congruency in what you say and what you are observed practicing? And, would you willingly follow someone you did not trust or did not find as credible?

Quantum Leaders realize that the more balanced they are in these four dimensions, the more likely they are to gain and sustain the willing followership of individuals in their organizations. Balanced leaders are "whole" people. Whole people create equilibrium in their world just as the forces of nature provide balance in the natural world. Organizations perform at optimum levels when the majority of their leaders and followers are whole people.

Lesson Four: Make the "LeaderShift"

This is one of the most practical and powerful lessons we have learned in terms of consistently gaining and sustaining willing followers. The experience in our organizational interventions and training programs consistently affirms that leaders must temporarily shift out of their personal comfort or preference zones. This flexibility of action is the only way people can successfully meet the challenges of leading during times of uncertainty.

We call this ability to meet the demand in front of you the "LeaderShift." The metaphor is based on the gearshift in an automobile. Imagine a standard transmission in an automobile and the floor-mounted gear shift knob. There is a visual imprint on the top the knob that usually displays five forward gears, a reverse gear, and neutral (see figure 14.2). In our work with organizations, we ask clients to imagine that they are at a stoplight at the bottom of the steepest hill in San Francisco, California. We tell them that the light just turned green. We then ask them if they can successfully drive their car up the hill in fifth gear. They of course recognize that this would be impossible or at least extremely difficult. People realize they must shift their transmission into first gear if to successfully climb the hill. They might prefer to drive in fifth gear, but they cannot do so to get up the hill.

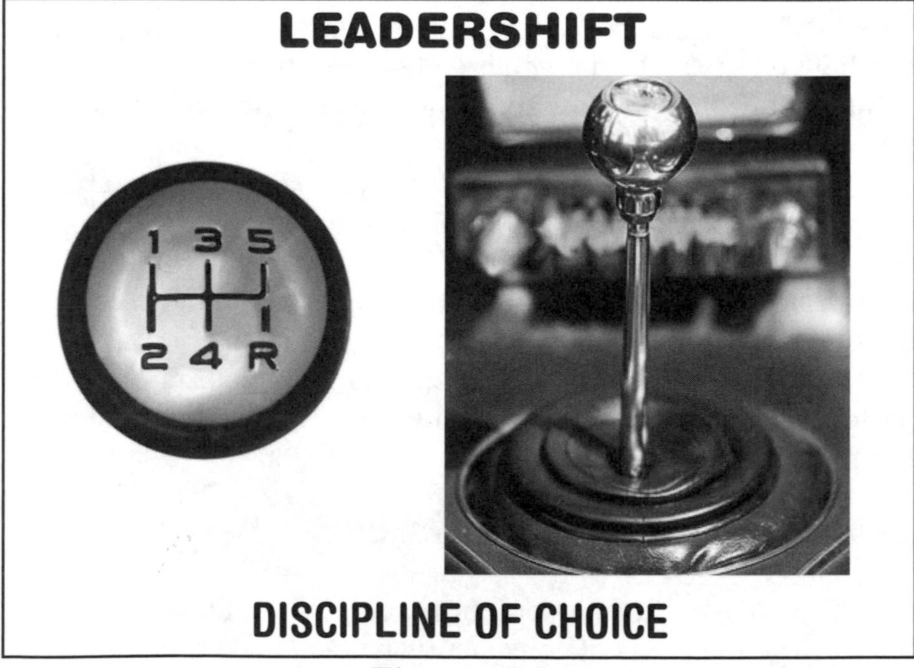

Figure 14.2
The Leadershift

The driving metaphor reflects a leadership reality we have observed. People know they have to shift their thinking and action to lead. However, many find it difficult to do so because they have a preferred "gear" or way of functioning. They like to lead others or drive the leadership process, based on preferences, or a "gear," that they are used to and in which they have a greater degree of comfort.

Just like we have to shift from one gear to another to navigate along a changing highway, successful leadership depends upon our ability to shift into other, perhaps non-preferred gears. Think of your own experience. A situation arises and you are at the "moment of truth." You have to step up and take the lead. In some cases, to succeed you have to do something different, try something else, or shift out of your established range of comfort.

This gear shift metaphor applies when we attempt to influence someone to follow us. The Quantum Leadership Model explains that you have to "meet people at their level to lead them to yours." In some cases, your preferred gear might be the one that works with specific followers. In other situations, you will not attract followers unless you temporarily shift out of your preference zones to meet follower's needs at their level.

Our experience tells us that making the appropriate shift is difficult. That is why a foundation in fact based models and holistic self-knowledge is important. In addition, we expose our clients to a variety of different situations to help them first recognize the need to shift and then experiment with alternate choices. With proper coaching and development we find that participants can assess situations more effectively and respond more appropriately.

Apply this lesson to your own life. What are your preferred ways of dealing with people and situations? How frequently do you perform "spontaneous right action" which is an automatic response that results in a desired, positive result? Do you recognize that you have alternate ways of interpreting and responding? Can you call upon a varied repertoire of actions that provide you with appropriate choices for the situation? And, how willing and able are you at actually stepping out to make the shift to an alternate way of responding?

An automobile has only a few gears and the shift from one to the other is set based on the physical machinery of the gear box. Humans are much more varied and complex. This diversity could create a countless number of choices or shifts one might have to make. It sounds almost too daunting to consider! However, we have found a fairly simple and practical template to guide the direction of ones choices. This is our next lesson.

Lesson Five: The Symbiotic Relationship

Lesson Five builds on the LeaderShift concept. What gear are you typically in when dealing with others? Answers to this question can be gained from greater self-awareness. What gear might be useful to gain and maintain willing followers? The concept of symbiosis offers a way to respond to this question.

Symbiosis is Greek for "living together." Symbiosis can describe various degrees of close relationship between organisms of different species. In some symbiotic relationships both parties benefit. This is known as mutualism. In other symbiotic relationships, one party feeds off of another. Parasites and predators fall into this category.

Our experience in organizations reveals how this phenomenon of nature also occurs in the work world. Relationships, between leaders and followers, managers and subordinates, and peer interactions are symbiotic. The positive and negative realities of symbiosis are revealed very clearly in an activity we call "Best Boss-Worst Boss." We ask people to work in small groups and generate lists of the behaviors, practices, beliefs and characteristics of the "best" and "worst" bosses they experienced in their work careers. The results are virtually always the same whether participants represent lower, middle, or upper levels of the organizational hierarchy. Table 14.1 summarizes the most common descriptors of "Best" and "Worst" bosses.

Table 14.1: Best Boss Worst Boss Descriptors

Best Boss		**Worst Boss**	
Trust	Strategic	Controlling	Distrustful
Honesty	Approachable	Micro-manager	Dishonest
Integrity	Passionate	Dictatorial	Abrupt
Respect	Fun	Abrasive	Yells
Compassion	Energetic	Cold	Distant
Empathy	Politically Savvy	Disrespectful	Non-communicative
Commitment	Inspiring	Uncaring	Manipulative
Good Communicator	Responsive	Angry	Arrogant
Coach	Hard Worker	Abusive	Unapproachable
Courage	Clear goals	Overly-emotional	Apathetic
Visionary	Knowledgeable	Liar	
	Mentor	Lacks knowledge	

When we ask participants if they would willingly follow these bosses, the answer is always the same. People want to follow "Best Bosses" and only want to comply with "Worst Bosses." Leaders and followers represent a positive or mutually beneficial symbiosis. Leaders offer direction to serve the needs of followers. Followers support leaders because they gain value by doing so. Best bosses create a symbiotic relationship that transcends their rank or title. Participants say their Best Boss would have influence even if she or he did not have rank or title. They were "Leader Bosses."

Worst Bosses also create a symbiotic relationship but it is based purely on the required interaction of superior to subordinate. Participants respond with an emphatic "NO" when asked if they would willingly follow Worst Bosses. Participants explain that such bosses would not have any influence without their formal title of authority. This clearly tells us that these worst bosses simply used positional power (predatory symbiosis) to command and control others. They get what they want without concern for their staff. In many cases, worst bosses abused their position to gain value for themselves at the expense of their subordinates (parasitic symbiosis). Subordinates comply because they must do so to maintain their job and/or avoid being abused.

We have also found that the "Best" list applies to descriptions of peers, co-workers and subordinates with whom people want to work. The "Worst"list relates to those with whom participants find to be difficult peers, co-workers and subordinates. What we have come to recognize very clearly is the symbiosis of leadership: people want to follow and are eager to support those who exhibit mutual trust, respect, care and concern, regardless of rank or title. These descriptors directly reflect the Nine Natural Laws and core skills and frameworks of Quantum Leadership. We have also found in our follow-up work with participants that those who apply the Quantum Leadership model create more positive, mutually satisfactory relationships with others and therefore have more positive influence.

Apply this lesson to yourself. Assess the quality of symbiosis you have with others. To what extent would others describe you as a best boss, coworker, subordinate, or partner at work? Do others perceive you as a person focused on mutually satisfactory goals and on their needs, interests, and values? How skillful (able to make the LeaderShift) are you at behaving in ways that reflect best boss behavior?

Lesson Six: Adapt and Evolve with a Road Map to Guide Your Growth

In the natural world, animals and plants survive through successive generations based on their ability to adapt and evolve. That ability is "imprinted" in animals based on their instincts. It is structured within plants based on their natural growth cycle. That is why apples do not grow on banana trees. And, it explains why you cannot grow an apple tree without the proper environment. In a way, animals and plants have an established road map that guides their growth and development. Their map is automatic, fixed, and based on set laws of nature.

A large percentage of human growth is also automatic based on the map of our DNA. However, humans have the ability to make choices not based on instinct but on intelligence. Humans can weigh their options when competing choices confront them. They do not simply wither and die because of a lack of some nutrient like a tree without water might die.

We have found that those who are the most effective Quantum Leaders adapt and evolve by creating personal and professional development plans to assure their growth and success. Following this final chapter is a template for your Individual Leadership Development. Pick an area in which you want to improve based on what you learned from the ideas within this book. Choose an improvement strategy based on the action ideas at the end of each chapter. Work your plan until you master that skill or recognize the value in altering your plan to become more skillful.

Ask two or three colleagues that know you well and that you trust to be your coaching partners. We have used this approach for participants that have attended our training programs for the past 20+ years. Results indicate that over 68% of our trainees complete their initial development plan based on six month follow-up research with these individuals in the form of structured personal interviews. If you are serious about becoming a quantum leader, it is essential that you create your own development plan. Photocopy the attached Development Plan template or go to The Leadership Group Web site at: www.leadershipgroup.com and download it. You can also order our other publications from the website or learn about additional action ideas that can help you to develop into a Quantum Leader.

Lesson Seven: What Happens After You've Tried Everything?

Over the years we've heard countless times from trainees and coaching clients that they've tried "EVERYTHING" to improve their leadership skills and that "NOTHING WORKS"! If you believe that statement to be true then give up! There is no need to even try if NOTHING WORKS!

We believe that no one has ever really tried everything. We also have found that some actions that are applied are not executed very skillfully. And, we have even noticed that an action that might not yield desired results in one situation would be very effective in another circumstance.

If you are feeling frustrated and at your wit's end, regroup and try something else. Review again the over 200 action ideas of this book. What haven't you tried? What else could you try? Consider why you have not tried something. Could it be related to your "preferred gear?" That is, it would require making a LeaderShift out of your comfort zone that you have not been willing to make?

Make a commitment to action and do something different! Do not accept that you are at the end of your rope. Get some help if necessary. Talk to a trusted ally - one with whom you have a symbiotic relationship that benefits you both. Expand self-awareness. Read a book with examples of what works and why. Consider if you might need to work on an alternate dimension first to enable you to succeed. For example, review your physical capabilities before working on one of the other dimensions.

In the natural world, animals and plants pass on their genes to continue their species. Those that have the most robust and adaptive genes continue their bloodline. Those that do not adapt, cease to exist. In the natural world, only the strong survive. In the Quantum Leadership world only the committed and most skilled survive to make a difference. Are you committed? Do you care enough to make a positive difference in your personal and professional world? It's time to put on your NIKES! You know what comes next.......either just do it or become extinct by doing nothing. Even if your physical body continues to exist, your mind, heart, and spirit will already have died.

The choice is yours! Choose as if your life depends on it!!! In the end it does. There is no abdication in the Quantum World, only infinite possibilities. Is it possible you'll make a difference? Let us know! Share your evolutionary leadership journey with us at:

Warren Blank: leaderwb@aol.com
Aaron Brown: abrownleads@aol.com

We would love to tell your story in our next book!

Individual Development Plan

My Name: ______________________________ Today's Date __________

★ What Skills/Attitudes/Competencies will I work on over the next 3-6 months, and how will I achieve my goals?

★ What motivation or help will I need from my "peer coaches/counselors?"

My Signature _________________________ Phone _________________

Peer Coaches/Counselors:

1. __________________________________ Phone _________________

2. __________________________________ Phone _________________

3. __________________________________ Phone _________________

Follow-up Dates ____

THE LEADERSHIP EVENT

Now that you have learned about *"The 9 Natural Laws of Leadership"*, discover how to apply it in the "Leadership Event" Model!

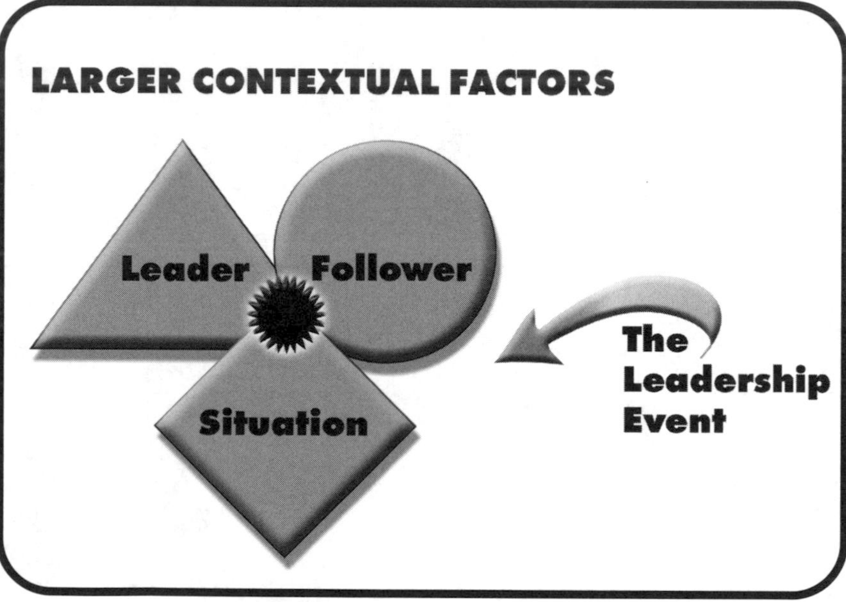

Components of the Leadership Event

◆◆◆

Bibliography

The American Reader, ed. Diane Ravitch. New York: HarperCollins, 1990.

Bandler, Richard, and John Grinder. *Reframing*, eds. Steve Andreas and

Connirae Andreas. Moab, Utah: Real People Press, 1982.

_______. *Frogs Into Princes*, Moab, Utah: Real People Press, 1979.

Bechloss, Michael. *The Crisis Years*. New York: Harper-Collins, 1991, pp.527-528. The idea of ignoring the second letter has been attributed to Robert F. Kennedy in most texts. Bechloss clarifies that it was Bundy's idea and that Bundy graciously allowed RFK to have ownership for the idea as an act of support for RFK's political career.

Bolman, Lee G., and Terrence E. Deal. *Reframing Organizations*. San Francisco: Jossey-Bass,1991.

Blank, Warren. and Aaron Brown. *The Leadership Event: The Moments of True Leadership that Move Organizations*. Vero Beach, FL: The Leadership Group Press, 2004.

Blank, Warren. *The 108 Skills of Natural Born Leaders*. New York: AMACOM, 2001.

Blank, Warren. *Leadership for Smart People: The Five Truths*. Vero Beach, FL: The Leadership Group Press, 2006.

Bridges, William. *Managing Transitions*. Reading, Mass.: Addison-Wesley, 1991.

Brooks, Michael. The Power of Business Rapport. New York: HarperCollins, 1991.

Buell, Barbara. "Businessland Seems Stuck in No-Man's-Land," *Business Week* (July 2, 1990).

Capra, Fritjof. *The Tao of Physics*. 2nd ed. Boston: New Science Library, 1985.

Carroll, Paul. *Big Blues: the Unmaking of IBM*. New York: Crown, 1993.

Chandler, Clay "The Man Who Bought IBM." *Fortune* (December 27, 2004).

Chu, Chin-Ning. *The Asian Mind Game*. New York: Rawson Associates,1991.

Collins, Larry, and Dominique Lapper. *Freedom at Midnight*. New York: Avon Books, 1975.

Douillard, John. *Body, Mind and Sport*. New York: Harmony Books, 1994.

Dumaine, Brian. "Toughest Bosses," *Fortune* (October 18, 1993).

Farnham, Alan. "State Your Values, Hold the Hot Air," *Fortune* (April 19, 1993).

Gergan, David. "Lip Balm for Bush," *U.S. News & World Report* (July 9,1990).

Gilder, George. Microcosm: *The Quantum Revolution in Science and Technology*. New York: Simon and Schuster, 1989.

Goswami, Amit. *The Self-Aware Universe*. New York: Putnam, 1993.

Graves, Jacqueline M. "Leaders of Corporate Change," *Fortune* (December 14, 1992).

Greengard, S. "Eye for an Eye," *American Way* (April 1990).

Gross, Ronald. *Peak Learning*. Los Angeles: Tarcher, 1991.

Hamel, Gary, and C. K. Prahalad. *Competing for the Future*. Boston: Harvard Business School Press, 1994.

Heisenberg, Werner. *Physics and Philosophy*. New York: Harper, 1971.

Huey, John. "Managing in the Midst of Chaos," Fortune (April 5, 1993).

________. "America's Most Successful Merchant," *Fortune* (September 23,1991).

Jenks, James M., and John M. Kelly. *Don't Do: Delegate!* New York: Ballantine, 1985.

Keller, Maryann. *Rude Awakening: The Rise, Fall, and Struggle for Recovery of General Motors*. New York: Morrow, 1989.

Koestenbaum, Peter. *Leadership: The Inner Side of Greatness*. San Francisco: Jossey-Bass, 1991.

Kroc, Ray. *Grinding It Out: The Making of McDonald's*. New York: Berkeley Medallion Books, 1977.

Labich, Ken. "Why Companies Fail," *Fortune* (November 14, 1994).

McCall, Morgan W, and Michael M. Lombardo. "What Makes a Top Executive?" *Psychology Today* (February 1983).

Mehrabian, Albert. *Silent Messages*. Belmont, Calif.: Wadsworth, 1971.

Nanus, Burt. *Visionary Leadership*. San Francisco: Jossey-Bass, 1990.

Pascale, Richard T. *Managing on the Edge*. New York: Touchstone, 1991, p.114.

Penrose, Roger. *The Emperor's New Mind*. New York: Penguin Books, 1989. Penrose argues that consciousness is needed when we face "non-algorithmic" situations, i.e., situations that require characteristics such as common sense, judgment, understanding, and artistic appraisal. Penrose also argues that consciousness is not needed when situations are automatic, programmed, or dictated by rules that can be mindlessly followed. He explains the need for consciousness in the leadership arena, in the unpredictable situations where no established guidelines exist.

Peters, Tom, and Nancy Austin. *A Passion for Excellence*. New York: Random House, 1985.

________. and Robert Waterman. *In Search of Excellence*. New York: Harper, 1982.

Phillips, Don T. *Lincoln on Leadership: Executive Strategies for Tough Times*. New York: Warner Books, 1992.

Pofeldt, Elaine. “Food for piece.” *Fortune*, December 27, 2004.

Pritchard, Peter. *The Making of McPaper: The Inside Story of USA Today*. New York: St. Martin’s Press, 1987.

Ray, Michael. “The New Business Paradigm,” New Traditions in Business, ed. J. Renesch. San Francisco: Berrett-Koehler, Publishers, 1992.

________. and Rochelle Myers. *Creativity in Business*. New York: Doubleday, 1986.

Reich, Robert B. *The Work of Nations: Preparing Ourselves for 21st Century Capitalism*. New York: Knopf, 1991.

Rice, Faye. “Champions of Communications,” *Fortune* (June 3, 1991).

Robbins, Anthony. *Unlimited Power*. New York: Fawcett Columbine, 1986.

________. *Awaken the Giant Within*. New York: Summit Books, 1991.

Saporito, Bill. “A Week Aboard the Wal-Mart Express,” *Fortune* (August 24, 1992).

Schlender, Brent. “The iPhone on training wheels,” *Fortune*, November 26, 2007. P. 54)

Schein, Edgar H. *Organizational Culture and Leadership*. San Francisco:Jossey-Bass, 1990.

Schlesinger, Arthur. *A Thousand Days*. Greenwich, Conn.: Fawcett Publications, 1965, pp. 756-757.

Secord, Paul F. “The Role of Facial Features in Interpersonal Perception,” *Person Perception and Interpersonal Behavior*, eds. R. Tagiuri and L. Petrullo. Stanford, Calif.: Stanford University Press, 1958, pp.300-315.

Senge, Peter. *The Fifth Discipline*. New York: Doubleday, 1990.

Sherman, Stratford. “Leaders Learn to Heed the Voice Within,” *Fortune* (August 22, 1994).

Stewart, Thomas. “The King Is Dead,” *Fortune* (January I, 1993).

Swanson, Gerald, and Robert Oates. *Enlightened Management.* Fairfield, IA: MIU Press, 1989.

Taylor, Alex III. *"Why Toyota Keeps Getting Better and Better,"* Fortune (November 19, 1990).

________. *"The Nine Lives of Jüürgen Schrempp."* Fortune (January 10, 2005).

Thompson, Charles. *What a Great Idea*! New York: HarperCollins, 1992.

Peters, Tom, and Nancy Austin. *A Passion for Excellence.* New York: Random House, 1985.

Tichy, Noel M., and Many Anne Devanna. *The Transformational Leader.* New York: Wiley, 1990.

Townsend, Robert. *Up the Organization.* Greenwich, Conn.: Fawcett Publications, 1970.

Tully, Shawn. "Why Go for Stretch Targets?" *Fortune* (November 14,1993).

Vaill, Peter. *Managing as a Performing Art.* San Francisco: Jossey-Bass, 1989.

von Oech, Roger. *A Whack on the Side of the Head.* New York: Warner Books, 1983.

Wallace, Robert Keith. *The Physiology of Consciousness.* Fairfield, IA: MIU Press, 1993.

Wenner, Jann S. *"Why Bush Won."* Rolling Stone (December 9, 2004).

Wheatley, Margaret J. *Leadership and the New Science.* San Francisco: Berrett-Koehler, 1992.

Wooden, John. *They Call Me Coach.* Waco, Tex.: Word Books, 1972.

Zohar, Danah. *The Quantum Self.* New York: Morrow, 1990.

Zukav, Gary. *The Dancing Wu Li Masters.* New York: Bantam Books,1980.

Zuker, Elaina. *The Seven Secrets of Influence.* New York: McGraw-Hill, 1991.

About the Authors

Warren Blank is President of The Leadership Group, a firm formed in 1986 with offices in Vero Beach, FL and Chapel Hill, NC. The Leadership Group clients include over 50 Fortune 500 firms and more than 80 different government agencies. Warren has a Ph.D. and MBA from the University of Cincinnati, an M.S. in Education from Indiana University and a B.A. from the University of Akron. He is the author of *The 108 Skills of Natural Born Leaders* (AMACOM 2001), *The Nine Natural Laws of Leadership - 2nd Edition* (Leadership Group 2006), *The Leadership Event* (2007) and *Leadership Skills for Managers* (American Management Institute 1995), and many articles in professional journals. Find out more at LeadershipGroup.com.

Aaron Brown, based in Denver, Colorado, is President of LEADS Associates which provides Leadership Education, Assessment and Development Services to individuals and organizations. Aaron has over thirty years of progressive management experience both in the public and private sectors. He has successfully designed and delivered hundreds of leadership training programs to over 30,000 participants. He is co-author of *The Nine Natural Laws of Leadership*, *The Leadership Event*, and the forth coming book, *People Won't Follow Leaders They Don't Like.*

Concluding Note from the Authors

Congratulations on reading our book and creating your 9 Natural Laws Individual Development Plan.

We invite you to continue your development and expand the quality of leadership throughout your organization. The Leadership Group and LEADS organizations offer training seminars, consulting workshops, and speaking services to organizations to create a leadership culture. You can also contact us for additional copies of the "9 Natural Laws of Leadership. Other titles available include:

1. *The Leadership Event*
2. *Leadership for Smart People*
3. *The 108 Skills of Natural Born Leaders*

Contact us at:

Warren Blank
The Leadership Group
505 Beachland Boulevard
Suite 223
Vero Beach, Florida 32963
919-656-3344
LeaderWB@aol.com

Aaron Brown
LEADS Associates
P.O. Box 371316
Denver, Colorado 80237
303-718-1358
abrownleads@aol.com

INDEX

The Natural Laws of Leadership Self-Assessment

Developed by:
Warren Blank and Aaron Brown

Directions:

The purpose of this self-assessment is to help you understand yourself as a leader.

This is not a test. There are no right or wrong answers. Please provide the most honest responses you can.

Respond to each question using the following scale:

Not Very Descriptive			Somewhat Descriptive			Very Descriptive
1	2	3	4	5	6	7

If you have any questions, please contact Warren Blank by telephone at 919 656-3344 or via e-mail at leaderwb@aol.com.

To what extent is each statement descriptive of your ACTUAL BEHAVIOR AT WORK:

Assessment:

____1. I gain the willing support of others when I make suggestions to take action.

____2. People frequently follow my lead when I offer courses of action.

____3. I openly support other's ideas when they make suggestions that help achieve desired outcomes.

____4. I do not hesitate to point out when other people offer good ideas.

____5. I recognize when several people offer ideas that others support to help a group be successful.

____6. I notice that more than one person typically gains the commitment of others when people work in groups.

____7. I can influence others to support my ideas evens when I do not have any formal authority over them.

____8. I can gain the willing commitment of others because they trust me as a person.

____9. I step forward and provide direction when others are uncertain about what to do.

____10. I seek ways to resolve problems and take advantage of opportunities even if it is not my job to do so.

____11. I take the risks associated with offering courses of action in difficult situations.

____12. I support other's actions in risky situations when I believe in the ideas.

____13. I accept that, in some situations, others may not follow my initiatives.

____14. I do not get discouraged when some people do not want to follow my lead.

____15. I never take for granted that I have all the information needed to resolve problems or exploit opportunities.

____16. I challenge myself to more effectively process information about situations that require action.

____17. I understand how my beliefs, values, and assumptions shape my perceptions.

____18. I continuously seek ways to enhance my capacity to be more expansive and inclusive in how I perceive, interpret, and evaluate situations.

____19. I develop positive relationships with others at work.

____20. I ask others for their ideas on how to deal with challenging situations.

____21. I recognize and reinforce others who take the lead to fulfill my organization's mission.

____22. I clearly demonstrate to others how my ideas support their needs and interests.

____23. I continuously seek out opportunities and obstacles so that I can take action to improve situations at work.

____24. I embrace the risks associated with offering ideas as a energizing challenge.

____25. I focus my attention on those who will follow rather than lament about those who do not follow.

____26. I clarify expectations in ways that help others understand the need for specific courses of action.

____27. I ask others for feedback about my strengths and weaknesses.

____28. I work on all dimensions, my physical and mental capacities, social skills, and system of beliefs, to enhance my effectiveness as a leader.

____29. I make the shift out of my "comfort zone" when it is necessary to work through challenges.

____30. I use a personal development plan to improve my leadership effectiveness.

Scoring:

Add up your scores for each of the 3 item sets noted below (e.g., the first item set is 1, 2, and 19). Rate your total for each set against the following scale:

Very Effective: 18 - 21
Effective: 14 - 17
Need Some Improvement: 10 - 13
Need Substantial Improvement: 9 or less

After completing your rating, review the brief statements that clarify the importance of each of your score in each area.

_____ **Items 1, 2, 19 - your score describes how well you fulfill Natural Law 1.** A leader has willing followers.

_____ **Items 3, 4, 20 - your score describes how well you fulfill Natural Law 2.** "Leadership" is a field of interaction, a relationship between leaders and followers.

_____ **Items 7, 8, 22 - your score describes how well you fulfill Natural Law 4.** Leaders rely upon influence beyond formal authority.

_____ **Items 9, 10, 23 - your score describes how well you fulfill Natural Law 5.** Leaders provide direction outside the boundaries of organizationally defined procedures.

_____ **Items 11, 12, 24 - your score describes how well you fulfill Natural Law 6.** Leadership involves risk and uncertainty.

_____ **Items 13, 14, 25 - your score describes how well you fulfill Natural Law 7.** Not everyone will follow a leader's initiative.

_____ **Items 15, 16, 26 - your score describes how well you fulfill Natural Law 8.** Consciousness, one's information processing capacity, creates leadership.

_____ **Items 17, 18, 27 - your score describes how well you fulfill Natural Law 9.** Leadership is a self-referral process. Leaders & followers process information from their subjective, internal frame of reference.

_____ **Items 28, 29, 30 - your score describes your evolutionary capacity to lead.** Leadership excellence demands an on-going commitment to continuous improvement over a long period of time.

Take Action to Improve!

The Nine Natural Laws of Leadership 3rd Edition provides a complete description of what it means to be a leader. The "Field Guide" at the end of chapters 2-11 suggest specific action choices on how to take the lead more skillfully.

To make overall improvements, read the entire book!

To make targeted improvements, first read Chapters 1 & 2 to get an overview of what it means to be a leader and then read Chapters 13-14 to gain perspective on how to take effective leader action. Then read the specific chapter noted for each item set below and apply the associated action ideas in those chapter's Field Guide

_____ **Items 1, 2, 19 refer to Law 1.** A leader has willing followers.

Leaders who succeed understand that they must gain willing followers and building positive working relationships is essential to gaining other's support. Read Chapter 11 and apply the action ideas suggested in the Chapter's Field Guide.

_____ **Items 3, 4, 20 refer to Law 2.** "Leadership" is a field of interaction, a relationship between leaders and followers.

To create "true leadership" requires being willing to follow as well as lead and asking others for ideas is one indicator of a willingness to follow. Read Chapter 3 and apply the action ideas suggested in the Chapter's Field Guide.

_____ **Items 5, 6, 21 refer to Law 3.** Leadership occurs as an event.

Leaders realize they cannot be the only ones who gain willing followers; they support others who also create "leadership events." Read Chapter 12 and compare your actions in terms of whether you are leading or managing.

_____ **Items 7, 8, 22 refer to Law 4.** Leaders use influence beyond formal authority.

Leadership influence is NOT based on position power, rank, or title. Leaders gain commitment and inspire willing support. Read Chapter 8 and apply the action ideas suggested in the Chapter's Field Guide.

_____ **Items 9, 10, 23 refer to Law 5.** Leaders provide direction and operate beyond the boundaries of organizationally defined procedures.

Leaders lead when there is a need: when others do not know what to do or established procedures do not exist or apply. Read Chapters 6

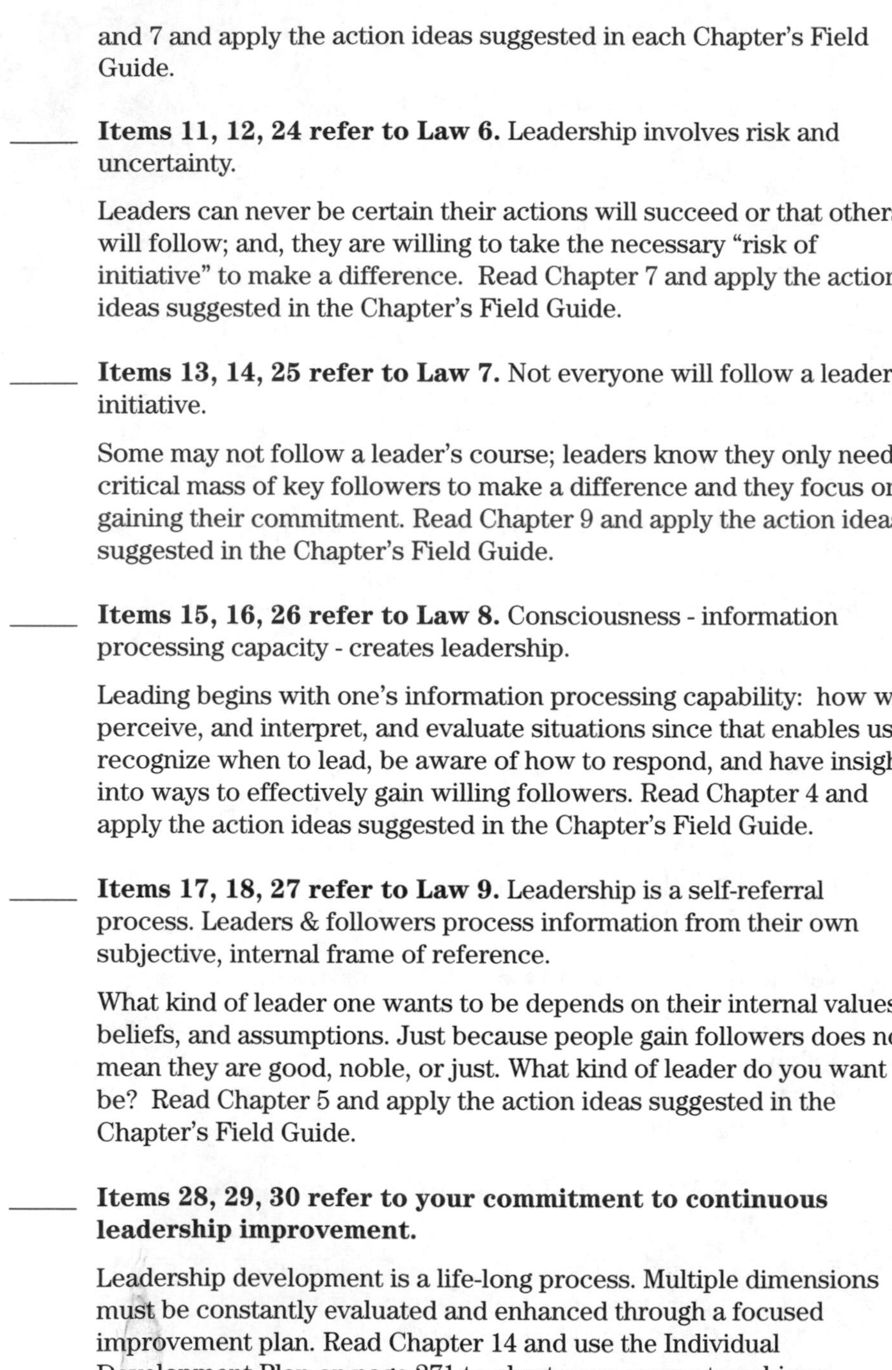

and 7 and apply the action ideas suggested in each Chapter's Field Guide.

_____ **Items 11, 12, 24 refer to Law 6.** Leadership involves risk and uncertainty.

Leaders can never be certain their actions will succeed or that others will follow; and, they are willing to take the necessary "risk of initiative" to make a difference. Read Chapter 7 and apply the action ideas suggested in the Chapter's Field Guide.

_____ **Items 13, 14, 25 refer to Law 7.** Not everyone will follow a leader's initiative.

Some may not follow a leader's course; leaders know they only need a critical mass of key followers to make a difference and they focus on gaining their commitment. Read Chapter 9 and apply the action ideas suggested in the Chapter's Field Guide.

_____ **Items 15, 16, 26 refer to Law 8.** Consciousness - information processing capacity - creates leadership.

Leading begins with one's information processing capability: how we perceive, and interpret, and evaluate situations since that enables us to recognize when to lead, be aware of how to respond, and have insight into ways to effectively gain willing followers. Read Chapter 4 and apply the action ideas suggested in the Chapter's Field Guide.

_____ **Items 17, 18, 27 refer to Law 9.** Leadership is a self-referral process. Leaders & followers process information from their own subjective, internal frame of reference.

What kind of leader one wants to be depends on their internal values, beliefs, and assumptions. Just because people gain followers does not mean they are good, noble, or just. What kind of leader do you want to be? Read Chapter 5 and apply the action ideas suggested in the Chapter's Field Guide.

_____ **Items 28, 29, 30 refer to your commitment to continuous leadership improvement.**

Leadership development is a life-long process. Multiple dimensions must be constantly evaluated and enhanced through a focused improvement plan. Read Chapter 14 and use the Individual Development Plan on page 271 to chart your course to achieve leadership excellence.